CHESS CRUSADER

confessions of an amateur chess player

Carl S. Portman

Acknowledgements

As Clarence the angel wrote in the inside of the book
Tom Sawyer in the film *It's a Wonderful Life*,

No man is a failure who has friends.

Many hardy souls have helped me to shape my life in the past and the present. This applies both at and away from the chessboard. I extend my love and gratitude to them all. With particular thanks to Jeremy Smith who was there at the beginning, Ray and Angela Hale (who will be there to the end!) and all the crew at Halefest, John Lenton, Richard Archer, Trevor Brotherton, Glyn Pugh, George Viszokai, John Cox, Bernard and Jean Crowhurst, Kevin Thurlow, Jovanka Houska, Caroline Pigden, Dave and Helen Ross, Gary Blain, Steve and Julie Lucas, Timothy Betts, Janet Marshall, Terry and Gill Turner, Richard Palliser, Tao Bhokanandh, Malcolm Pein, Richard Beckett, Neil Staples, Keith Freshwater, Ben Graff, Ben Aubury, Antonia Hedges, Raymond Keene, Stuart Conquest, Karla Harris, Veronica Freeman, and the unnamed lady who led me from the garden of innocence – we may not have been the best, but you probably taught me the most! Thanks even to my enemies, who also shaped who I am today. Without you, I could not be me.

To those who have passed on to the next life, but shone a beautiful light into mine, I remember Meyrick Cox, Jeff

Cox, Nancy Cox, David Everington, Colin Roberts, Laurie Brokenshire, and Patrick Moore.

In a group sense, I wish to thank everyone in the UK Armed Forces Chess Association, NATO Chess, The Shropshire Chess Association, the English Chess Federation, and all the chess clubs I have ever been a member of.

I am always indebted to Chess & Bridge of London who have supported me in my many chess ventures over the years. It is greatly appreciated.

I am grateful to James Essinger and The Conrad Press for believing in me and taking on the publication of this book. I want to single out my wife Susan for her love and support, despite suffering a horrifying and incurable cancer during the writing of this memoir. She above all knows me best, and it is the love that we share that makes the days so special, regardless of how we feel physically. Susan, I feel incredibly blessed, privileged, and fortunate to have shared some of your life. It was what I always wanted. Thank you.

Finally, I want to thank you the reader. You have spent your hard-earned money on this book and I am most appreciative of that fact. I hope therefore that you enjoy the read and get value (and maybe a few laughs and tears) for your pennies.

For Rose, Sid and Mum
I hope that you would have been
proud of me in some way.

Foreword by Jovanka Houska

It takes a lot of courage to open up your own personal Pandora's box of memories, take pen to paper and tell your story to the world. So, it is with the utmost pleasure and pride that I write the foreword for one of my dearest friends Carl Portman's book *Chess Crusader*. As you will soon find out for yourself, dear reader, Carl is gifted as both a natural entertainer and storyteller. Although this memoir is primarily about chess, the tales in it are filled with a frank and refreshing honesty that will literally have your heart racing with adventure. It's a story of a life well lived with adventure, adversity, happiness and love in a way that is so uniquely Carl.

I find it quite curious how lifelong friendships can start from nothing more mundane than a chance encounter. Rather fittingly, I first met Carl in the quaint town of Llandudno, home of the British Chess Championships 2017. It was a hot summer day and I was standing at the entrance of the drama theatre Venue Cymru trying to figure out where on earth the tournament playing rooms were. With no chess posters in sight and four endlessly long corridors to choose between, I did what any self-respecting lazy person would do. I grabbed the closest passer-by to ask for directions.

Now the story could have ended there. But this stranger merrily declared that he also didn't know the location of the playing hall. Together we set on a joyful mini-quest, exploring long corridors and opening unknown doors with childish delight. Although that episode probably lasted no more than five minutes, I weirdly knew that I had found a new friend. It will come as no surprise to tell you that this cheerful stranger was none other than Carl Portman.

Now if I was to be truly accurate, it was actually in 2018 that I really got to know Carl when he approached me in an email (that included references!) about a weekend of chess training at his house. It took me a nanosecond, to give that invitation a resounding yes, no references needed – I trusted my instincts.

Carl sporting a fine moustache, and studying some crazy lines with IM Jovanka Houska – nine times British Women's Champion, at Carl's house in 2018.

I am not exaggerating when I say that that chess weekend was one of my highlights of 2018. In the dreamy setting of the English countryside and to the sound-track of Carl's beloved heavy metal music, we immersed ourselves in the world of thirty-two wooden pieces and sixty-four squares. Amidst all the joy and laughter, I somehow managed to forget the closet full of poisonous spiders and even became fond of Carl's distracting handlebar moustache! I credit that uplifting weekend with Carl, his wonderful wife Susan and our canine study companions Dickens and Darwin with helping me achieve one of my best Olympiad performances.

Although the reminiscences I have mentioned are some of my cherished memories, I am not the only one that holds Carl in such high regard. In 2015 he won the ECF President's award for services to chess, a tremendous achievement only reserved for the true stalwarts of the game. There is one area however, in Carl's chess career which is unparalleled and that is his tremendous work as ECF manager of Chess in Prisons. In 2017 Carl wrote a remarkable book called *Chess Behind Bars*, a ground-breaking guide to chess in prisons.

It's a role that Carl was born for. It takes a lot of guts to brazenly walk into some of the UK's toughest prisons and happily duel over the chess board with some scary inmates. Yet this is something that Carl does with no fear just pure pleasure! It is a testament to Carl's infectious love of the game and dedicated hard work that his letterbox is filled with hundreds of letters from prisoners detailing their life-changing experiences, all thanks to chess.

I will let you; dear reader turn the page and enjoy Carl's extraordinary story in his own words, but as a final aside I want to leave you with some words that Carl gave me that I now live by.

'Be a first-class version of yourself, never a second-class version of anyone else - OWN IT!'

Jovanka Houska
Bergen, Norway, March 2021

Contents

Acknowledgements   5
Foreword by Jovanka Houska   9
Introduction   17
Caissa's kiss (or, how I found chess)   23
Childhood   30
School and chess   51
Work and women   80
USSR 1990   107
A man barely alive (AMBA)   124
Correspondence chess   141
Floreat Salopia   147
Germany   171
Hello, this is England calling   196
Saints and sinners   230
Armed Forces chess   254
Coaching   278
Chess in prisons   296
My next move   313
Games selection   319
About the author   344
Bibliography and useful addresses   346
Index of names   348

'You must take your opponent into a deep dark forest where two plus two equals five and the path leading out is only wide enough for one.'

Mikhail Tal

World Chess Champion 1960-61

Introduction

My life will be very strange to a great many people. It has been one of tremendous struggle.

I am not referring to the normal, everyday challenges such as relationships, paying the bills, health, work, kids and life aspirations. I am talking about chess.

This memoir is about my life as an amateur chess player. Let me just clarify the difference between an amateur and a professional. I am happy to use the *Concise Oxford English Dictionary* definitions here:

> *Amateur: One who practices a thing only as a pastime.*
> *Especially unpaid.*

> *Professional: Of, belonging to, connected with a profession.*
> *Paid.*

I have always found this to be quite contentious. Whilst some people get paid, and are therefore deemed to be *professional* I have known amateurs with a professional mindset and professionals with an amateur mindset. It all depends on the individual. I am indeed an amateur player. I have had a career and life away from the board even though I have been paid to play chess from time to time!

How does playing chess make me feel? Well, I am not going to say that it is better than certain other pleasures in life, but it lasts longer, and there is no guilt. For me, it is as black and white as the board itself. On one hand, the sheer brutality of the game metaphorically tears at the flesh. It rips off layer after layer until the bones become exposed. Once laid bare the following question must and will be answered. 'Who are you?' We cannot escape the truth that lies before us on the chessboard. Are you going to fight, or walk away? Are you a crusader or a cream puff?

On the other hand, chess is a game of infinite beauty. Its complexity and richness have always amazed me. It is a kaleidoscope of strategical and tactical possibilities. Chess diverted me from a potential life in the gutter. I have learned to treat the two imposters of victory and defeat just the same, which has stood me well in life. I do not exaggerate when I say that like being in love for the very first time, competitive chess makes my heart hammer away, and in those moments at the board I feel truly alive. My body and mind are at their most absolute. When I am playing chess, the world around me is invisible and all that matters is the game. I neither want nor require anything else. Not food, drink or company. I enter a zen like state. All competitive chess players do.

Understandably, most of my friends have little concept of what it has been like to spend a huge chunk of a life in bitter struggle over sixty-four silly little squares, often against perfect strangers. Whilst my pals were relaxing at weekends, enjoying nice walks, picnics, watching TV or going out for a meal, I was engaging in psychological warfare, attempting to impose my will on opponents who wanted to do exactly the same to me.

There is no place for rainbows and teddy bears and reassuring hugs. It is about testing yourself and being tested. It is about hunting kings and winning battles. Where else can you do that of a weekend?

Chess is not for everyone, but for the millions who play across the globe it is the mental nourishment they crave. The 'everyone is a winner' mentality does not apply in chess. Everyone is a participant for sure, but chess is a meritocracy and there *are* winners and losers. That is the very nature of competition. I am not the best chess player in the world, nor am I the worst. I am just a chess player and a small fish in a very big pool. It has been my obsession since 1976 and it will remain so until death itself delivers the final checkmate. Even then I might try and do a deal with the devil as Antonius Block did in the famous film *The Seventh Seal*.

I have played chess on trains, boats and aeroplanes. I have played in doctor's surgeries, hospital beds, hotels, castles, gardens, health spa pools, military barracks, rainforest huts and even open fields in deep, crisp snow. I cannot begin to imagine how many hours of my life I have sacrificed for this game. The chess community is swollen with fascinating characters and I have been fortunate to have met so many. A chess set speaks all languages after all, and the world can unite around that one.

I have not shied away from being honest in this memoir, I have told it like it is. My opinions (like moves on a chessboard) are my own and I take full responsibility for them. I may change a name here or there simply to protect the guilty, or indeed the innocent.

Why would you read this book? I am not a grandmaster or a celebrity after all. I am but a coffee-house player in my own way. However, I believe that both chess players and non-players alike will relate to something similar in their own lives amongst these pages. It may offer food for thought. This memoir is about finding something life-changing in one defining moment. It reveals how I became rich without money.

The most valuable things in my life have not been material. Cars, houses, money – they all played a part of course but it is the things that I *did*, not the things that I *owned* that mattered.

And of course, it is first and foremost about the people in a life that make all the difference. I grew up on a council estate in Birmingham and managed at some point to captain my country at chess. I am fiercely proud of that and it makes me happy. No more or less than that. We should all be happy about something.

I must say a few words about the chess community. Be of no doubt, chess players in general are a bloody strange brew. I can spot a chess player in a crowd, with great ease. They are usually holding a carrier bag, the contents of which no one wants to discover. They are probably wearing a Christmas jersey, despite it being August, and they will be wandering around aimlessly with seemingly no idea about what direction to go in.

Chess players are often socially awkward and uncomfortable with jokes, especially if they are deemed as politically unacceptable. Many also believe that a bus timetable is a mathematical question. Many cannot drive (that would involve anatomical dexterity) and finally but most importantly some of the chaps could not pull a woman if their life depended upon it. A sample chat up line would be something like 'would you like to come back to my place and look at my pawn collection.' Oh dear.

Yet these are my friends, acquaintances, mentors and sparring partners. They are my brothers and sisters in the struggle. Chess players have a sturdy intellectual carapace. They think a lot and usually consider what they say before they speak, as they would a move at the board. This is not only wise, but creditable. Chess players are surprisingly good at being objective and finding a balanced view. After all, the game demands that we consider the other person's point of view, for if we do not, the consequences could be dire. Further, chess players understand what the battle is like when the first pawn is pushed. Therefore, they are *of* me and I respect each and every one of them for that. We all seek the truth; we all want to find beauty and we are all inextricably linked in our quest to be creative. The feeling of winning is reward for us all.

Undoubtedly, I have made a few enemies in chess, and I do not dismiss them lightly. I learn more about myself from my enemies than my friends. We need the darkness to find the light.

It was Alexandre Dumas who said that friendship consists in forgetting what one gives and remembering what one receives. I hope then that this memoir, illustrates clearly how my heart is brimming over with the love and affection for all that I have received from chess and chess players.

Do not read this book if you are devoid of a sense of humour, or you are easily offended. That is the modern snowflake ethos, but I come from a different time, indeed a different century. Since this is about my life, I must tell it as it is not how someone wants it to be.

Three things cannot be hidden. The sun, the moon and the truth. The harsh reality of the truth can be uncomfortable. This memoir might expose uncomfortable issues for some, (cancer, alcoholism, domestic violence) but that is life, and I believe that we should stand and face our demons head on, otherwise they win. Now it is time to turn the page for you are about to witness a beautiful union.

Carl Portman
Oxfordshire April 2021

Caissa's kiss (or, how I found chess)

May you, just once or twice in your lifetime see something infinitely rare and strange and beautiful.

Pamela Brown (from Natures Gifts)

As I stood in the school playground with my worn-out shoes, light blue blazer with a ripped right pocket and a poorly knotted necktie, the rain hammered into my face like a squadron of tiny nails. It was freezing cold and therefore a significant influence on my decision not to join my pals playing football. Those were the days when a bit of rain was not the signal for everyone to rush inside. We were robust back then, and I played football (not *soccer* as the Americans insist on calling it) in all weathers.

However, it was not to be the case on that day. Something didn't feel quite right. What was I to do? I had to get inside. The chilly air sent a shiver up my still developing spine. I could have slipped into the library since that was nice and warm, and a pretty girl who was sadly not a classmate sorted through the books with a cheery smile that made me feel happy, but I had heard about a chess club that met at lunchtimes, so I decided to go and visit the nerds and the geeks (we called them spazzers in those days; kids can be so cruel) to see what the fuss was all about.

I still recall ascending the stairs in the block and reaching the geography room. I wrinkled my nose and peered through the little pane of glass in the door. Sure enough there they were. Several kids of all shapes and sizes and one teacher were bent double over chequered boards with heads in hands – thinking. They were not even moving. They were as statues, frozen in time. Suddenly one of the kids jumped up, confirming that there was indeed life within.

I tentatively opened the door and peered inside. 'Aah, Portman' said the chess teacher Mr. Lenton, who also happened to be the deputy head of the school. 'Come on in, do you play chess? Do you fancy a game?'

He was a bit scary was John Lenton. He had sinister eyebrows and a gaze that could melt Kryptonite. He wore one of those black cape things that Mr. Chips wore in the film *Goodbye Mr. Chips* and he also walked around school with a clipboard, taking names. Mr. Lenton had this uncanny knack of appearing in the corridor just at the moment that you decided to run not walk. He used a Parker fountain pen which wrote in brilliant blue ink and he also coveted a red pen, which he used for reminding him of important things – and for taking those names. I appeared on his naughty list just once and I had to stand up in assembly to the ridicule of hundreds of other pupils. It transpired that the *offence* was committed by my brother Lawrence, so he actually penalized the wrong Portman, but I will forgive him that for all he has done for me since. He actually loved his profession and the kids, and he was damned good at what he did.

'No sir, I don't actually know how to play,' I replied.

'Well come in Portman and watch. Sit down and don't make a noise.'

If I had made a noise it would have been easy to hear. It was like a library in there. All I could hear were clocks ticking. Tick, tick, tick, tick. It seemed so loud, and it emanated from several weird looking clocks – called chess clocks. These are actually two clocks in one and they set time for the players – if you run out of time, the consequences are severe – you lose the game. Time and tempo are everything in chess. I guess they are in life also.

Other than that, it was silence. Perfect, wonderful, beautiful silence. No-one was shouting or swearing, nothing. It was absolutely deafening! I was to learn later that the chess club could actually be a very noisy place but not when there were serious games between members, or inter-school matches. Then it was quiet. This was clearly one of those days.

I am often asked why I play chess, and one of the things I have treasured the most is the tranquility. Chess removes me far away from the madding crowd. It acts like some form of transcendental meditation as I fall into a hypnotic state where the noise and grind of everyday life vanishes. I sometimes feel as if I have entered some kind of spirit world.

Whether I am playing a club match or a weekend tournament, there is an opportunity just to think, and to withdraw within myself. It's just me and the board. Where else in life is one allowed to be so creative? Is it not fantastic to see that the position at the board is but a physical manifestation of an intellectual battle between two determined protagonists?

In life, we have to follow rules and social expectations. Walk slowly, don't park here, keep off the grass, no entry, private keep out, members only access. Life is full of restrictions imposed upon us by other human beings. Well that is not the case on a chessboard. Whilst there are obviously rules for the game, it is your battle, your playground. You will create your own magic. You can play a placid game or recreate the wild wild west!

I did not know it then, but I know it now. The moment I stepped into the room on that first day at the school chess club - *she* was there. I was about to be seduced by a notorious temptress and I was only twelve years old. Like millions before me Caissa came to enlist me into her army of devotees. Caissa is the Goddess of chess, first mentioned during the Renaissance by Italian poet Hieronymus Vida. Later In 1763, at the age of seventeen, a chap called William Jones wrote the poem 'Caissa' based on Vida's work, giving a mythical origin of chess that has become well-known in the chess world.

In the poem the nymph Caissa initially repels the advances of Mars, the god of war. Spurned, Mars seeks the aid of the god of sport, who creates the game of chess as a gift for Mars to win Caissa's favour. Mars wins her over with the game. He wrote...

> *O'er hills and valleys was her beauty fam'd,*
> *And fair Caissa was the damsel nam'd.*

Further, in the book, *The Golden Dozen*, by Irving Chernev he outlines the nine *muses* (or if you like, qualities) of Caissa dedicated to the aspiring chess master. They are:

Imagination, Understanding, Accuracy,
Confidence, Caution, Courage,
Ambition, Patience, Memory

I am often given to wondering that those at the very top have all of these muses, but lesser players are missing one or more. Each may cosset their own view.

One thing is for certain. On that day, she hypnotized me with that black and white board. The sixty-four squares each had a purpose. The bishops, kings, queens, knights and pawns seemed to be charged with energy, coming alive the moment that they were touched. Note that there are four knights in chess, and chess is a game of war. The four horsemen, I thought – this is an apocalyptic game for me! Even today several decades on I can still recall the smell of the plastic chess pieces. I was completely smitten with the way that they looked and felt and how they moved in such mysterious ways. Of course, the best chess sets are made of wood, but they are much more expensive and my school - Charlton School – was a secondary school in Telford, with enough financial struggles of its own. Plastic would have to do.

Chess is an inexpensive game fortunately, and the plastic sets are fine. I knew then, in that one sacred hour that chess and I were going to be friends for life. I picked up a knight and felt the contours of it. My finger touched the horse's mouth and I half expected it to snort hot breath at me. The tactile element of the game cannot be replicated on today's computers. I still remember smelling that knight. Fresh plastic! When you put all thirty-two pieces back in the box the collective smell was quite lovely. It sounds like some kind of fetish, and that I go around smelling plastic all day. I do not. But that day I was getting to know the chess pieces before I even knew how they moved. Maybe this was love at first sight. Or maybe love at first knight.

I was twelve years old and chess was my earliest epiphany.

For the rest of my life, I would be a soldier of Caissa and spread the chess gospel on my crusades in schools, prisons, other organisations, and many social settings.

To get in training for my quest, I would play chess constantly over the next four years at school. I had a yearning to be as good as I could. I quickly became obsessed with the game and the sheer joy of learning and playing. Here, I could fight someone without throwing a punch or getting the slipper for it.

Yes, those were the days when pupils were physically beaten if they wandered from the path of conformity. You got the cane, the slipper, a wooden board rubber at the back of the head, a slap or hit with a wooden ruler. I am not talking about Victorian England here; this is the late 1970s and early 1980s.

It seems so primitive, yet the threat in my case was always greater than its execution and although I was no angel (I once set fire to a kid's trousers with a Bunsen burner because he said Aston Villa were rubbish) I never received the slipper or the cane. It is true though that one psycho teacher called Mr. Clements smashed my hand with a ruler for underlining a heading. He was a sadist for sure and probably long gone now.

Many teachers in the UK were as sadistic at the time in my personal view, and they vented their own frustrations and repressions on the kids. I saw kids get slapped and punched and I even saw one given a fat and bleeding lip. Mark my words, it simply made us more resilient. There were no snowflakes back then.

In 1979, Pink Floyd wrote, *We don't need no education; we don't need no thought control. No dark sarcasm in the classroom, hey teacher leave those kids alone* in their epic album *The Wall*. Millions of kids could relate to that, and they still do.

Chess would therefore be my mental opiate; the living embodiment of disappearing down the rabbit hole. I played it in class, on the bus, in exams, in the toilets, in the playground, the chess club and in my room at home.

It would be the one thing I could turn to when the horrors of home life was raging around me. What a gift this was, from nowhere. Chess would never let me down. *She* would never let me down. Caissa had found a new recruit and I was a loyal and willing soldier – or crusader if you will.

Childhood

Children who are reared in homes of poverty have only two mealtime choices – take it or leave it

Anon

If childhood was a car, mine would be a Reliant Robin. I am reticent to talk about those days because they were mostly wretched. Such memories remain within me, quietly raging in the shadows. I am opening up now because it offers context as to how influential, if not critical chess has been, and remains in my life. Someone once told me that you have to know where you came from to know where you want to go.

I am not one to blame my childhood for things that I do or don't do today. As an adult we can make our own choices. Yet it is a fact that character when young is forged by the people you meet and the experiences you have. If you have a loving family, supportive friends and teachers, you are likely to be happy and grow intellectually and emotionally. A bit of money helps grease the wheels too. If you have one parent, no support and live in a violent, loveless, chaotic shithole then you are certainly going to be affected and life could take you down nefarious pathways. Luckily, some of us – and I am one – have enough strength of character to take all of the bad stuff and recycle it into something more positive. I stress though that I suppress a great deal – it does not disappear.

165 Grange Farm Drive in Birmingham. The house where I was born.

I was born at number 165, Grange Farm Drive in West Heath, Birmingham in February 1964. It was a council house and my grandparents, Sid and Rose lived there for many years. I have no idea why I was not born in hospital but I see from the records that the weather was mild but foggy. Information about my childhood is very sketchy, but I was actually born Carl Stephen Knight and my natural father's name was Frederick. I know nothing more than that. He left me and Mum before I could even walk, and I never saw him again.

My mother Sandra, was always ultra-defensive when I asked about him and she closed down any conversation immediately, stating that he went loopy and ended up in a mental institution. I have often wondered if that were true, and if so is his DNA responsible for some of my own character traits? However, since *Daddy* did a rain check on my life I will never know. I just know that I was born a jackdaw and I have never pretended to be an owl. Mark this though – I am actually an English Knight, and that is official.

31

I have never felt compelled to try to find Fred as I believe that you cannot miss what you never had. He might well have been locked away in a straitjacket, but he might also have been an inventor, I do not know, and I do not care. He wasn't there for his family – that's all there is to it. His actions say more about him than I ever could. I have one photograph of him holding me in his hands at Cofton Park. I was going to include that photograph in this book – but he doesn't deserve the space. Soon afterwards, he and Mum conceived my other blood brother Lawrence and then good old Fred disappeared (he did a Bobby Fischer – look him up). I always wondered what part, if any my mum played in the break-up. I shall never know.

My Mum in the late 1950's. She was attractive, intelligent and vibrant.

My mum was very intelligent, and she could complete a crossword in minutes. She was quite good-looking, and at some point dyed her hair blonde as many did back then. Her sense of humour was excellent and she had the most infectious love of, and almost supernatural connection with animals.

Another thing about Mum was, she taught me manners, and that has always served me well. She was especially keen to ensure that whenever I walked on a pavement with a member of the opposite sex, the lady walked on the inside, and the man walked nearest the oncoming traffic! That was the man's job – to protect. Please and thank you, the proper use of a knife and fork and to always carry a handkerchief. These were important lessons early on, and I am amazed to see how many people today eschew these basic niceties. Further, Mum taught me how to write properly. I did not need school for that – parents surely take more pride in teaching their own children how to accomplish this fundamental task.

The great city of Birmingham is where I grew up until the age of 12. I must have had an accent because people tell me they can hear it even now. My mum was as a single mother for many years and brought us up on a council estate in Northfield. I respect her for that. It was a rough area but as with many such places we could rely on a small but select group of people who helped out. We would be babysat by any number of strangers including *auntie Lesley* who wasn't our auntie at all but Mum's best mate.

There was no central heating, no television and no transportation. We walked everywhere and one of my earliest memories is stepping out with Mum on a freezing cold winter's day, somewhere near a red telephone box. We almost walked into it, because it was a tremendous pea souper of a day. The fog in those days seemed to be all pervasive, and it appeared every other day in winter.

You couldn't see the cracks in the broken and weed-infested pavements in front of you. I vividly recall the fog being punctuated by little red Chalwyn paraffin lanterns that used to hang from makeshift barriers that road maintenance workers had left. I used to gaze into the twinkling lights, lost in the cosy glow that the lamp contained within. I was shivering but mesmerized. It was warmer in those lamps than in my house – if only I could shrink and snuggle up inside one to get warm. I keep one at home today for nostalgia.

I can vaguely recall a couple of men appearing into Mum's life (not together!) and staying over at our house in Ingoldsby Road. One was called Rob and he was a lorry driver and he seemed nice, but he was not around for long. He had jet black hair smoothed down with lashings of Brylcreem. Unfortunately, Mum was one of those women who fell for barbaric men. Whether she liked the thrill of being around them or not I will never know.

At some point she must have had a liaison with a black man because my older brother Andrew was of mixed race. I say *was* because he died at a relatively young age. In those days he was referred to as 'half-caste' but these days the term 'mixed race' is apparently appropriate. It doesn't matter to me – he was always *Andrew* first before anything else. The problem these days is that we tend to judge people by a colour or religious persuasion before we even get to know the actual person. That's a pitiful social failing in my view, and it needs to stop. We should label jars, not people.

In any event Andrew and I always got on just fine and we grew up without any problem at all. Why shouldn't we? Having a *black* brother was never an issue and we never talked about it ever being one. True, there were some nasty things said to him at school (kids are cruel) but Lawrence and I defended

Andrew to the hilt of course, getting into some feral scuffles on his behalf. On one occasion a lad went way too far and called him a nigger, so we gave him a right good hiding I am afraid. Unsurprisingly, he never said anything about Andrew again.

Andrew and I had some great laughs and when people talk to me today about black issues I actually have a pretty good understanding. I must stress though that Andrew himself never ever considered himself to be a victim. He was admirably robust and could easily handle himself in a scrap. In his older years as an adult, he never once said to me, 'It's because I am black.' He just got on with life. Not everyone can do that, I understand but he certainly did.

He loved his music and I would hear him playing his cassettes on his little portable recorder in his bedroom. One day I heard these doom-laden chords emanating from his room. I ran in and asked him what it was. 'Electric Funeral' by Black Sabbath,' he replied. That was it, I was hooked. It just blew me away. He also loved playing 'Close to the Edge' by YES, 'Potato land' by Spirit and any Thin Lizzy that he could get his hands on.

I wonder now if he was influenced by their black front man Phil Lynott. I saw Black Sabbath live on 9th January 1982 at Bingley Hall in Stafford on the Mob Rules tour. It is the first live music I ever attended and it was orgasmic. When the band hit the stage to E5150 and Mob Rules, and the illuminated cross appeared before our heads I could have died of ecstasy right there. Tony Iommi smashed out the chords and they reverberated around my rib cage, as I was standing just a couple of yards from the stage. 'Jesus – what the hell is this?' I thought. Ronnie James Dio fronted the band then. Ozzy Osbourne had left for a solo career, but both were equally brilliant in their own way. I owe Andrew an unpayable debt for the music.

Aside from any issues he may have had regarding colour, I had my own abuse to deal with without a dad around, being called 'an illegitimate child' by the adults and a bastard son by the kids. As I said, kids are cruel. As an adult I came to realise that there is no such thing as an illegitimate child – only illegitimate parents, but it was a real stigma back then. I also dealt with the fact that no one ever came to school to a parents' evening for me, and the kids were quick to notice that.

Andrew died of alcoholism in August 2001 and Mum died of the same disease in September 2001. Both died in Shropshire. I never attended any of the funerals. I was living in Germany at the time and I recall being told very late and I had no time to get back and, in any event, JTB (read more later on) would be there and I was spoiling for a fight. I decided it would be best if I did not attend. I was still bloated with suppressed rage.

I never attended Sid's funeral either, but I did attend my nan's. They died within a short stretch of one another. Sid of cancer – he smoked like a chimney – and Rose literally died of a broken heart. I will never forget her burial. Nan was as old-fashioned as they come but very tolerant of new faces in her community especially the West Indians and Caribbean's with those tremendous accents and strange culinary delights. We marvelled at the linguistic complexities of some of the words.

Rose would have been delighted when on arrival at the cemetery we found the vicar to be of Jamaican origin and she was fantastic. I recall that it was pouring down with rain. She said some apt and lovely words for Nan and finished up looking at the heavens as we all got drenched. You have to imagine the next line in a Caribbean accent, but she closed with:

'I think Rose would agree that gettin' soaked out here is pointless and we would all be better off goin' inside and havin'a cuppa tea.'

Classic stuff. Nowadays everyone gets so uptight about racism but sometimes there are just light-hearted moments with no malice that show that our differences and cultures can be amusing and shared, and that they can bring us together all the more. Take note, society and stop getting so bloody uptight.

I miss them all of course and I have barely anyone left by way of family. They might as well have all died together in a plane crash. I still have my half-sister Fiona who is very precious to me. I cannot be bitter, because as I will reveal, I met some fantastic people through chess who acted (whether they knew it or not) as mentors and inspirational figures to me.

In essence Sid and Rose were the people I cared about the most as a kid and the ones who looked out for me and my brothers. Nan and Nandad (as we curiously called him) were the most decent and beautiful people I have ever met. Sid never swore once, and Rose was the same. She originated from Scotland and once professed to washing the shirts for Celtic Football Club. She said she pegged the shirts out on the line and neighbours had to pay her a penny to come and look at them.

She also used to get us on April Fool's Day each year telling us some crazy story. The best one was that a big black crow was in a pie in the oven. We rushed to look only to find out that we had been fooled yet again.

Sid would have his little phrases such as, 'Pennies to the poor

I fling, and pull them back on a piece of string.' He always chuckled at that one.

Friday nights were the best. Mum walked us through West Heath Park to Nan's house at Grange Farm Drive, where we would stay over, and we would have treats. Usually, we kids would have a chocolate bar – called a bar six. Nan would have a bottle of stout and a packet of chicken crisps. Then we would watch *Land of the Giants*, and if we were really good – *The Persuaders!* Roger Moore was good, and the women liked him, but I adored Danny (Tony Curtis) with his brown leather driving gloves, fast cars, sparkling eyes and enviable natural ability to be attractive to the opposite sex. I really wanted to be like Tony Curtis.

On the Saturday morning we would rush out of bed into Nan and Nandad's room. Sid was always up at 5am so Nan was always on her own in bed for a while. Sid shaved early every day. He was a tail gunner in the Second World War, so my uncle Terry (who was also in the RAF) tells me. Sid religiously wore a shirt and tie even at weekends. We would jump on the bed and cuddle into Nan as she drank her morning tea. Sid doted on her and would always say 'Rosy Lee (*tea*) Rosie?'

I never knew anyone drink as much tea as that man. He would consume quantities on a Brobdingnagian scale each and every day. The very act of making tea for his wife gave him immense pleasure.

Each summer he would take us blackberrying down *The Gulley* which was a narrow lane near the house. I still recall the smell of the various plants in the hedges and the sound of the bees going about their business, burying themselves deep into the blackthorn and wildflowers. On occasional warm and sunny Sundays, we would go for a walk to Kings Norton park. We would have fifty pence each and buy ice cream then go on the Helter-Skelter.

These were simple pleasures, but those moments were the best of my childhood and happened all too rarely. The highlight of it all was when Sid took us to The Mop Fair at Turves Green in Birmingham which is held every October. I was mesmerized by the coloured lights, the goldfish hanging in bags of water (a practice now almost disappeared, thankfully), the smell of candy floss and toffee apples and the big one – the pig roast on the spit. We never had any, but it was certainly something to see.

I have no idea what Mum did when we were dropped off at Nan's – and I don't wish to know. We were just happy when Friday night came and our time at Grange Farm Drive began.

Nan would cook us egg, chips and beans in her famous old chip pan. Bloody hell they were good. No, they were the best. She could cook a splendid Sunday roast too. Without all of that sustenance we would have been skeletal, it's quite true. My grandparents were that special breed of people who had nothing, yet gave us everything. They had one holiday every two or three years if they were lucky, spending a few days in Weston Super Mare where they would always bring back a plastic boat for us to play with in the bath. I can still smell the plastic on that boat. Just like with the chess sets, plastic seems to evoke differing memories. I am beginning to worry myself now!

Not that we had many baths. I can honestly say that there were occasions where we sat in the sink and had a wash down. I can still feel that now, really cold on the testicles, I can tell you. I mean, I must have been about four or five years old or

39

something, but it absolutely happened. On a Monday, Nan did the clothes washing using some dilapidated old mangle while we sang a few silly songs. The favourite was 'Congratulations' by Cliff Richard. I have always loved that tune. Nan would make up daft verses that would not rhyme and I would say 'Nan, that's not how it goes.' She would chuckle as she put her aching back into the mangle work. It was magic.

Nan and nandad (as we called him) in Birmingham in the 1970's

We had religion in our house, but it wasn't anything to do with God. It was football. My team was, and always will be Aston Villa. When you come from Birmingham you support Aston Villa or Birmingham City. It usually depends on what area you live in but also who gets to you first as a kid. My Uncle Terry and Nandad did that job. I would talk Villa with Sid for hours. Terry hated the blues, or *blue noses* as we affectionately call them. He sat me on his knee one day and showed me two posters. One was of the Blues team, (known also as *Small Heath* by Villa fans) and one of the Villa, or *The Vile* as the blue noses call us (are you following?).

He pointed to the Birmingham City one and said that if I ever came into the house with one of *those* shirts on I would get a good hiding. He pointed to the claret and blue shirts and said that this was the team I would be supporting from now on. He actually took me to my first Villa match (thanks for not being there *Dad*) which was at St Andrew's - the home ground of the enemy! We even went in the Blues end. He was absolutely crazy. We could not shout for fear of being beaten to a pulp but will never forget him saying to me, 'This is the enemy sunshine. This is what you are up against. Feel it. Listen to them. Animals they are.' He was almost frothing at the mouth.

I was scared shitless. I was a kid. Even worse, I distinctly recall being knocked over by a gigantic police horse outside the ground. Its breath stank and its eyes were bulging at me. Uncle Terry was furious. Anyway Villa won, of course, which made it all worth it.

My team play at Villa Park and the partisan part of the ground is called The Holte End. That's the only place to be, with almost 14,000 other people singing a song of unity – 'Holte Enders in the Sky.' It is sung to the tune of the Johnny Cash song, 'Ghost Riders in the Sky.'

I have been a true *Villan* since that day and as with any football fan I have had my fair share of tears of joy and despair. For the record, my favourite player has always been Andy Gray. He would put his head where angels would fear to tread, and he bagged lots of goals as a result. They don't make 'em like

Andy anymore. Villa have won every cup that a domestic club can – including the European Cup (now Champions League) in 1982. We are one of only five British clubs ever to win it. Are you listening Birmingham?

Some of my neighbours are Blues fans and I have particularly good sport with a chap called Kenton who gives every bit as good as he gets. He and his wife Nicola are the very best of people, as is their wider family, but football is football and when we discuss that – the gloves are off for us both. There's no love lost but we will be first to buy one another a pint of beer. In my view there is nothing wrong with tribal warfare and as a 'Holte Ender In The Sky' I will always stand with my claret and blue army. If you don't understand, don't worry, I am not seeking approval.

I really ought to mention that the current manager, Dean Smith was a boyhood Aston Villa fan and his father swept the terraces. Further, Smith is a chess player. Indeed, he was West Midlands school chess champion. There are many analogies between chess and football with tactics and strategy, attack and defence, psychology and preparation.

Do not forget that whilst footballers are individuals, they must work as a team. The same can be said for the chess pieces. They each have their own strengths and weaknesses and working together should bring out the very best of them. Unity is strength after all.

Finally I mention the concept of space. Of course, footballers crave this on the pitch and it is desirable in order to maximise possibilities. The same in chess; having space to play is very beneficial – and the question of how to 'make space' is a long and protracted one. If every Aston Villa player learned chess, perhaps we could once again become the kings of Europe. Leave me alone to dream will you please?

Now it is time to deal with the huge, scrofulous elephant in the room. The room of my childhood.

Mum met her next husband and my then (not only disowned but never owned) stepfather John Portman, or as I like to refer to him as *John the Bastard*. I shall refer to him as JTB from now on. When they met, we moved from Birmingham to a pretty but isolated little village in Shropshire called Kynnersley. I was twelve years old and it was 1976, the red-hot summer. We lived in a tied cottage because JTB was working on a farm.

A born psychopath, the man was a wife and child beater with a highly volatile temper, brought about by his lack of intelligence and self-respect. The coward was quick to punch and kick out, at one stage knocking several of my mother's teeth out and fracturing her jaw and arm. She occasionally had black eyes, swollen arms and bruises everywhere, saying each time that she had fallen. Of course we kids knew differently. When you are a few feet away from your mother getting punched and beaten but you are too young and weak to stop the assailant, the memory becomes a scar. I wanted to kill him, even when I was so young.

He hit me and Lawrence mostly, but I refused to cry. I remember kneeling on the floor once and I sneezed. JTB kicked me in the head for doing it. I told him that when I was older, and he was vulnerable I would kill him. That got another beating, but it felt bloody good to stand up for myself – and I have been doing so ever since, so I thank him for that. I can tolerate pain for myself, but when I see others being abused I start to get very upset, very quickly.

I despise bullies and have a special loathing for men who abuse women and kids. Mine was only ever physical violence, nothing sexual but it is abuse just the same. There were no helplines back then. No mobile phones. No counsellors. No one to talk to. You just got on with it. You either found a backbone or you crumbled. We are much more aware of abuse these days, and people do some incredible and much under-valued work to support victims of domestic violence. I take my hat off to them. These are the people who should get an OBE or such award.

Even today abused people slip through the safety net. Professionals can and sometimes do miss the signs. Kids still get beaten regularly and are half-starved. Women get raped and beaten. It happens under our very noses, maybe even next door to you. Sometimes society sees it and sometimes it chooses not to. I beg of every reader, if ever you suspect that someone is being mistreated, damned well challenge it. We raise money for kids in Africa yet the child next door to you might also be starving and injured. If you do not condemn it, you condone it.

Looking back I have always tried to go to the aid of any vulnerable person; especially those who are victims of an abuse of power. I would become an official Trade Union representative at work many years later just so that I could protect some of the team who were in my view being abused by bullying management. I just won't tolerate it.

In this respect I particularly related to the words of Reverend Edward Smith Ufford which said...

Throw out the lifeline across the dark wave;
There is a brother whom someone should save.
Somebody's brother! O who then will dare
To throw out the lifeline, his peril to share?

My childhood is really not something I blame when things go awry. Indeed, it taught me valuable lessons. I don't have to be that miserable bully – that loser. I can be whatever I choose to be. I can be a better person.

I do not remember a single happy Christmas with JTB around. I only recall one pathetic excuse for a camping holiday. Clarach Bay in Wales it was. Home life was dreadful. There were no hugs, no kisses and no one said they loved anyone – ever. Mum never even ate with us – she couldn't bear to. In the end she turned to alcohol, perhaps unsurprisingly. The village had one Working Men's Club and nothing else, not even a little shop.

A milk van delivered our eggs, bread and milk twice a week. A bus ran from the village to town (Wellington) on Thursdays and Saturdays and Mum would sometimes catch that. True she would return with some food but there was always plenty of alcohol and cigarettes in the carrier bags too. She worked behind the bar at the club and as the customers would often buy her drinks she quickly developed a taste for it.

Cider was the great favourite. We had barely any money, and I remember being hungry for much of the time, '*stealing*' bread occasionally from the cupboard. The slices had always been counted, and if there was one missing, or a bit out of one the good hidings would come from JTB. School dinners were my saviour, and without those I think I would have been seriously mal-nourished.

That is also why today in 2021 the footballer Marcus Rashford has my full support for demanding of politicians that kids have meals in schools and even during the holidays. It's a lifeline and I have been there. Kids really do go hungry in the UK today and it is not their fault. It is not just Africa that has hunger – it happens right here, today.

Although life at home was largely wretched, the introduction of chess shone a brilliant light in the darkness. Chess diverted my attention from the misery of violence and alcoholic rages, and I became immersed in a silent world of concentration. I was lucky to find a friend in the village in Jeremy Smith. He was just a bit older than me and we shared a deep love of football, playing as we did in his garden and the big field adjacent to his house. I also used to go round for the occasional game of chess with him. His house was much warmer than mine and the conversation was always fun. We have always loved farming (tractor and combine harvesters are brilliant, right?) and indeed he went off to America to be a combine harvester driver in the vast fields of Montana. We are back in one another's lives again now and share a love of photography in addition to many other subjects.

Back then it was all about chess. Two worlds had collided, my home battles and my chess battles. They could not have been more contrasting. I should say that I don't blame my mother. Who am I to ever know what she endured? But JTB will never be forgiven. He left her, of course when she needed help the most. He soon found another woman to control and abuse. His day of reckoning will come, and I want to be there. It seems cruel and grossly unfair that he still lives despite the passing of my mother, and just about everyone else. He did have two children with Mum. Jonathan was the golden boy and we have not spoken for decades.

Fiona is the only girl and the only family that I am still regularly in touch with today. She is a generous and gentle soul who sacrificed her own childhood looking after and nursing Mum when she was dying of alcohol poisoning over many months. While all the young girls were out playing Fiona was changing urine-stained bedding and watching over Mum who was skeletal and beyond reach in so many ways. She was still mischievous like the Mother of old, and her deep love of animals kept her going but too many of the lights had gone out. I could not reach her. I could not save her. No-one could.

Though I previously mentioned that Fiona is my half-sister, that is only in law. There is nothing half about her. She is my sister and that's an end to it. Mum decided that Fiona should be named after all of her aunties. It must be quite amusing for Fi when she is asked for her full name. It is Fiona Rosina Elizabeth Mary Ann. Very funny.

At some point, I don't know when, my name was changed from Knight to Portman. I don't know if Mum did this officially or not, but I resented it and still used Knight for a while. After all, there are knights in chess, so it was an appropriate name for me. I have often toyed with the idea of reverting to my birth name, but both the Portman and the Knight men were losers. Maybe I will change it one day to something weird like *Chessman*. Yes, *Carl Chessman* sounds fine to me. Maybe I should just have one name like Sting or Prince. I wonder what that name would be? Boomslang, I quite like that.

I lived at Kynnersley from age twelve until I was sixteen (almost seventeen) when I suddenly left home. I did so not because of the violence, but for a completely different reason. Life, like chess, presents us with unexpected moves and we have to make decisions about how we respond.

At school I never sought or wanted a girlfriend. I was not interested in girls. The best sex education lesson I ever had was observing the monkeys in the enclosure at the West Midlands Safari Park. The two loves of my life were chess and football. There was simply no time for anything else. I did fancy a couple of gorgeous girls in my class, but I was never going to ask any of them to go out with me, so to speak. I had a fear of rejection with girls. If I did not ask, they could not refuse. That negative attitude cost me in my formative years but that's another story.

Anyhow, whilst at home in Kynnersley one day at the age of sixteen just after I left school, there was a knock at the door. It was a woman who lived in the village. She was about thirty-four years of age, had one young child, and she was going through a divorce. She was blonde, and very attractive. She had to go to a business meeting in Shrewsbury urgently. Could my brother Lawrence babysit her son until she returned?

'Carl will do it; he is the oldest brother home at the moment,' said Mum.

So up to the lady's house I went and that night would change my life. Bear in mind that I had never even been out with a girl at this point in my life. No heavy petting, no French kissing – none of it. What a shock to my system – not to say my hormone levels then when she arrived home, went upstairs and then came back down in a black basque and suspenders.

My eyes were not the only things on stalks. Sex is an animal instinct. Despite the fact that we humans are weak and feeble when we are born, when the moment comes for our first sexual coupling we instinctively know what to do – or I did anyway! I had read about foreplay. I heard a joke on TV once where a working-class bloke from Yorkshire tried to explain it. He said, 'I just tell the wife, brace yourself Effie, I'm coming in dry.' That was foreplay he said.

I knew from a young age that there was more to it than that. Take your time they said. Explore each other's bodies they said. Yes, right. Well, they did not have this woman to contend with! When you are sixteen, foreplay lasts for about five minutes and you just want to release the tension as quickly as possible.

I will spare the gory details, but I was seduced within the hour and lost my virginity. I had in the space of sixty minutes transformed from a boy to a man, in my own mind at least - and I threw away my beloved Subbuteo football figures just to prove it. Everyone remembers their first time but my second was more memorable. The woman had an MGB GT and I got the gearstick stuck somewhere I shouldn't. Life had certainly changed. This woman had given me wings and I was flying high. It is only as we get older that we appreciate the subtle notion that the chase is very often much better than the catch.

Mum gave me an ultimatum that in effect was never going to be anything other than a one-way ticket. Stop seeing this woman or move out of the house. What kind of a choice was that? Testosterone was my new master, and it drove me to the brink of madness, as it does with teenagers. The ultimatum was no threat to me but an opportunity to leave 2 Kynnersley and the grief behind forever. I packed a bag immediately, leaving most of my few belongings in my bedroom (which anyway I

49

had to share with one of my brothers) and I never looked back, literally. I was in love, or so it felt. I was invincible.

The trouble is, when you are a teenager, your decisions are often not made in your head, they are made in your pants. You need someone to be there to advise, guide and support you when you are throbbing with testosterone. All I had was chess but then again that was all I wanted. Well, that and sex. Preferably more of the latter. I was young and as energetic and crazed as a puppy. I thought that I could never be unhappy again.

I was wrong.

School and chess

Looking happy in my Charlton School uniform in 1979.

Charlton School was a damned good school in the 1980s. The teachers cared about the pupils and they worked hard. For my first year we had a headmistress called Mrs. Rafferty. She wore a lot of pink, had purple and blue hair at some stage and walked a ferocious-looking bulldog around the school. She reminded me very much of Mrs. Slocombe from *Are You Being Served?*. She was replaced by Roy Tromans. He was a dead ringer for Herbert Lom, the actor. Some thought he was okay, and others painted him as, 'A complete bastard and I hope they name a public bog after him' if you read the rather unflattering comment on Twitter.

He was definitely autocratic, and sometimes patronising and condescending, but he played chess, so I liked him. Indeed, he used the acronym CHES as the school motto. It means *Courtesy*, *Honesty*, *Endeavour* and *Self Discipline*. I was always annoyed that he never added another 'S' on the end, so as to properly complete the word chess. What about *Self-control* or something like that, I thought. Anyway, he always played the same chess opening if he could, the ultra-sharp Max-Lange attack. The first few moves are as follows. 1. e4 e5 2. Nf3 Nc6 3. Bc4 Nf6 4. d4 exd4 5. O-O Bc5 6. e5 d5 7. exf6 dxc4 which is uncompromising, and quite frankly a little mad.

Perhaps chess players do play in the style of their own character after all. Looking back to my school days I can honestly say that I enjoyed it, probably because it took me away from home, thus I could eat some decent food (I loved sponge pudding with hundreds and thousands on the top of the icing), see friends, play chess and be safe. I was a fairly attentive, enthusiastic kid and I did not get into much trouble at all. A few scuffles here and there maybe, but never any detentions, not once. Some say I was never caught.

I must remark though that one of the downsides to having no help, encouragement or support at home, was that I did not do as well at school as I should have. This can have a big impact on a child's life. I still have my school reports and I showed them to my wife recently. Bottom of the class at mathematics, but top of the class at English. Why so? My honest view is that my almost-retired maths teacher seemed to have lost her lustre, whereas my English teacher - Mrs. Davies - was brilliant and shiny. She was enthusiastic, encouraging and challenging. We studied *Cider with Rosie* and *Fahrenheit 451* which introduced me to literature and fuelled my imagination.

I cannot just blame or praise teachers. Even at a young age we still have some responsibility for ourselves. Kids can often wind teachers up. I like to think I never did this, but who knows. Teachers have a very difficult job so I bear no malice.

I loved words, and I never liked figures. I was afraid of numbers and triangles and graphs and the X and Y axis. And just what is the point of algebra? I have never had to use it in my adult life. What is the use of algebra when you are driving a tractor, cleaning out a monkey enclosure, throwing a rugby ball or operating a ski-lift? I still shudder even though years later I passed examinations in accountancy and quantitative studies at degree level, first time! I did it to prove to myself that I could. Once again I refer to chess. If at first you don't succeed, set up the pieces and try again.

I admire people who are good at maths and the world needs them, but it is just not for me. People say that you have to be good at maths to play chess. I refuse to subscribe to that school of thought. It's nonsense so if you are bad at maths don't worry about it – just play chess and have fun. If you are good at maths then play chess and do some long division, just to keep your hand in.

I spent too much time looking out of the window apparently and I always 'had the potential to do so much better,' if only I wanted to. In my haste to be first to finish and to please I made mistakes. I was apparently a pleasant lad, who could do better. I missed countless days at school, not because of truancy, which

I never committed once but because I stayed home. This did not help my education.

Either Mum was too pissed to help me get ready or perhaps there was a bruise or two that would be too visible. The school bus came and went many times and I wished I had been on it. Instead, I stayed home in the gloomy house. Mum would sleep all afternoon and leave a note telling me what time I had to wake her up. 'Wake me up at five and no noise,' was the regular note.

At home one day, I had a massive fight with Lawrence (we were like Cain and Abel) and as he hid in the toilet after punching me in the face I went after him in an incendiary rage. The door was half panelled with opaque glass and I guessed where his face was. I smashed my fist through the window connecting beautifully with his chin which almost knocked him out. Unfortunately, as I drew my arm back a huge shard of broken glass tore into my wrist and cut it open at the main arterial vein.

The blood began spurting out in a crimson fountain. Mum was out cold in bed in another alcoholic daze as I ran to her squirting hot blood all over her face. She managed to tourniquet my wrist and a neighbour got me to hospital in his rusty old pick-up truck. There was blood all over the house, which by now looked like a murder scene. I lost a lot of blood that day and frightened myself and Mum. She went berserk at us for fighting again and I had several stitches in my wrist and my arm in a sling. She made me go to school the next day *as punishment* but there was a game on at the chess club, so I was where I wanted to be anyway! More chess please. Incidentally, I still have a fine arrowhead scar on my wrist to remember that day. As for Lawrence, I got my own back, smashing a beer glass on his head. We were never meant to like one another, and we never will. You cannot choose your family after all.

Glenn Wood was my best pal at school. We were in the same class throughout the years and we both played football together, although our choice of teams was totally incongruent. We should really have been enemies. He supported Wolverhampton Wanderers whilst I was blessed of course to follow the mighty Aston Villa. In sporting terms, we were probably *frenemies* as the word goes today. If he had been a blue nose we would never have stayed friends. Shout out to our form teacher, Mrs. Nelson who helped nurture our friendship by having us sit together in lessons. She could see that we were good for one another.

We both loved chess and we were fiercely competitive. Our games became personal challenges, school term after school term. We asked no quarter and we certainly gave none, ever. We even played chess in our end of terms exams – passing a piece of paper back and forth with the moves written on. We also swapped football cards in one exam. I needed the German goalkeeper Sepp Maier and Glenn had him in his collection. I cannot remember what I gave him for Sepp (who is a legend) but I think I had to submit two cards in exchange.

Glenn would leave school to join the Royal Navy. He was excellent at maths and I think he worked with radar systems or something. I met him once many years later and we went out to paint the town red. He ended up painting my foot yellow and green as he vomited over it after drinking way too much. I thought it was most unedifying and we never kept in touch after that.

My other big friend was Paul Myers. He lived in the village next to mine – Preston upon the Weald Moors - and we played chess on the school bus morning, noon and night. I still have the pocket set that we used. We had some tremendous games too, and we passed countless hours on four wheels enjoying the royal game.

We kept ourselves to ourselves, always sitting in the middle of the bus. The back seat was *owned* by the bus bully and his acolyte mate. I shall refrain from printing his full name here, but it was Stuart. Each day he would send his knucklehead pal down the bus to call someone to the back to be *duffed up* as they say. Paul Myers and I were largely left alone until one day there was a tap on my shoulder.

'Portman, it's your turn. Get to the back of the bus.'

'Leave me alone' I said, 'I just want to play chess.'

'Chess is for dicks – get to the back of the bus.'

The clown wasn't having it and he insisted that I go, or it would be worse for me. Honestly, I never caused any trouble at school, but I tell you, I had enough hidings at home and this prat wasn't going to have his share as well. I knew instantly what I was going to do. There was no backing down. There was only a single course of action to take. I gave the chess set to Paul and told him I would be back in a minute. He looked worried but I told him with a smile not to be.

I walked to the back and sat down next to Stuart.

'Are you ready for this?' he said.

I did not even answer him. Chess teaches us that the element of surprise can be the difference between winning and losing. I immediately let fly with my fists in a rapid-fire succession into his rib cage and stomach – knocking the stuffing out of him.

He was stunned. I carried on, pouring my pent-up rage upon him. I felt unstoppable as the red mist fell, and he never even had the chance to hit me back. Not once. It felt good – worryingly so. I must have landed fifteen or twenty blows when he gasped, 'okay, that's enough now.'

It was too late. I had the bloodlust. I felt massive, stronger with every punch. I carried on with a few more for good measure – by now totally enraged. I felt like I could really damage him, and I stopped. He was lucky that day. I remember saying something like:

'If you ever call me, my mate or anyone else on this bus to the back seat again I will smash your face in, okay, you cowardly little shit?'

He agreed sheepishly. 'That goes for you too,' I said to knucklehead who was sitting on the seat in front, equally stunned. When it was Stuart's turn to get off the bus he could barely move. He never asked anyone to the back again to my knowledge, and he kept well-away from the *boring* chess players. I was so proud of myself and I think the chess players were elevated in the eyes of the schoolkids. Kudos.

When I got home I told Mum what happened. She gave me a right roasting for fighting, but added that she was proud of me for sticking up for myself. I wasn't hard, I was just mad and nothing would stop me teaching that bully a lesson. I think she knew that I had to react in such a way. This was the beginning of my policy on standing up to bullies of all forms whether at home, school or work. Bullies are cowards, it's as simple as that. If you are being bullied, the only course of action is to stand up to them. If they take your dinner money on Monday, they will be back on Tuesday so stand straight and look 'em in the eye. You are much more courageous than you think. Trust me, you really are.

Back to the school chess club where the magic began. It was now my second home. That geography room, adorned as it was with maps of the world, weather system chart and storeroom full of chess equipment was a haven. The very act of taking my opponent's pieces and of checkmating someone gave me a real and lasting sense of accomplishment. Mind you I got beaten enough times too, and I wasn't so keen on that. Defeats tend to linger in the mind, sometimes for weeks, months and years.

Occasionally, a lost game can have such a devastating impact that you never forget it. I had to learn how to bounce back after disappointment and loss. Chess is painfully brutal. You are on your own with your feelings. Some people walk away and don't play again because defeat is too painful. Some kids have even committed suicide.

Mr. Lenton ensured that we could play in an orderly way, learning how to think and not to speak in the quietness of the room. Because of chess I improved at geography. I studied the maps of the world to see where chess began in India and Persia, moving to the Middle East and Europe. I could soon picture a map of the world in my mind, which helped in my exams. Chess was also helping me remember things. I had to recall chess openings (or suffer the consequences), and this was an instantly transferable skill. My mind was getting better at retaining information. I even improved a little at maths!

I cannot remember from where I obtained my first chess set, but I did have a plastic set and fold up board. I also bought a book, from a shop called John Menzies in town. I still have that book today. It was *Chess* by R.F Green which was first published in 1889 but I had the 1975 edition. When I read the introduction to that little tome I was hooked on chess literature. He stated:

It (chess) has emancipated itself from every social restriction and surmounted every national custom and prejudice; it has survived every political change and every distraction of fashion and is, today, more widely known and practiced than any other game in the world. Who, in view of these facts, making the slightest claim to culture, can afford to neglect it?

Chess has no barriers to background, gender, (dis)ability, age etc, and it really is a cultural pursuit. One can play it anywhere in the world as it speaks one language. I quickly grasped the rudiments of the game, at least the rules. Chess is easy to learn but you will never master it because it is so complicated. There are millions of possibilities, and you cannot anticipate everything that your opponent will do. Try to accept that your chess should be fun and that you can aspire to improve. Forget any ideas about mastering it. You won't. You cannot *decide* to become a Grandmaster either. That requires hard work, commitment and talent and even then, there are no guarantees and success, like life – isn't linear.

We had a school chess ladder where you challenged the people immediately above you – up to three places. I began at the very bottom and had a burning desire to get to the very top, I wanted to be the best player. I wanted to prove to myself that I could do something better than anyone else. Someone would be proud of me – if not myself then maybe Mum.

I am referring to the years 1976 to 1980 here. Back then, in

Kynnersley we had a rented television where you had to insert 50p in the meter box on the back to watch anything. A few hours passed before time ran out and then *boof* – the 'telly had gone' as we used to say. A man would visit every few weeks to empty it and we got a rebate of a few pounds – which was immediately spent on cider and cigarettes for Mum and JTB.

The absolute highlight of the week for me was watching a chess programme called *The Master Game* on the BBC. Actually, it was a series, running from 1975 to 1981, and miraculously there seemed to be no opposition to me watching it. At the time, it was the world's only televised international chess tournament and it seemed primitive by today's standards with the pieces being moved by a man in black gloves using some kind of glass table and mirror system. Yet it was a very popular programme and it served as nourishment for my soul. As long as I could watch that, I could handle anything that life threw at me. It was my language, my world.

There were top British masters such as Nigel Short, Tony Miles, Jon Speelman, John Nunn, and George Botterill. The latter incidentally smoked a rather splendid pipe. The foreign contingent included Vlastimil Hort, Viktor Korchnoi, Bent Larsen, Jan Hein Donner, Walter Browne and my hero Anatoly Karpov – who was at the time the reigning world champion. William Hartston was an excellent commentator (and player) and decades on would be the co-inventor of the TV programme *Gogglebox*.

I particularly relished the 1977 Master Game final where Karpov played Tony Miles who was a fellow Brummie (a slang name for a person originating from Birmingham) and Karpov won it in the third game after the first two were drawn. There was some controversy in the endgame when during terrible time trouble Karpov had promoted a pawn to a queen but there was no extra queen to hand, so they played on just using the pawn as a queen. This is not allowed under chess rules and technically the game could have been stopped but it wasn't and Karpov won it. Here is the final position.

It looks weird to have a pawn on the first rank but remember it is a queen, and therefore Black is checkmated.

In any event this was a fine effort from the Englishman. He would go on to secure a world-famous victory against the almost invincible Karpov at a tournament in Sweden in 1980 with what looked like an insulting opening played by a beginner. He replied to the first move of 1.e4 with the ludicrous looking 1… a6. Karpov must have been shocked. So shocked that he never recovered, and he lost the game. Commentators went mental, and they wanted to call the opening the Birmingham Defence but it was eventually christened the St. George Defence.

I learned a tremendous amount about chess from that series. When to attack and when to wait. When to swap off pieces and when not to. When and where to castle. I improved my opening and endgame knowledge also and tried all sorts of tricks back at school, sometimes with excellent results and sometimes with awful ones. The difference was, the likes of Grandmaster Nigel Short understood strategy.

He was playing chess but I was only making moves. There is a world of difference. He saw the bigger picture, but then he was a prodigy. I was still being potty trained by comparison, but it did not diminish my enjoyment of the game one jot. I knew then that I should strive to be a first-class chess version of myself, not a second-class version of someone else, who may or may not be a grandmaster.

Some of the Master Game series can be purchased on DVD and I recommend that chess fans obtain a copy. This is history. Some of the episodes have been lost by the BBC much to my chagrin. There was one other game that stuck in my mind from the final series in 1981. The controversial American Walter Browne played Argentinian Miguel Quinteros in a fantastic swashbuckling game where the South American put both of his bishops *en-prise* (able to be taken) in a Sicilian Najdorf (Poisoned Pawn) game. Somehow that game was drawn but it was one of the best fighting draws I had ever seen. I remember thinking, 'If this is what chess could be like then I have a very long way to go, but I am going to enjoy the journey.'

Back then in 1981, I didn't have enough understanding of the game to know how to improve in a disciplined way. There were no chess coaches, and no computers to use, so I did what everyone else did and learned from books, magazines, newspaper articles and other stronger players. Naturally, the school chess teacher Mr. Lenton helped, but he had a big class to deal with and face-to-face time was very limited.

I became utterly spellbound with chess personalities from the past. They all had such fantastic names. Who were they? How did they get so good at chess? We never learned this amazing stuff in class. Some of the people sounded other-worldly. The likes of Eugene Alexandrovich Znosko-Borovsky (1884-1954), Efim Dmitriyevich Bogoljubov (1889-1952), Saviely Grigoryevich Tartakower (1887-1956) and Aaron Nimzowitsch (1886-1935), held me captive on many an evening. A chess book became as dear to me as any object possibly could be. It was a bible, a resource, a mystery, an adventure, and I could disappear inside its pages. I was never so happy, to feel so totally alive as when I was looking at chess books.

I gradually worked my way up the chess club ladder and became one of the stronger players. However, there were still others to try to beat. Glenn and I were about the same strength and we could beat one another on any given day. Then there was Andy Knight and a lad called Ivan Watkiss. Standing above all was Gary Cook. He was the best player and was winning the school championship at will. Despite several efforts I could not knock him off his perch and there was only one term remaining before I had to leave school as a sixteen-year-old in 1980. I had one more opportunity to stand on top of the pedestal. Yet how was I to do it? The answer was to be found almost literally on my very own doorstep.

Home life aside, I loved living in Kynnersley. I enjoyed

woodland walks, cycle rides (using someone else's borrowed bike) and strolling in the fields talking to the cows – which was very therapeutic. Yet in the village there was something else that caught my eye, and only after dark. There was a big house at the top of the road called Crown House. Late at night, set against an inky black sky, I could often see a single light shining in a small window. It emanated from an Anglepoise lamp under which a lone figure sat toiling away studying something, head in hands for hours on end. Who was he and what was he doing?

I made it my business to find out and I befriended his brother Meyrick with whom I have enjoyed a lifelong friendship. He went to Eton College and I went to a secondary school but the beautiful thing about our friendship was that none of that mattered. There was no elitism, no snobbery, and no jostling for position. We were just best mates.

He would write to me from Eton College telling me about his latest escapades. They got the matron's dog drunk on gin, made poison darts, and even drove a hovercraft over a field. Nothing was beyond Meyrick. We got into all sorts of mischief back in Kynnersley. One time we had catapults made from tractor tyres which we strapped around our waists. They were huge things that operated like the old Roman ballista. They could take half a brick. Once, we did a joint lobbing and two huge rocks hurled onto the top of a neighbour's roof, bringing slates crashing down.

'Fucking hell, we better scarper,' Meyrick would say. Funny how Carl always got the blame. I mean Meyrick went to Eton, he could not possibly do such terrible things could he? It will have been that Brummie secondary school ingrate. Yeah, right! Don't judge people by their upbringing and education I say.

Meyrick tragically passed away during the writing of this memoir after a tremendous fight against cancer. He was only fifty-six years of age. He was born in the same year, just three weeks later than me. I attended his funeral virtually via computer, because the Covid regulations did not allow me to attend. He was cremated and I wept when the music played to see him through the final curtain to the Summerland. It was 'Shine on you crazy diamond' by Pink Floyd. This was poignant because it was the song that Meyrick and I used to sit and listen to as kids. It was our favourite. He knew damned well that I would hear it one last time with him.

Remember when you were young?
You shone like the sun
Shine on, you crazy diamond

Goodbye dear friend.

I always thought that I would go before him (I choose 'Jerusalem' for my final song) and my dear ones seem to be disappearing all around me. These are the people who helped forge my own character. Surely, we are all a reflection of the friends that we choose. Am I to be the last man standing? I don't want to be old and alone – it is my one remaining fear. Surely I would have the courage to pull the plug if it got desperate? Who knows? All I know is the fact that I am losing more of the people I love and cherish. Worse still, unless I die first there's more of it to come.

I write more eulogies than I do best man speeches these days. Death and the resulting loss to all is brutal. It is unremitting, horrifying and totally unavoidable. With every year that passes the reaper throws his grenades ever closer as he walks towards me. Well, sod him. Not yet. Not yet!!

It was Meyrick's brother John, who was the lone figure in the window. His surname is Cox. Yes, John Cox, the chess master. He lived in my little village at the arse end of nowhere! I couldn't believe it. Talk about serendipity. John also learned his trade from books and magazines because as I say, you did your own work then without a chess database. I recall that John studied endgames for hour upon hour.

He repeated practicing chess endings until the patterns were well and truly memorised. John is now an International Master (IM) but back then he was a FIDE Master (FM) which is one level below. FIDE (Fédération Internationale des Échecs) is the organization that runs chess and awards titles. I say *awards,* but they have to be earned to a strict system which involves playing others of a certain strength. If you want a title you will have to beat stronger players. In essence to get to a Grandmaster you have to have been a FIDE Master and International Master first, and only when you can compete with (and beat) players at grandmaster level do you have the chance to become one yourself.

John was absolutely brilliant with me, and we soon became friends. I would have been a complete patzer (weak player) to him, but he always found time to patiently answer my questions. He often played the English Opening and I studied this for a while hoping to play a bit like him. This choice is one of positional chess, not aiming for quick wins, but playing the longer game. I was amazed when he moved pieces backwards and I thought he was retreating. Only years later when I improved at chess did I realise that he wasn't retreating at all

– he was merely attacking from a different direction as skillful players do.

Chess is a tremendously difficult game and any player who wishes to seriously improve must make sacrifices, and I don't just mean at the board. There is no way around this. One of the greatest sacrifices is time. One has to give up vast chunks of time to study and John did this diligently and willingly. In the early 1980s he had played and beaten the then World Champion Anatoly Karpov in a simultaneous exhibition, and he beat Grandmaster Leonid Shamkovich at Lloyds Bank Masters in 1981. John is also a former British U-18 Champion. I was (and remain) full of admiration for him, and he has always been down to earth and approachable. Mind you – he is an Arsenal fan so he is not quite perfect!

I asked John to help me with some chess ideas to play in my forthcoming battle at the school chess club. I was determined to beat Gary Cook who just needed a draw to take the title. John was kind enough to look at some openings with me, and we did so whilst listening to 'Armed Forces' by Elvis Costello and The Attractions which is an album John very much enjoyed. I particularly liked the elephants on the cover. John's sage advice made me feel for the first time like someone was on my side, in my corner. Of course, I had to sit there and play the moves myself against Gary Cook – no one could do that for me, but it was so useful to have some ideas to take to the board. I felt prepared.

Thus it was that on 18th March 1980 the battle began. I cannot begin to tell you how important this game was to me. For one thing, Gary was a prefect, as was my pal Glenn, but not me. I paid a price for not attending school often enough or maybe because I was just not clever enough. However, I could forge my own pathway to glory and become the school chess champion of which there was only one. The champion won school honours and was therefore awarded a special tie to wear. Even prefects could not touch you if you wore one of those.

It was a very exclusive club, and it is hard at a young age not to think of the prize, which then influences performance. I wish I had the knowledge and (at least some of the) wisdom of my later years. I know now that one should never focus on the money – play the game and if you do that the prize will take care of itself.

I admit that I was nervous. Just as I never asked a girl out for fear of rejection, I did not want to think about how rejected I would feel if I did not win this title.

Gary was not only a fine chess player, but a lovely lad and we had great respect for one another. We had played many friendly games and by now he was only a little better than me. The chess club was buzzing in those years. Mr. Lenton had developed it so that being a member was quite cool.

One of the girls in my class even began talking to me about chess and I think she quite liked me. Unfortunately, it wasn't the girl that I fancied, and she had a big shock of frizzy hair that reminded me of Leo Sayer, and it scared me, quite frankly. Imagine kissing that girl, I thought – I could get lost in that jungle. She started to get a bit too *full-on* for my liking and I avoided her at all costs.

I started to wonder if we were going to have one of those 'You show me yours and I will show you mine' moments but thankfully it never came to that. Anyway, I had already been there, showing Karen Whittingham my *pixie lamp* when I was twelve years old at Preston school just before I went to the big school. I took a quick glance at what she had before running off, giggling.

I was White in the game and I opened with my king's pawn. I played 1.e4. Gary replied with 1...c5 and we entered the Sicilian Defence, indicating that he was ready for a fight. This is an aggressive and combative opening and it is extremely sharp. The gloves come off right at the start. The battle was on.

As the game continued, the other chess club members looked on in silence. All too soon, lunch-time was over, but we had not finished. Indeed, at that very point after thirty-three moves we were dead level. All Gary needed was that draw so he tried hard to exchange queens to make the job easier. The queen is the most powerful piece on the board. I had to win the game, so a draw was not enough. I had to keep the queens on but moving her away could be worse than exchanging her. What to do?

We both wrote the position down, as did Mr. Lenton, and the game would resume the next day. I went home that night, playing Paul Myers on the school bus. He had been watching the game, but we never spoke about it. He knew I would not do so until it was over. That night I got my chess set out and started studying the adjourned position. No-one needed to make a sealed move[1] so I was free to select what I wanted. This was the position.

---

1   A sealed move is one that has to be written down and sealed in an envelope prior to the game resuming. That move is binding on the player but it is not known to the opponent

It is a level game. Today with the use of powerful chess software one can put this position into the computer and it will tell you that as it stands the armies are equal. The engine wants to play the white knight to the e7 square giving check or even exchange queens. Back in 1980 we just used our little grey cells.

The computer suggestion would have been no good to me. I needed to win. What would John Cox do? He would work at the position. I burned hours into the night on the position and decided on a plan. It was risky but as they say in Russia the man who does not take risks never gets to drink the champagne. Again, I had to suppress dark thoughts of failure. I have since learned that the only failure is if we don't begin something. I knew that failure was part of life but I did not want it to be this time because I would not get another opportunity to be school champion. It quite literally was now or never. I needed this in my life.

I was going to set a trap. I wondered if Gary would be looking at the position seriously or would he just have thought it was going to end in a draw? In the position shown Black has two bishops on a very open battlefield which is very powerful. Material is level but who is trying to do what? White has two horrible, doubled pawns in the centre but some activity too. What would Gary expect me to do? He would select two or three obvious moves, but I knew there was no way he would look at the one I was going to choose.

I went to sleep with the position buried deep within my head. Caissa had truly blessed me with this game but cursed me too. I remember my nerves that next morning whilst in class studying history. For some reason we were being taught about Adolf Hitler and the fact that he was born in 1889 in Austria.

I was thinking, how come a man from Austria presided over Germany? How come he wanted blue-eyed blonde people to be the master race, but he had dark eyes, black hair and the most ridiculous moustache I had ever seen. It is right that young people should be curious and ask questions.

Apparently, the teacher's answer of 'stop asking questions Portman' was not really helpful for my learning.

My mind wandered back to chess, and lunchtime was soon upon us. Gary and I arrived at the club and shook hands. I think we both felt the pressure. I had respect for him but also a tremendous inner belief that I could win the game. Would my trap work? If it didn't and I lost I had no idea how I would react. Mr. Lenton called for quiet as a few ruddy-faced urchins arrived to see the bloodbath, and he told us to begin. I exchanged a quick glance with Gary and then played my move.

34.Qb1!?

Yes, my queen went to b1 and in chess terms the exclamation mark and question mark after the move signify that it is *interesting* but not necessarily good. This move was as much about psychology as calculation. Both are important in chess. Gary raised an eyebrow, almost imperceptibly. I knew then that he had not considered this move. I had guessed his next move in the context that all he needed was a draw so he was likely to try to offer the queen exchange again.

He ruminated for what seemed like a lifetime, then reached out and picked up his queen, placing it on b5. Bloody hell, he's played it. He failed to see the danger and walked into my trap. I took the queen off immediately, and he recaptured the queen with his bishop. He missed my next move – the one I had studied under the light of the bedroom door (I kid you not) at home the night before.

I played my rook to b1.

Gary rocked back. He had to lose one of his glorious bishops. He couldn't save them both. The game continued 36...Bc4 37.Rxb6 Bxd5+ 38.Bg2 Bxg2+ 39.Kxg2 and then totally flustered he committed his final sin and played 39...Rd5 attacking the knight. I replied immediately with 40.Ne7+ forking his king and rook, winning the latter. He played 40...Kf7 obviously not seeing my next move which was 41.Nxd5 and Gary resigned. We shook hands and he said 'Well done' which was typical of him.

I did it! I was the school chess champion.

This was the first time in my life that I had achieved something truly special. When I stood on stage at assembly and received the massive chess trophy (engraved with my name of course) and the honours necktie I could not have been prouder.

In a sense, that moment has never been eclipsed. I was allowed to take the trophy home for one day to show Mum and she was as pleased as punch.

I gave the silverware a seat of its own on the school bus next to me and Paul Myers and even the bus driver congratulated me. I think the penny dropped then that if I worked at something, results would come. I put the trophy up by the telly for the night and stared at it as if to say to JTB, 'you'll never win anything in your life, you loser.'

I lost that priceless necktie a long time ago. I believe Lawrence destroyed it. He hated me having anything. I was often invited back to Charlton School by Mr. Lenton to give simultaneous displays against the chess club of the day. It was an honour and a thrill to do so. I even played in a wheelchair after having a broken leg. This was my way of giving something back to the Charlton School chess club.

There were other memorable moments in the chess class, such as the first time I actually beat the teacher, and playing against former British Champion Alan Phillips in a simultaneous exhibition at the school. I lost but enjoyed the game and he was very

A broken leg never stopped me giving a simul for the kids. You play chess with the brain, after all.

73

nice about it. I will always be indebted to John Lenton. I think he knew how difficult my home life was and he knew that chess was my escape.

He drove me (and the chess team) to away games in the school's league and we visited Shrewsbury school and had tea and cake – something I never did at home. It was lovely. It was exciting. Chess was opening doors to new people and places and broadening my mind. At some point, Mr. Lenton asked if I wanted to go to a proper chess club – one that had adults as well as youngsters. Of course, I said yes. I do recall that he took me there for the first visit. It was GKN Sankey chess club, in Shropshire. This would be a sacred church for me over the next few years.

TELFORD JOURNAL THURSDAY, JUNE 14, 1990   5

Chess player Carl Portman (26) (centre right) visited Charlton School in Wellington to play 15 simultaneous games of chess with the Charlton Chess Club. Carl, secretary of the Coddon Chess Club and a former Charlton pupil takes part in these challenges to help promote chess to youngsters within the county. The club is pictured with deputy head Mr John Lenton (centre left).

Giving a simultaneous exhibition at my old school in 1990.
John Lenton, who taught me chess is standing next to me.

As a twelve/thirteen-year-old I was still a kid, and I used to get various lifts to the club in the early days but not very often. Some of the club members were extremely kind. Every Friday I would enter the big glass double doors to be greeted by the sights and smells of the club. I could always smell stale beer and cigarettes which was not surprising since they had a bar – but there was a games machine to the right, in one corner.

Readers of a certain age will remember when Space Invaders first arrived on the market. This primitive but totally compulsive game with its flashing lights, little green monsters and strange sounds when the gun was firing kept me enthralled and I just had to play it every time before I ascended the next flight of steps into the chess club room.

I always bought a glass of pop and a bag of crisps. I learned that GKN stood for *Guest, Keen and Nettlefolds* and the club was used chiefly for workers at their factory but the chess players came from all backgrounds. GKN could be traced back to 1759 and the industrial revolution, working in tooling and component manufacturing. The club had substantial sturdy wooden chess boards which I always used to set out early to get merit marks with the adults – another case of me thinking ahead. The pieces were plastic, which was a shame.

There were some formidable characters and I remember Alan Knight who always smoked a pipe at the board. He was a super aggressive and most excellent player. Lou Prescott was in his eighties and could recite Shakespeare at leisure. He too smoked a pipe and when I played him there were half spent matches all over the table and the board. His hands were not steady and sometimes I could barely see him through the fumes.

Several players smoked cigarettes and even a cigar or two, so the room was a real fug by 9pm most evenings. There were yellowed nicotine-stained curtains and warm wet circles from beer mats on tables across the room. Forget health and safety regulations back then. Kids got smoke blown in their faces by adults who did not want to lose at any cost. We learned to hold our own though, and not be shrinking violets.

Amusingly, there was a schoolteacher at the club who professed to hating kids, and another teacher who insisted on playing the Pirc Defence for decades, refusing to change to anything else even when he was defeated time and again with it. Sometimes you just have to try something new at the board. I recall a few stand-up arguments between adults as well. Occasionally they were vicious and at one time someone threatened to stove in another member's skull with one of those heavy wooden boards. I saw an actual fight once – the climax of years of previous bad-blood between the two protagonists. I was used to aggression and violence however so unlike some of the horrified kids, I wasn't at all fazed. I must have been conditioned to it but still it was not the sort of thing that should be happening in front of kids at any place.

It was all about the chess for me and I just loved going to the club. I ached for the days to pass to Friday again when I could once again spend time away from home and lose myself in the happy hours with Caissa. I should remark that back then the adults freely played the kids and helped them where they could. That still happens at clubs today of course but nowhere near as much as I would like to see.

There was one chap at the club called Syd Bricknell who was really great with me and the other youngsters. We used to play, and he would invent daft words to describe a move. After I played 1.g4 once (call it the exuberance of youth) he said, 'my word young man, what a hippogenarious move.' I loved that word, and used it to describe weird moves for years after. I sometimes shared it with juniors when I began coaching decades later, and they loved it too. Thanks Syd. You are not forgotten. Incidentally there is an actual name for that 1.g4 move which is equally comical...The Grob.

How should I describe the next hero? George Viszokai is Hungarian and a former wrestler. He lives for chess. He looked after us kids and ferried me around to endless tournaments. He had a zeal for the game that was incredibly infectious, and in those days he always seemed to play the Caro Kann opening as Black as if it were his best friend. He cossetted an unshakeable faith in that opening and I think he still plays it. We had some great laughs at tournaments I can tell you. I can exclusively reveal now, many decades on, that he was also responsible for an outrageous incident when me and a couple of other juniors were in his car about to leave for a match.

He always drove Mazdas did George, and they were always nice. When setting off to a match one black and filthy winter's night he reversed into a fellow club member's car, causing it a bit of damage. He looked at us kids with his serious face and said, 'Don't say a word about this to anyone kids, have you got it?'

'Yes Mr. Viszokai,' came the instant reply. Well he was a wrestler after all. Who was going to mess with him? Besides, we were not keen on the owner of the other vehicle, because he was a big head, thus he deserved all he got. Twisted logic, I agree but that's kids for you.

We lads stuck together, particularly me and Richard Archer. There was also a boy called Kevin Brotherton and also Phil Darmanin who was a dangerous player, but not serious about his chess. He was one for the ladies and with good reason – he had the gift of the gab and the good looks to back it up. He was a really lovely lad and I always liked him. We ended up playing some Sunday league football together and he is the only person I have ever known who gleefully claimed responsibility for a horrible smelling fart that went off in the changing rooms – even though it was one of my pals that did it. That was Phil's way of being one of the lads and we loved him for it. As for Richard, we shall hear much more about this young man later.

I should also mention Glyn Pugh. He is another of life's affable and generous characters, who loves his chess. We played loads of games for fun and in serious competition. He liked to attack and would play c4, d4, e4, and f4, flinging his pen down onto the table in imperious fashion, in a demonstration of satisfaction. I was honoured to be best man at his wedding to Sandra, even though my bloody car broke down on the way. I had a second-hand SAAB 900 turbo and the head gasket cracked. That was ridiculously expensive to remedy, but the wedding was marvellous and he was and is a truly happy man. I played him online in a Shropshire match in November 2020 and we drew, so it was lovely to be back in touch.

The combination of school and chess club kept me going. I never entertained the thought that I would want to play chess for a living, I wasn't near good enough. However, I knew it would always be a part of my life. Already it had opened new vistas for me. I didn't need parents. I had what I wanted in my chess family. I was happy at the board, playing this wonderful game. I did not want or ask for anything else and as long as I had chess, life was enjoyable.

I had to develop that ruthless streak though. It is fair to say that after living in a violent household one might like to get away from it all and partake of something much more peaceful. Not so chess. It is bloody and unremittingly violent. I choose those words carefully.

Imagine it. Each time you arrive at your *battle station* (the board) and meet the enemy you know that you are there to defeat them. It matters not if it is a man, woman or a young child, you must prevail and crush their own hopes and dreams. That is what brutality is and I loved it, as did my opponents. Winning is a basic primal instinct and we all want a slice. To think otherwise is to be deluded.

The problem is that life often has other plans. Sooner or later two things are going to ride into town and challenge your stability, your safe and precious world. These two friendly foes are the opposite sex and money. The former can appear from nowhere, the latter you have to work for. That requires a job in the real world, not at the chess board. Both of the above are usually life-changing.

In my case, the former ended my childhood days forever.

Work and women

*Love is the only game in which two can play
and both can lose*

Anon

I left school in June 1980 and began work in July. Not for me a college or university. Don't be daft. Mum wanted money – hard cash pays for housekeeping which unsurprisingly manifested itself in bottles called Woodpecker Cider. In those days back in 1980 Margaret Thatcher's government was running something called a Youth Opportunities Programme, (YOP) later called a Youth Training Scheme (YTS). In my case the deal was that I would work my balls off for forty hours a week doing *general farm work* for the princely sum of £23.50, ten pounds of which I had to immediately surrender to Mum on pay day. I wouldn't have minded if she had used it for the purpose I gave it to her for.

Thatcher and her government did some nasty shit in those days and like every dictator she has her followers and enemies. Let us just take the mining community. What annoyed me most of all was that when they eventually capitulated after a long and bitter struggle for their cause, the government never replaced that work with anything for those communities. There seemed to me to be no opportunity for them to retrain or even have anything to retrain for. They were rear-ended, and many will never forgive Thatcher. Make no mistake, those communities still feel the pain today.

I recall when she died the outpouring of anger and the headline, 'Ding Dong the Witch is Dead' which was a real expression of hatred from some communities who had been left to rot. Sure enough, mining was costing too much, and it probably had to go, but to just leave people with no jobs and no hope is unforgivable. I am a proud Englishman but I have a massive respect for the Welsh miners and their families who fought and suffered and also gave to others when they were themselves in dire straits. Yet that was seldom if ever in the news!

Anyway, that is but one of my abiding memories of that time and I am no politician and there are differing sides to every story. They say there are three sides to every story. His version, her version, and the truth. I do have to say that there were some traits about Thatcher that I did admire – standing up to the Argentinians after the invasion of the Falkland Islands being one. Also, it must have been incredibly challenging to remain true to herself as a woman amongst so many men, many of whom wanted to stab her in the back. She reminded me a little of Elizabeth I of England.

Even before Thatcher came to power we had power cuts, and the never-ending quest to find candles. In the dark evenings when the power went off we would light the candles and drink Bovril. In the 1970s there were three-day working weeks, and bread strikes. One could queue for half a mile just to obtain a single loaf of bread and I stood in one of those queues in the bitter cold. It was like 1930s Russia. When I returned home with a loaf (success!) I was allowed the crust and I could warm my feet in the top half of the gas oven! I will never forget that. The headlines said, 'It's Breadlam out there.' It seems like another lifetime, but it wasn't all that long ago. Now we have the Covid Pandemic to send us all mad. One man eats a bat in China, and as a result people cannot hug their mothers and fathers, sisters and brothers. These are the times we live in.

Back to the job situation and I needed work quickly. There was a farm situated in the neighbouring village, therefore the locality was useful. I had no transport. I applied for a YOP job there. I wasn't interested in farming, or gardening but it was work. Lawrence enjoyed such agricultural endeavours, so he and JTB would often be seen nurturing some cabbages or carrots in the garden.

I should add that Mum was the worst cook in the world – she could boil the crap out of decent vegetables until there was nothing of any nourishment left in them. She would scoop the sad-looking things out of a pot, throw some oil spill disguised as gravy over them and liberally throw them in our direction – being careful not to actually ingest any of it herself. I loathed and detested Sunday lunch for just that reason. It was a gelatinous pile of inedible mush, that made me want to vomit. Sorry Mum – but you always knew I hated it and I had to eat what I left over for my tea. There's probably a helpline for this these days as well – Food Oppression Of Kids (FOOK) or something.

Yet Mum really did need the money and she insisted that further education was therefore not for me - so I went for the job and unsurprisingly I got it. After all, I was young and fit, I lived locally, and I could do all the shit jobs that no-one else would ever entertain. Thus it was that for six utterly miserable, soul-corroding months I weeded fields, painted rusty fences for mile upon mile, chopped sugar beet in freezing cold fields and of course mucked out the dairy every morning. There's nothing like the smell of cow shit in the morning to wake you up.

The worst was the sugar beet. Chopping tops off freezing lumps of beet all day in sub-zero temperatures affected me badly, but I stuck at it. I loathed it with every fibre in my body. Each night I walked home to immerse my hands and feet in a bucket of hot water to try to get feeling back in them. This caused chilblains and misery. I was not made for freezing temperatures; I prefer rainforests nowadays and I still love being outdoors.

I despised the owner and his wife, loathed his farm manager, and I had no love for the farm itself. They treated me like a slave. The only blessing was that whilst mucking out I got to drive the little red Dexter tractor. I enjoyed that and it was the only skill I actually learned. The rest was just cheap labour and the exploitation of school leavers. It happened across the UK at the time and Thatcher knew it.

I was going to write to her on behalf of young people everywhere to tell her where to stick her YOP scheme but instead I got another YOP job in a DIY shop, but I didn't last all of it. I disliked that job too – selling doors and paint and screws to people who really didn't want to be doing DIY anyway. I remember two things from that time. First my morning task. I had to open up the shop and turn on the eight-track cassette player.

Each and every sodding day it would always begin with the song 'Do you know the way to San Jose?' I came to abhor that track. It was like a form of torture. Nowadays when I hear it you will find me shouting out loud, 'Yes I bloody-well do know the way to San Jose' to the incredulity of those around me.

I must say that the owners, Stuart and Harry were always very good to me. Harry was a former copper who always wore a black v-neck jersey and a tie whilst Stuart was more of a wide boy. He liked women, fancy cars and Jimi Hendrix, especially the track 'Hey Joe' which he learned to play on guitar.

I can never forget one particular short, rotund customer called George. He was a regular, and he came in to purchase planks of wood. Lots of them. He had deep craggy lines on his face and a weathered look that suggested he spent most of his waking hours out of doors. He had the biggest nose I have ever seen on a human being. It was like a shark fin. It was so immense that I wondered how his head could stay upright. His nose actually set off the door alarm when he entered the shop before his body had set foot inside. One day I decided to ask George why he was purchasing so much wood, as it was costing him a fortune.

He told me that he was building a special shed for his birds. He kept Zebra Finches and Bengalese. Every time he said this, he did so with a lisp, and I can hear him speaking to this day. I asked him if he would have preferred to purchase a whole shed, as it would be cheaper, but he insisted that building something for his birds by his own hand gave him great pleasure. Fair enough.

One day, after the shed had been built George came into the shop. He approached the counter and asked for some planks of wood. 'I thought you had finished your shed,' I said to him. George looked at me and suddenly broke down. He began sobbing his heart out. Apparently, his shed had burned down, roasting all of his precious birds. There was nothing left but ashes on the floor. The poor bloke wanted to build a new one and start again but he was in no fit state. I refused to sell him any that day, but I spoke to the manager and we found some materials to give to George at no cost and we knew another chap who was handy, so he helped him build another shed. I left the job before I ever knew if he purchased any more birds. It was a very sad affair.

Oddly enough, chess helped me in both jobs. My silent obsession with the royal game got me through. Every day on the farm I carried my pocket set in my jacket. The garment in this case was my school blazer which I could not afford to throw away, so it finished its life covered in cow shit and tractor oil. In the fields, whilst weeding (thanks again Thatcher for giving me such great new transferable skills and wonderful memories!) I would get the pocket set out and study some chess openings or try to solve a position that I had set up from the night before.

I was feeling utterly dejected some days, standing in the middle of nowhere freezing my nuts off, but chess would never let me down – I always had a friend. I cannot tell you how important it was to me. I cannot begin to describe how the act of moving some little plastic pieces around a tiny chessboard gave me such happiness and hope.

I also had a little pocket radio where I would listen to Radio 4 whilst working. Every now and again chess would be in the news – almost always Anatoly Karpov. It was a thrill just to get a snippet of chess news. Nowadays we are swamped with it. One can have too much choice in the sweetshop.

I appreciate that Karpov is not the most exciting of chess personalities but at his prime in chess, he was virtually unbeatable. I would sit on that little tractor and dream, imagining what it would be like to be him, sitting at the board pretty much knowing that I wouldn't lose. I still completed my work tasks (to be fair to myself I have always had a good work ethic) but I tried to visualize games in my mind whilst doing it. I worked as hard as I ever have in my life on that farm for £23 sodding quid a week. I suppose that by enduring such dark days, it made me appreciate the better ones later on.

Chess featured in the DIY shop of course, when I would get my pocket set out at lunch-time or even in the quiet times, when I could just put it on the counter. You would be surprised how many customers commented on it and chess enabled me to strike up conversations that I would otherwise not have had. I loved telling people that I was a former School Champion if they asked how *good* I was. The naked truth is, in the great ocean of chess my swimming strength was weak. I had no delusions about becoming a grandmaster, having neither the talent nor support for it. I was knackered at the weekends when chess tournaments were on and I slept a lot to replenish my energy. Work was consuming my time and I already mentioned my introduction to the fair sex at the age of sixteen, so now *women* were in my life too which I shall come to presently.

My life would take a pivotal turn in 1981 when I applied for a job as a labourer at the local Ministry of Defence base at Central Ordnance Depot (COD) Donnington. It was *prima facie* just a job but was actually the beginning of my career. I would give 30 years of my life working in the UK and abroad for the MoD and it gave me so much in return. I thoroughly enjoyed my time, and I look back only with fond memories and no complaints.

I had stopped playing competitive chess at that time, save for the occasional game and I refrained from study to concentrate on other things. Looking back this was a terrible shame because they were key years that I should have been learning and playing in order to significantly improve.

The lady who seduced me had taken me in (in more ways than one) so I had somewhere to live but all of that came to a sorry end when I found her in bed with another bloke. I was devastated – and still just seventeen. I recall arriving home one day to find a Land Rover on the driveway. That was odd I thought, I don't own a Land Rover! The penny did not drop until I went upstairs and heard giggling from the bedroom. As I walked in all I saw was his buttocks. I don't know who was more surprised, him or me. He was well shocked to see me walk in and he apologised. I told him I didn't blame him as he probably did not know there was someone else in her life but *she* knew it, so I held her accountable.

He scarpered but I didn't get nasty. I was just devastated. I thought I would never be so unhappy again. Within a few days my bag was packed and off I went like Dick Whittington on his travels. I found some digs and became a lodger in a property run by a single elderly woman. Basically, she had a screw loose. My board included two meals per day and every evening almost without fail she would cook peas. It was peas with everything. I began to hate the things. One day I told her to stop serving peas, but she took umbrage. I then had carrots every other night for weeks after that. This lady had a nasty-looking scar on her face and I was curious as to how she acquired it.

It transpired that her only son was a paranoid schizophrenic and he had stabbed people including her. I came home one night to find her sobbing. Her son had been released from the mental hospital, returned home and hidden behind the curtains. When she got home he jumped out and apparently tried to murder her. Luckily, she dissuaded him from doing so and managed to call the police who removed him – about an hour before I arrived. She said he was coming back! I knew then it was time to leave and began looking for new digs.

I still had a chess set in my room and would occasionally play through some games played by greats such as Capablanca and Tal. The game was still close to my heart and it helped to burn time when things got depressing. I just could not settle. There was no stability in my life. I was lurching from one crisis to another. The final straw occurred when one morning I did not go into work because I was feeling unwell. There was a knock at my door and in walked the landlady with a female friend of hers. They both sat on each side of the bed asking me how I was. I knew what was coming and her mate who was probably in her fifties slipped a bony hand underneath the blanket and headed north towards my genitals. I sprung up like a jack-in-the-box and told them to get out, which they did, muttering to themselves.

Nothing was said at mealtime, but a week later I had found new digs not far away. In keeping with my life at the time, I ended up having a relationship with the woman who owned, and also lived in the house. It went really well for a while and there were genuine feelings involved. I was quite settled but the place was never mine. We argued a lot and on one occasion she produced a kitchen knife. I was no angel – but she was a real firebrand at times. At one stage she broke my favourite chess set – she knew where to hurt me!

Not surprisingly with all of this aggravation devouring my energy, settling to chess study was difficult and it languished on the back-burner. I was playing Sunday league football at this time instead, but I was still not able to settle and my natural rhythm was all over the place. I broke my leg again going in for another ridiculous 50-50 tackle and it took time to heal. My sunny disposition was becoming clouded. It was affecting my work, and I was given a written warning for too much absence and told to buck up. Thankfully, I did so because I was able to appreciate where my priorities lay. Without money I would literally be out on the streets. I needed clarity, not chaos.

Ultimately, I have my workmates to thank for saving the day. Upon joining the MoD I worked as labourer with the Royal Electrical and Mechanical Engineers (REME) and the older blokes were particularly kind to me.

I still remember my first day and being introduced to the team. Over the far side of the room was a man rocking back and forth whilst working away quite happily at his desk. I wondered what he was doing. 'Is that bloke alright?' I enquired.

'Oh that's Bernard – he listens to rock music all day, we leave him to it.'

Well I certainly didn't leave him to it. He was my first port of call and he became a very good friend, as did his wife Jean. He was quite a few years older than me, a former Barnardo's boy who joined the navy. He loved his metal and rock and would bring his radio cassette player in (which split into two neat speakers) and set it on his desk. He got me into all sorts of stuff and we went to some fantastic rock concerts.

We went to a Judas Priest gig at a small venue in Birmingham. It was bedlam. I lost my expensive watch - and Bernard - in a sea of sweat and blood at the front. It was fantastic. My ribs almost got broken but when Rob Halford tore into the music, nothing mattered except for escaping reality and bustin' it. Those were the days when I could go down the front and head-bang in the mosh pit – but I would need a respirator nowadays. Once a rocker, always a rocker and I still have it all in my head.

Bernard was a sensible, intelligent man who gave me sage advice. I learned a lot from him and I am blessed to have met him. I bought his SAAB 900 Turbo car at one point. Yes it was the one that later broke down at my mate's wedding but it was not Bernard's fault. The registration number began TNT and it certainly was dynamite. It pissed me off when I damaged it a couple of years later when I skidded on ice on my way to work at RAF Stafford. Cost me a sodding fortune it did. Thanks for the memories mate.

Naturally all the lads essayed the whole repertoire of jokes and pranks when I joined (go and ask for a long stand and a bag of sparks at the Quartermaster's store) but they saw something in me that no one at home ever did. It helped that I could give a joke as well as take one. I knew how to stand up for myself alright but if I am blessed with just one thing it is the ability to make people laugh and it works wonders.

I certainly gave as good as I got. I glued the cassettes into one bloke's radio cassette player (not Bernard's), put fish paste in people's cheese sandwiches and made endless spoof phone calls using different accents.

I used to work a fair bit of overtime and I became friends with a chap called Chris Cadman. We were a bit wild. One night in the warehouse we built up some wooden pallets up into a jump ramp – just like Evel Knievel used to do. Then we *borrowed* a moped belonging to John Oakley and decided to see who could land the furthest off the ramp. I was literally in mid-air when the MoD Police came into the building. They used to do regular security checks with their ferocious Alsatian dogs, and they chose my building that night. I was a cocky git back then…

The copper said, 'And what the hell do you think you are doing?'

I said, 'I am jumping off this ramp on a moped, what does it look like I am doing?'

That was it. I got reported and my boss gave me a right dressing down and a verbal warning. He was a lovely bloke and I felt bad, but go easy on me, for I was young and needed to let off steam. What reader has never felt the same? Incidentally, John Oakley was none too impressed either I can tell you.

I was not the one responsible however when a brown paper bag was found in the building and we all had to go outside in the freezing weather. This was a time when the Irish Republican Army (IRA) was active and suspicious packages could be a bomb, because then we were a 'legitimate' target in their twisted view.

We called the bomb squad from Hereford and the offending bag was investigated but it did not need to be blown up. One of the lads had left a bag of pornographic magazines for a pal. The offender had to admit to it and he got a written warning for that stunt. I also recall that we called the bomb squad out because someone heard something ticking in his locker. This time they blew the whole bloody set of lockers up with all our stuff in it. The offending article? A clock – stupid buggers. One of the lads – an Indian fellow called Amrik – was beside himself when he heard the controlled explosion in the building. He had left his curry lunch in the locker and that ended up all over the wall with fragments of metal. You have to laugh.

Although I did not do well at school, I wasn't stupid, and I was a quick learner if something interested me. I absorbed and retained information easily. Chess helped me again by training my memory. I became interested in what the chaps - and indeed two ladies - were working on. Generator sets and oscilloscopes were quite fascinating, and I learned the NATO stock numbers for these items off by heart.

I was helping the lads put kit together ready to distribute to the military who were fighting in the Falkland Islands, so it had to be done correctly. Our mantra was, 'The right kit, at the right place, at the right time, in the right condition.' That has always stuck with me. Logistics became my profession and again I used to think about this at the chessboard. It was important to know when to bring up supplies for an attack on the king and when to move resources elsewhere. Think about it; move the right chess piece to the right square, at the right time for maximum effect. *Et voilà*.

One day the men had a *serious word* with me during a tea break. They said that I had a good brain, that I was a decent lad and that I was totally wasted labouring for them. Why didn't I go into the warehouse environment and work my way up the shop-floor chain to management? I wanted to continue working for them because they had become family to me, but I knew that I had to get on – earn more money and explore my potential.

With a genuinely heavy heart, I applied for a storekeeper assistant grade two position a few weeks later and I got the job. My career began from there. When there were jobs to learn, or cover was required for an absent person, many of the staff said they wouldn't do it as 'it was not my job.' I took the opposite view. I would undertake as many extra tasks as I could in order to learn new skills. Then, when there was overtime work available guess who had the skill set to do various tasks? My strategy literally paid off and I was earning lots of extra money. I progressed from being the newbie to one of the more skilled members of the team pretty quickly. It always pays to be positive – in a warehouse or at the chessboard. I also made friends with the lads in the carpenter's shop and we played chess every lunch-time.

There would be a crowd of blokes round watching the games. They loved it. No-one could beat me but one day I slipped up and a chap called Dave squeaked a draw. He went mad – running around the storehouse shrieking, 'I did it. I got a draw.' It was hilarious. One of the other lads wore a ridiculous-looking wig. It had nothing to do with cancer or illness, it was just vanity. I was playing him at chess one day and his rug slipped down over the front of his eyes as he was considering his move. I thought he was being attacked by a hamster. I fell about laughing, I just couldn't help it. I wish I could play those lads again now, I suspect some have long since parted ways with this life.

Something else happened during that tea break. I had saved some money as a result of the overtime, I never got into debt and I lived by my nan's mantra, 'Pay as you go, if you can't pay don't go.' One of the lads called Lance was very cool. He was young and good-looking with a huge moustache and a bright yellow TR7 car. He loved photography and making money and he also had a gorgeous girlfriend. He played guitar very proficiently.

It was Lance and a couple of the other chaps who convinced me to haul my ass out of digs and buy – not rent - my own flat. I did so. At the age of nineteen I owned my own bedsit flat in Telford, paid for by myself – with no handouts. I was damned proud of that, and I still am. It was built by Barratt homes (who I have always detested I am afraid) and it cost me the sum of £14,850. I never missed a mortgage payment although I had virtually no money for food. In 1983, interest rates were up to 13% (Thanks again Thatcher) and it was crippling me. I literally ate beans on toast for weeks. Friends kept me fed by coming round with goodies. If I bought shopping for myself it was usually waffles and Fray Bentos pies.

I met my future wife in my flat, but more on that later.

It was not long before the heavy metal posters appeared on the walls, including the likes of Judas Priest, Deep Purple, Rainbow, Rush and the Scorpions. Above all I worshipped at the altar of Ozzy Osbourne and Black Sabbath. Ozzy was from Birmingham and supported my football team, Aston Villa. Not only this but his music resonated with me.

People might take the piss now but he went from working in an abattoir and having nothing to having more money and success than most people could ever dream of. Who is laughing now? He used to make me laugh, and God alone knows I needed it. One day whilst touring in Hamburg, Ozzy painted his face purple for a prank. However, he had not realised that he used indelible ink and had to walk around Hamburg for three days with a purple head. Thus, a huge image of Ozzy adorned half of one wall in my flat. As a young single male I needed a of a female model up on the wall and Maria Whittaker was the order of the day back then. It was tasteful mind, there were no nudes in my flat – as my visitors would testify. The power of suggestion has always been more interesting than *the reveal* I find.

Heavy metal was my soul mate of course and I feel part of a privileged family whenever I indulge. The people that love rock and metal are first class. I always preferred mixing with them as opposed to the pretentious wankers that were into The Style Council or Duran Duran. Rock chicks (as we used to say) were way more interesting and had more depth to them.

The narcissistic pop girls had little substance and kissed like mudskippers. They would talk about clothing and make-up, whilst the rock ladies, though fewer in number by far in society would engage in a discussion about Tolkien or the artist Roger Dean. Rock lyrics weren't all about love and lust – they were about life and death. If you get a chance, listen to 'Forgotten Sons' by Marillion. There's something to give you goose bumps. Music has to have some meaning as well as rhythm.

I profess however to liking Dexy's Midnight Runners. *'Come on Eileen'* is an absolute classic. I will throw in *'Money for nothing'* by Dire Straits, too.

Back then, I desperately wanted a guitar. Lance happened to live in the same street and he owned a gorgeous black Hondo Pro-Am II electric one which he put up for sale but I could not stump up the cash. Fortuitously for me, his washing machine had broken down irreparably and I owned one. We made an exchange. I had to get my washing to a local laundromat, but that guitar was good. I can play a bit but not proficiently. Well, not everyone who owns a Lamborghini can drive, can they?

I affixed two very substantial speakers to the wall, accompanied by a rather neat Pioneer hi-fi system. The flats were built in blocks of eight and two of the neighbours were partially deaf. My mate Kevin Norris occupied another one. Directly opposite me was a woman called Pat. 'Pat in the flat' as I lovingly called her. Down the corridor was a chap called Roy.

He was a bin man (that was the technical term back then for a refuse collector) and I have to say that he too had an extraordinarily big hooter (nose) but unlike George's from the DIY shop this man had a dewdrop forever poised at the bottom of his. It must have been the same dewdrop for years as I never saw it fall off although I kept staring at it when I spoke to him, willing the thing to be liberated. It stressed me out staring at it.

He and Pat were both in their fifties and were almost certainly indulging in some nefarious sexual practices several times a week. I often heard moans and groans from the end of the corridor and after I had established that no-one was being murdered, the penny dropped. Occasionally it sounded like a herd of migrating wildebeest, and I could not tell if Pat was having an orgasm or an asthma attack, but I at least had my hi-fi to drown it out as the walls were cracker thin. I would crank up the Pioneer and headbang around the room, playing out front as the lead singer of a band, to an imaginary arena of 20,000 people.

I am now in my fifties and I still unashamedly do that! I used to sing into the air microphone and then offer it to the audience – which was the fridge – to sing the chorus. Jesus, that must have looked weird. The year 1983 was tremendous for rock music and I vividly recall playing Ronnie James Dio's *Holy Diver*, Iron Maiden's *Piece of Mind* and Ozzy Osbourne's *Bark at The Moon* for hours. It was wonderful. I have been to endless classical concerts and cultured events such as the ballet and the opera and they are enjoyable but heavy metal is still my preference.

I digress. Pat was a lovely lady, but she scared the hell out of me. Every time I opened my door, she would open hers. She must have been hiding behind it, listening. The woman was a predator and she could freeze the blood in my veins.

She was definitely up for naughty pleasures, but alas I found her to be quite repulsive in that respect. She had wild staring eyes, a permanent wetness on her lips and I could not help but notice that her huge breasts hung down to her waist and swayed in metronomic fashion from side to side when she walked.

I only ever entered her flat once – and that was the first and last time. Let's just say I was suitably uncomfortable with her hospitality, and the strange looking item on her coffee table, which worked optimally with the aid of several batteries. I think I nervously told her one of my favourite jokes of the time. 'Did you hear about the Irish woman who used a vibrator for the first time? She knocked three of her teeth out!' This served only to arouse Pat, and as she smiled I swore that there was a tooth missing. I made a swift exit.

My young and nubile pal Kevin was also a prime target, but he too employed the same strategy with Pat. She wasn't so much a cougar as an old lioness, but we loved the bones of her, honestly. Thankfully Roy was our saviour, desperate as he was to inject some kind of passion into his life. If they were happy who the hell were we to deny them?

The other flat owners were rarely there. It was fabulous. I could play my music nice and loud. My friends knew whether or not I was home before they even arrived at the door. Oh yes, at some point a strange girl called Jackie moved in directly above me. I think the best way to describe her was *neo-gothic*. She was attractive, at least she had beautiful green eyes, but she also had a large, yellow-fanged Alsatian which deterred me from visiting her, although I admittedly did so a few times at her request. The girl had no conversation in her at all – and seemed to have a proclivity for colds. She studied lycanthropy, and when she ate meat she really tore into it. What with her and that dog, I decided I would rather stay alive so I remained as aloof as possible.

I admit it, my flat had red light bulbs. Whilst I distinctly understood that this was also the colour used by prostitutes worldwide to tout for business, it gave my flat the sort of doom-laden look that I wanted. Don't be misled though, my flat was always spic and span as my wife can testify, but it needed a bit of atmosphere. It wasn't unseemly at all.

Something else I owned that was red was a little Honda moped which I always parked in the hallway. This was my only mode of transportation and I travelled to work on it wearing carrier bags fixed with elastic bands around my feet when it rained. I could not afford any protective clothing. I had this ridiculous orange, open-faced helmet that made me look like a big berry. Seriously I must have looked like an absolute tit on that bike. I think it was only 50cc or something. One day a grizzled old man on a bicycle overtook me going up a hill. I was hugely embarrassed and immediately resolved to get a car.

I ended up with a Mini which I bought off a mate who turned out to be gay and he tried it on with me. We actually put the engine back together first. He would give me the car for free if I jumped in the sack with him. I paid him the money instead! Each to their own but I liked the ladies thank you. A free car could not change my primal instinct. Anyway, it was a rust bucket. It would barely start even when I pulled the choke out. I pushed that sodding thing around Telford for three months and it always broke down at traffic lights. Transport was an issue for years.

I used to get a lift in with Kevin from the flats, but he drove like a chimp. He could barely see, and his little green FIAT ended up in the hedge with us in it on more than one occasion. The thing was a death trap, and the door would suddenly fly open if he went over seventy miles per hour, but I needed the lift so I learned to hold on.

We had some epic laughs Kevin and I, but trouble always found him. One night we were sitting in a pub and there was this beast of a man in a sheepskin coat sitting having a beer at the table by us. He had a broken nose, a black eye and fists like jackhammers. He also had a bulldog which was snoring away at his feet. Kevin was referring to the bulldog when he said very loudly, 'God, you're fucking ugly' but the bloke thought he meant him. He sprang up and drew back ready to knock Kev into the next week, but it took all my guile to talk him out of it – and it cost me a pint.

He was not so lucky another time when he insulted a girl. She punched him in the face, knocking him across a table. His face was badly cut as she had a sharp ring on her fingers. Ouch. I found it hilarious and it taught him to be more respectful to the ladies. I wonder where he is now. Probably getting up to mischief. He loved his music too, and a bit of chess so we played often for fun.

I do miss Kevin and those carefree moments where spontane-ity was the order of the day. We went on holiday to Sidmouth in that jalopy of a car. We had virtually no money, in fact I remember I had precisely £17 for the week. We slept in the car in a field. At about 3am Kevin screamed his head off and almost gave me a coronary. He had awoken to a faint noise at his windscreen in the dead of night, and opened his eyes to find a huge white ghostly face at the window. He almost shat himself. It was the big fat head of some curious sheep that had wandered across in the field and was blinking like an idiot through the window.

He was always easily scared was Kev, so he started the car, slammed his foot down and drove to a layby where we had a kip. We had breakfast at the Little Chef which cost me a third of my holiday money, so we drove back home. He refused to sleep out for another night, and we had no money for hotels. Aye, those were the days. I called him the ovine oracle for weeks.

I should confess that in those days I fancied myself as a bit of an actor as well as a joker. I auditioned for the part of a policeman in the play *A Wild Goose Chase* at The Little Theatre in Donnington, Telford and I got the part. That was in November 1984 when I was only twenty years old. To be absolutely honest, I read the script and saw that the copper kissed a girl in the opening scene, and I caught sight of the girl who was going for the part!

Luckily, we got along swimmingly, and the opening scene saw us kissing rather vigorously on a sofa and I remember the first night, which was always for the old-aged pensioners. The front row didn't expect such an erotic opening scene when the curtain went up and we heard some audible gasps as Claire and I kissed passionately. It is quite hard to do that in an acting sense, but we were both young and hardly needed practice.

I thought I heard one old lady in the front row say 'disgusting' as the kiss lingered on and I absolutely loved it. It gave me a real kick. I have always liked to shock so this was right up my street. Later on I found myself in the chorus line in *Calamity Jane*, which I did not enjoy but it was fun whilst it lasted. Maybe one day there is a final performance in me. I would absolutely love to play Ebenezer Scrooge. I always preferred him as the miserable sod. Charles Dickens was a genius.

My amateur dramatics day.
On the couch with Claire just prior to the kissing scene.

Back then I was also knocking about with a local rock band called Phantom. A neighbour called *Baz* was the lead singer and he was a bit of a head case. The band had a tour bus, which was really an old coach driven by the most miserable bastard you ever met in your life. Derek and his mate Arthur did all the cable work and were forever shouting out in a Brummie accent, 'Who's got the fuckin' gaffer tape?'

Anyhow, Phantom performed several gigs around England

and I went along to help do the pyrotechnics and other roadie tasks. This consisted of placing small incendiary devices that exploded in old steel milk churns, carefully situated by the side of the stage. Barry was also a fire eater so the fans got plenty of bang for their buck. One day we had to do the Mill Inn at Oswestry. The crowd were students, and they had been on the lash for a while before we arrived. They actually sat on chairs at the front and they were almost all wearing white shirts. I told them they better move back because there would be a big bang and also lots of fire later on. 'Fuck off mate,' they said, 'We've paid our money and we will stand where we like.' Well, I did warn them. I packed something a little extra into the milk churns just for the gobshites, and halfway through the set... BOOM!

When the smoke finally cleared there were several forlorn figures standing at the front, half blinded, temporarily deaf and covered in crap. The smoke alone had ruined their clothing and the white shirts were now black. It was brilliant!

I slept in the tour bus – which was no fun, freezing my balls off at 4am in Rochdale or somewhere, listening to Derek and Arthur, still rowing. I would walk the streets in the early hours just to get off the bus. Even then chess was useful. Unsurprisingly I always had a pocket set with me and I would sit somewhere on a city wall and play chess in the cold and the half-light.

We moved on to a place called Bristol Granary and the gig went well. Afterwards I remember dancing with a girl on the table of the local pub. She had stripped down to her knickers and bra after I dared her! Her pants were green and white striped. In those days there was confectionery on the market called Pacers and they were similarly green and white striped so I nicknamed her Pacer. I took my leather jacket off and joined her for a head bang on the table. It was all good fun and no-one was hurt. Yes, we were all pissed. Those were the days. The tours were fun but very hard work. The band had a lot of kit to lug around. If you've ever seen the film *Bad News* it was just like that.

Back home in Leegomery, Telford, I asked a girl from work to come round to my flat. I liked Sandra and at some point intended to ask her out for a drink, though I absolutely knew she would say no. We worked in the same department. She had lovely blonde curly hair which gave her the rock chic look but unfortunately she never liked that sort of music. She visited my flat one evening accompanied by a friend (probably for safety!) called Susan Watson.

As soon as Susan walked in my heart missed a beat - she had brought fish and chips! What a girl. Did I forget to mention that I also instantly fancied her? I couldn't keep my eyes off the girl. From the moment she stepped in the whole room changed. She brought colour and laughter into my flat. She wore autumnal clothes and had the most beautiful brown eyes. Susan was like no other girl I had ever met, and I soon learned that she was strong-willed and had values and integrity. She knew her own mind, and I liked that. She was sizzling hot! Eventually I would summon the courage to ask her out but she would refuse, saying she wanted us to be just friends. That was a good start as far as I was concerned. I would rather have her forever as a friend than lose her after a month as a lover.

Chess came to my rescue yet again, having taught me how to play the long game. I took this to extremes with Susan though, waiting decades to ask her out again when the opportunity arose. This time she said yes. Did I mention that she is now my wife? Checkmate! The message to all you lads is never to give up on your girl. If she is worth the fight, then fight you must. The labyrinth of love is as complex as the labyrinth of chess but the fight is most pleasurable.

Sue clearly remembers my flat, the music, the weird lighting and our first meeting. I was nineteen and she was almost seventeen. We would go out for drinks as pals on many occasions and have a real laugh. Jeremy would come too. Sue and I trusted one another, and we enjoyed each other's company. Nothing has changed in that respect. I know that I have loved her from the very first second.

I have always preferred the company of women and I was always lucky enough to have Susan to take my arm if I needed to go to a function with a lady and she would ask me to go with her to parties when she required a chap to accompany her. It was purely platonic with no strings attached and it worked for us. In my personal view, women are infinitely more interesting to talk to than men. They have a broader range of subject matter and they pay attention to detail.

As for men, what was it that Woody Allen famously said? Oh yes, 'Women need a reason for sex, men just need a place.' Spot on Woody. He also said that he never made the chess team because he was too short. After all these years I think I might just have a notion as to what a woman likes to see in a man. Apart from being trustworthy and loyal, he needs to be a good listener and have the capacity to make her laugh.

When I look back at photographs of my flat, I note that I always had a chess set ready on the table. I still studied, especially in the still of the night when the world was asleep and I could draw the energy from the world. The chessboard seemed to come alive with more clarity after midnight, I don't know why.

I was obsessed with blitz chess (five minutes per player for the whole game) and when Richard Archer visited we would stoke up the heavy metal and play chess for hours. We seemed to have a penchant for Anthrax, and the track 'Efilnikufesin (N.F.L)' which if you read it backwards is rather comical. The trick folks is that you've got to play it loud – and we certainly did. Richard has always been a bit stronger than me at chess, but we shared some ridiculously creative games during those years, not necessarily by skill, many positions occurred by chance but this was pure unadulterated fun. Richie is a Yorkshire lad now, having moved away from Shropshire decades ago.

Ultimately it was Richard's enthusiasm for the game that made me want to get back to it. Life took me away from chess for a while, but it never took chess out of me. I owned an apartment, held down a secure job and even had some time on my hands. I needed to stop thinking about women (easier said than done) and work at my game. I was beginning to get the urge to play again. Caissa was calling. I built up my chess book collection, committed myself to more study and I even began playing correspondence games. Regrettably though, I had missed several crucial years that I could never retrieve. Even learning at twelve years old was way too late. You really need to start at about eight and have a support mechanism if you want to have any chance to shine in the chess world.

That aside, the past was the past and I decided to have another go. I dusted myself down and asked myself what book might help me to get back on track. It had to be 'Anatoly Karpov's Games as World Champion 1975-77' by O'Connell and Levy. Karpov once said, 'Happiness should always remain a bit incomplete, after all, dreams are boundless.' I could not agree more, and I wanted to dream again.

Karpov rekindled my inner chess flame again. I took a holiday and stayed for a few days in a caravan for isolation. As the rain lashed down on the roof, I sat inside, nice and snug, digesting the games in that book. To be fair, he was not a world champion for nothing. Game after game appeared on my chessboard as I became dazed and confused swimming around in the comprehensive ocean of his brilliance. Karpov would make a move that I only understood several moves later, when the smoke had cleared. He never used computers back then.

He was a child of the Soviet Union for sure, one of Leonid Brezhnev's communist favourites. Chess in the Soviet Union had always fascinated me. I had a thought. Why read about it when I could actually go? I had a few pennies put by after all. I resolved to go to the USSR at some point. I needed to save a bit more, buy a very warm coat and get my passport sorted out.

Then it was *Zdravstvuyte Moskva*.

At work in the early 1990's. I am standing, third from left.
The missile always pointed towards Russia!

USSR 1990

Have you ever thought that Adam and Eve were Russian?
They had nothing to wear, nothing to eat but an apple and
yet they were told that they were living in paradise.

Anon

It would be 1990 before I visited the USSR – as it was still known at that time. I went for a few weeks' holiday with my then girlfriend, Gill. None of my friends, family, or even anyone I had met had ever visited the country. The Chernobyl disaster had occurred only four years earlier and yet Kiev was on my itinerary. People thought I was crazy. I probably was. I had seen the pictures of horrifically deformed adults, and children with swollen heads and twisted limbs.

The children were placed into orphanages and the images that we as a nation saw on television depicted a grisly horror story unfolding, with grotesquely deformed babies and kids dying half-starved in cots; cold, afraid and lonely. It was utterly desperate and one of the saddest portraits of humanity that I had ever seen.

The truth is that although this was meant to be an organized small group holiday I had other ideas and my own agenda. This may sound a bit selfish but Gill was totally supportive and knew that chess would be the main focus for me. I would have gone alone, but she wanted to go too so that suited us both. I wanted to do two things in particular. The first was to visit an orphanage in the Ukraine to donate something and the second was to visit Moscow Central Chess Club on Gogolevsky Boulevard.

I had always had a fascination with Russia and the Soviet Union. Its history is very rich and troubled politically, socially and economically. It has incredible architecture and art, not to mention the astonishing topography and the wide variety of wildlife. How about the sheer diversity of people and their lifestyles? Amazing! Then of course there is the chess. When I was a kid, if you had told me I would visit CCCP and the chess club in Moscow, I would never have believed you. I never even thought I would travel in an aircraft. Mind you with Aeroflot at that time I wished I never had.

The itinerary included visits to Moscow, Leningrad (it was only afterwards changed to St Petersburg in June 1991), Kiev, Tbilisi and Yalta. I visited during the very same month that Mikhail Gorbachev became President. His tenure was 15th March 1990 to 25th December 1991, and it ended with the unpredictable and unhinged maverick Boris Yeltsin being elected. It was indeed still the USSR when I visited because it only dissolved on New Year's Eve 1991 with Yeltsin at the helm. Therefore, I was one of the last tourists to visit the USSR at the age of twenty-six. I guess I feel a part of history in that sense.

We landed at Sheremetyevo International airport, and when the aircraft door opened, we were greeted by an icy wind, light snowfall and two military armed guards with what looked like sub-machine guns. They escorted us with a scowl into the terminal building.

I was a little nervous about this trip. I was of course working for the British government, and the Ministry of Defence had a red list of countries that staff were forbidden to visit unless they had clearance and permission. Luckily, I did obtain the blessing of the MoD, but I had to have a brief with ministry officials before I left and a debrief upon my return.

It was real cold war stuff. I was told to be aware of anything *suspicious* such as being followed. I should be careful what I ate and also be very wary of prostitutes. I should not invite anyone to the UK. It might sound ridiculous now but it was suggested that I should check my room for bugging devices. What drama. I wasn't a spy but people were nervy at the time! This sounded like Bobby Fischer versus the Russians with all the suspicion he had about being bugged. I was no Bobby Fischer, but I might have had some information of use to the Russians. Who knows? They were not 'friends.'

Officials were particularly keen to know why I was visiting. Why the USSR? Why not Spain like everyone else? I told them it was a chess holiday but they were suspicious of this. 'So, you're going to spend time with the Russians and play chess?' they enquired.

'Yes of course,' was my honest reply. They accepted it, but they were far from convinced.

I am sure they thought that they had some sort of communist in their midst, especially when I told them that communism was a great idea in principle but it did not work in practice. Mind you, capitalism has a lot to answer for as well, but that is another story. Luckily, I wrote a chess column for the main in-house magazine of the MoD so they had proof that I was indeed a chess player. I could have paid a price for my puckish behaviour and got the red *rejected* stamp for my trip, but they could not find a valid reason not to let me go and in any event, their tip about the prostitutes did come in useful as I shall reveal.

Standing in Red Square, Moscow in 1990
just before the fall of the USSR.

The visit began in Moscow – a place that I had read so much about in my chess books as a kid. I will never forget the moment we arrived at Red Square and I first set eyes on St Basil's cathedral. I actually shed a tear. This is one of the most iconic buildings in the world and there it was before me. I was so happy to be able to go inside and explore. I remember a lot of steps. It was built on the orders of Ivan the Terrible between 1555 to 1561. The building symbolizes a giant bonfire rising up to the heavens. No one knows who the architect was, but legend has it that Ivan had him blinded, so that he could never build anything as beautiful again. That's gratitude for you. At the time, the international view of Russia was almost always dystopian but there is such beauty, one just has to look. Here I was, Carl Portman the council estate Brummie, standing in Red Square, Moscow. I remember thinking, 'would my grandparents be proud of me or would they not like me being here?'

Our tour guide was Natalia Krivlenkova and she knew precisely what strings to pull to make things happen. Who could ever forget first meeting such a woman? She was wearing a blue denim jacket and a white tutu. I do not lie. She also wore dark sunglasses and thick rubber boots. She looked like she had been made out of spare parts, but this was Russia, and anything was possible. It transpires that she was a gem, but she did ask some strange political questions occasionally, so I gave considered answers. I wondered if somehow she knew that I was a government worker. I certainly did not tell her the truth when she asked, 'Tell me what job you do?' You see, there really are times when it has to be acceptable to lie.

Natalia had organised a tour of the Kremlin. There were four other people in addition to me and Gill, and when we arrived at the entrance, the armed sentry took an instant dislike to a chap called Ralph. He was a smashing fellow emanating as he did from Nottingham but the sentry refused entry as I would rib him about later. They not only refused but they took him aside to inspect his bags and documents. There was nothing that Natalia could do to assuage the guard.

We gained entry and once inside I stared in wonder at some of the world-famous Fabergé eggs. Photographs were forbidden, and many years have passed but I think there were three on display. They were gorgeous, and exquisite. The bright blues and greens and golds were mesmerizing. There was also a fantastic chess table with an ornate set. It was as ostentatious as I thought it would be and having seen the crown jewels in London and the Palace of Versailles, it compares favourably. It is a stupendous and mesmerizing building.

Next up was a stroll across the square to see Lenin (That's Vladimir, not John as some wag once thought) lying in his mausoleum. I was instructed to go to the front of the huge queue of half-frozen people which snaked around the square, but I felt this was unfair and chose not to. Anyway, he was dead, there were plenty of other things to do than see an embalmed body – even if he was famous. Mind you, he was fond of chess, and I read that he was a very bad loser.

I had arranged for Natalia to take me to the Moscow Central Chess Club on a private tour, which she dutifully did. This would be the most exciting aspect of the trip in chess terms. We arrived by taxi at Gogulevsky Boulevard and the chess club, to be met by the deputy director Anatoly Fyodorovich who took me around. I only spoke a few words of Russian and his English was limited so I was grateful to Natalia for interpreting.

I saw the chess tables where Spassky and other famous Russians had played. This was the club where so many Soviets learned their trade as they ascended the international chess summit. Chess was the tool to beat the world over the head with. It was a cultural, intelligent and sophisticated game played by everyone from bourgeois government staff to the proletariat factory workers.

All schools taught chess as part of the national curriculum. Soviets played chess from cradle to grave and if they were really good, they were plucked out of the education system to further develop in Pioneer Palaces. I imagined such a thing occurring in England in our own education system, or at least setting chess problems as homework to get the brain working.

I was given a cup of thick black coffee and a fancy little cake. In return I gave the gentleman some pencils with the UK Union Flag on, which he really cherished. One could not carry much into the Soviet Union and I wanted to give some little gifts, so pencils, notebooks and bubble gum were the currency of the day.

I had a nice tour of the building and recall it being a bit dark and drab, but I could sense the history in the air. I went into an ante-room and saw who I believed to be Alexander Khalifman in some kind of coaching session. I did not ask, but I am certain that it was him. I did not play chess against anyone regrettably as they seemed to have kept the doors open just for me (and Gill) to visit, which was jolly decent. There was no-one else around. It was over all too soon, and I would love to have spent a few hours playing chess there. It is my intention to return and do just that one day.

Back outside, people were selling chess stamps and booklets, so I purchased some as souvenirs. It was chess nirvana. On the way back to the Kosmos hotel, Natalia gave me a very brief tour of Moscow. I am afraid I almost caused a scene. As we drove, she pointed out the Lubyanka Building - Headquarters of the KGB. Straight away I got my camera and took a snap from the car. She said that photography was forbidden and that now we could be followed as they had people watching from the building. I told her to put her foot down, which she did, and we thus avoided any interviews under the anglepoise lamp! She was noticeably nervous though.

We popped out of the car for a while to visit the famous Moscow Metro with its many chandeliers and beautiful tiles.

Opened in 1935 this was the first underground rail system in the Soviet Union. The interior décor is representative of different styles such as Art Deco, the Empire style, gothic as well as Russian folk patterns. It's been bombed a few times and had suffered from fires so it is no place to hang around, but it is absolutely gorgeous and a must see on any visit.

The very first McDonalds restaurant had opened just eight weeks earlier in Moscow and we drove past a queue of shivering people waiting to get a taste of this decadent western delicacy. I had read about an elderly couple living in a tiny Moscow apartment. They had very little money, but the husband queued for hours in the snow to get his first ever Big Mac. Once he had secured it, he trudged home, ascended the flights of stairs breathlessly and shared half of the food with his wife. Apparently they loved it. This is what marriage is about – such moments of bliss.

There were plenty of chess sets for sale and I bought a couple, along with some magazines and a chess clock. It was paradise really. I did not have long in Moscow unfortunately, but Natalia would accompany us to the other places on the trip and she was indispensable. We kept in touch for a couple of years afterwards, writing to her in her home city of Leningrad.

For the rest of the tour she wore rubber and PVC. In fact she wore more rubber than a deep-sea fisherman. Her mind was as irregular as her dress sense, but she was an intelligent and engaging woman who was desperate to see more of the world. She wanted to come to England, but sadly this never transpired, at least not to visit me.

We journeyed on to Leningrad and in many ways I enjoyed that city more than Moscow. There was more stunning architecture at every turn, and my visit to the Hermitage Museum will never be forgotten. It is the second largest in the world, of monstrous size. It could take a week to get around it. The hotel room offered a view of the river Neva and the Russian cruiser Aurora. I took a walk in the crisp snow down by the river to see it up close. It was bitterly cold and I felt that I was in some sort of film set but it was worth it to see the ship that had taken part in the October revolution of 1917. I love history when you can touch it or see it. Books are fine up to a point.

Our group contained a lone female traveller. She and Gill befriended one another. Neither of them were into chess so they spent some time doing stuff together whilst I did even more chess. I did warn Gill what it would be like. Her friend had a shock of ginger hair cut into a bob and so many freckles that it reminded me of looking at the constellation in the night sky. I must be honest and reveal that I think a lady with freckles is very cute. Freckles, curls and a winning smile and I am hooked. The ladies were happy to team up for some side events and share some *girlie time* (for want of a better phrase) which left me some time to concentrate on the chess. Besides, Natalia and I were getting on famously too, discussing aspects of our own countries from a cultural perspective. No, I did not give any official secrets away and if anyone asked me, I worked as a logistician – but not with the government.

Natalia worked her magic for me again and arranged a visit to a Pioneers Palace and the chess club. My recollections are somewhat vague, but I know that we were met by a very classy lady who took me into a room adorned with chess sets. I was sat at a table and offered coffee and cake. After an explanation about how the palace operated she asked if I would like to play some chess. Would I? Start the clocks! I recall that we both won and lost a few quick games whilst several people appeared in order to see this English chess player.

Someone brought me some white fish. It was raw and tasted salty, but it would have been rude to refuse so I managed to eat it. We left after a couple of hours and I felt privileged to have been given some time there.

I did have one terribly embarrassing experience in Leningrad. Many of the shops are below ground level. I descended into one bakery and spied some biscuits at a glass counter. Oblivious to everything else around me I went straight up and the woman smiled and said something to me in Russian that I did not understand. Natalia stepped in and then I looked to my right to see a very long line of mostly middle-aged ladies queuing to get their weekly biscuit ration.

I was horrified and I immediately apologised to them, but they all insisted on me being served because I was a visitor and one from the United Kingdom at that. It would have been rude not to take the biscuits. Natalia told me to take them, which I did, and we left. I felt terrible but Natalia scoffed them without any guilt so at least I made someone happy. Those women were resourceful and strong-willed, clearly existing in a city where food was far from plentiful. We have nothing to moan about in the west. Some of us live like kings and queens compared to those women. Truly I admired them.

We journeyed on to Kiev. Regrettably, I never gained access to an orphanage. I think there were political reasons for this. A person from the west – looking at what was going on, it was still raw. Natalia tried; she really did. My protestations were met with a resounding *Nyet* so that was that. I gave her a few small gifts and some money in an envelope (I trusted her) to donate and she promised so to do. She wrote and said that she did so I have to believe that.

The other thing I remember about Kiev apart from the fantastic architecture (I love onion domes) was a trip to a monastery of the caves (Kyivo-Pechers'ka Lavra) where the shrivelled bodies of tiny monks were on display. It seems that humans have got bigger over the decades because these fellows were tiny. You could see hands, but not much more, thankfully. All rather macabre.

The building itself is eleventh century and a must see for anyone visiting Kiev. I did not get the opportunity to play chess here unfortunately, but I saw some people playing in a park. They were old men, wearing rabbit skin hats and thick military long coats, huddled over chess boards in the park. Snow was falling and it looked like a scene from a film. If you have seen *The Queen's Gambit* series on Netflix, then think about the final scene when Beth Harmon walks up to the players in the snow and you'll get the picture here. I desperately wanted to go over and say hello, but the light was fading and we had to get back for dinner. I purchased even more chess stamps from a kiosk before I left.

Kiev is a beautiful city, but the people were struggling for obvious reasons: politically, economically and socially. I vowed to return one day. Regardless of political situations across the world it is often the people that suffer. For some, capitalism did not work because the rich got richer and 20% of people owned 80% of the wealth. Here, communism seemed to deliver exactly the same result.

Distribution of wealth is critical for social cohesion no matter what ideological system or fancy name we wrap around it. I wondered what the hell these souls had to look forward to.

How would they look back on their lives? What made them genuinely happy or sad? What did they aspire to? What did they yearn for? What qualities were necessary to survive the daily grind? These are the people I wanted to have conversations with, to learn about their situation, but time would not permit.

We should be grateful for what we have, because there are people in the world suffering way more than we could ever know. Travel gives us an insight, a mere snapshot into the lives of others and only in that context, can we put our own lives into perspective. Travel then is truly broadening.

We flew on to Tbilisi, home of former world chess champion Tigran Petrosian, also known as Iron Tigran. It was a strange experience. The bathroom was the worst I have ever experienced, and I have slept in military transit accommodation so that's saying something. Whilst micturating, I particularly enjoyed trying to work out the actual species of the huge yet strangely magnificent cockroaches on the walls. Perhaps they were attracted to the damp, or maybe just the taste of urine.

At dinner on the first night, an unkempt man with several missing teeth kept coming over to our table to give Gill flowers. We thought that this was a very kind gesture and something that the locals did for visitors. After the meal we rose from the table and the man, now clearly inebriated, followed us to the lift and began tugging at my good lady's arm, trying to pull her away from me.

Apparently, the flowers were some kind of exchange for a sexual favour! That might be how they do business in Tbilisi but that was not for us, so we got into the lift pretty quickly. The now angry man was pulling the doors open with his bare hands and became highly aggressive shouting and trying to get

118

in. Gill was frightened. In a flash, and instinctively I punched him on the jaw and he fell back as the doors closed and up we went to the room.

We never saw him again. He was inebriated, and probably slept it off. The fun did not end there. I had to go to reception a short time later and as I got into the lift two women who I quickly deduced were *ladies of the night*, stepped in and began to accost me. One put her hand on my chest and the other was moving in for what looked like a kiss but I thought my wallet might disappear, so I pushed them away trying to be polite but they were determined. I got to reception then returned to the lift back to my room about ten minutes later. When the doors opened there they were again. They were dressed like the pop band Bananarama with thick make up and that sky-blue eyeliner that is so popular in Eastern Europe and Russia.

One of the gruesome twosome was revealing as much cleavage as she could without actually undressing and the other was trying to blink at me seductively, but her good eye was bloodshot, possibly from an excess of vodka. She was wearing yellow and black stripes and looked like a huge wasp. This vespine seductress and her pal exited the lift with me and started putting their hands on me as I walked up the corridor to my door. They were chattering away in their native tongue. When I opened my door and they saw another woman inside they disappeared pronto. Well, the MoD warned me about these furtive feline temptresses after all!

Chess remained top of the agenda for me. Natalia took me to a very large beige building and said that I would be playing chess inside. It was a scary looking place and I wondered if I might ever leave.

However, this is my kind of set up. The room was adorned with red, green and gold carpeting and looked very opulent. It was a long way from Grange-Farm Drive, and I felt like a prince. At that moment, as if they had been hiding behind a door, two smiling women walked in. One was clearly older than the other and they brought refreshment by way of tea with them. I honestly thought they were maids. One escorted me to a table and Natalia interpreted for us. They wanted to know all about me and why I was visiting. They were naturally curious. After some small talk I was offered the opportunity to play chess. Bring it on. I was loving the Soviet Union.

I played the younger lady first whilst the other watched on, as did Natalia. Now remember, I was 26 years of age and probably graded about 150. Not *that* good, but I could give anyone a game. However, the lady systematically took me apart. Game after game I tried to at least meet her on equal terms but she found ingenious ways to infiltrate my position. She was tactically quick but positionally brilliant. We played 5-minute blitz and I drew only one game.

Before I could catch my breath, the second lady took her place. She looked quite a bit older and I fancied my chances this time. I lost every game! Her endgame technique was brilliant. If I played an inferior move she would let out a little chuckle and raise an eyebrow. At one stage she enquired 'Would you like to take that move back?' There was no way that was going to happen as my pride would not allow it. I congratulated both ladies on playing excellent chess and said that I clearly had to work on my game.

As we shook hands one of the ladies declared that they were International Masters! The second player I went into battle against was Tamara Khugashvili. They were lovely people, and I won't forget their kindness. The cake was particularly tasty. Natalia drove me around to look at some of the local district but I did not enjoy Tbilisi as much as the previous cities. On reflection, I should have finished with a visit to Moscow, not begun with it.

Playing chess in Tbilisi at a Pioneer's Palace. This lady hammered me.

We boarded Aeroflot and flew on to Yalta, our final destination. It was a memorable flight. I have no idea if the situation has improved nowadays, but their safety record left a lot to be desired at that time. There were no overhead lockers where I sat, so people just put their bags on the table in front of us. Ours was like a dinner table with two people facing each other. I was strapped in facing passengers, as the crew would be.

Everyone was praying and making cruciform gestures with their hands. I was petrified. It's never really a good sign is it? When the aircraft took off, my heavy bag slid across the table

121

and slammed into the face of the woman praying opposite. It must have felt like a Mike Tyson upper cut. She just winced and carried on praying.

I only knew two things about Yalta. First of all it was situated on the Black Sea on the Crimean Peninsula, and secondly there was a war conference there in 1945 where Churchill, Roosevelt and Stalin met to decide how Germany should be divvied up after the war. I have one abiding memory of my first day on that visit. I was standing in the middle of a cobbled street and I suddenly I felt hot breath on my neck. I turned around with a start to be greeted by the face of the ugliest camel I have ever seen. It was a huge, unsightly beast. It was old and hoary, possessing big yellow buckled teeth, a bristled chin and breath that stank like a sewer. It had a big fat head and boggly eyes. Truly, the creature was grotesque.

When I turned around I scared it as much as it scared me and the even-toed ungulate suddenly jumped back with a start, as did I. We must have looked a right sight. In any event Natalia pissed herself laughing and said she loved the English because we are so funny. 'Yeah' I said; 'we don't get that many camels in the middle of Telford.'

What about the chess? Well, once again, I observed people playing in the park but this time I did go over and played a game against a small chap with soft brown eyes and a comical toothless smile. We played one slow game and I managed to win. A westerner in those parts was like an alien at that time and many people gathered round and shook my hand. I gave the man some pencils after the game and he was really taken aback. He loved them... then he started singing some kind of folk song, and his mates joined in. I wish I had filmed it.

Someone produced a bottle of what looked like aviation fuel and offered me a swig. I politely declined, worried that it might kill me on the spot.

And that was it. The trip was over. Both Gill and I thoroughly enjoyed it. It is true that whilst I have obviously focused on the chess, Gill and I did have a great time and shared plenty of sight-seeing together. We packed as much as we could into the days. We kept in touch with Natalia for some time afterwards but as with all these things, it faded. On the flight home I knew that I had only had a taste of the Soviet Union, but that one day I would return for the full course. That day is still waiting, and I am getting serious wanderlust.

Upon my return home I was summoned to the MoD debrief in which I was asked lots of inane questions like 'Were you followed?' and 'Did you tell anyone what your job was?' I mean if I were going to be naughty, I would hardly tell the MoD would I? Naturally, I talked about chess most of the time which seemed to bore them very quickly. To be honest, there were times when I thought that I was being followed but some of that could just have been silly paranoia. If someone was following me, so what?

I cannot leave the subject of the almost unfathomable Soviets without quoting from the chess book *The Soviet Chess School* written by A. Kotov and M. Yudovich. In an effort to illustrate the standing that chess had in Russia, the penultimate paragraph in the book says, *We call on all the world's chess players actively to join the struggle for the preservation of life on Earth, which is threatened by a thermonuclear catastrophe.*

Well, this was still the cold war after all.

A man barely alive (AMBA)

Give me health and a day, and I will make the pomp
of Emperors look ridiculous

Ralph Waldo Emerson

When I was younger I was a very active sportsman. In my early and mid-twenties I was running every day, playing two football matches each weekend in local leagues (take note you whining Premier League players), enjoying badminton every Friday night and even participating in the odd game of golf and cricket. I loved the competitive aspect of participation in these sports, just as I did at the chess board.

Your biggest opponent is not the other person, it is you. We learn this when we are pushed to our limits. We discover who we are when we are called upon to dig deep, when our bodies and minds ask that little bit more of us than we thought we could give. Sport was an integral aspect of my life. But to my huge frustration, good health has not been my friend.

I have a rare blood disorder which was discovered in my late teens, but it did not stop me doing my sport. I have haemolytic anaemia where my red blood cells break down too quickly – about ninety days instead of 120. I have a letter from the Haematologist, confirming that I am a mutant. My genes certainly are. My spleen is enlarged, therefore contact sport is ill-advised on doctor's orders in case it gets bashed.

Even with this knowledge, I could not give up my football. I played one game on the Astroturf at Lilleshall, in Shropshire. This huge bloke came out of nowhere and smashed into my spleen area with his knee as we jumped for a header. I knew something bad had happened as I could barely breath. Cue the trip to hospital and the local Accident and Emergency department.

After a short wait I saw a stunningly beautiful Indian doctor. She told me to drop my trousers and pants and then said, 'I am going to put my finger in your rectum, I need to feel what's going on, as there could be blood.'

As she inserted a very cold digit I recall getting over the embarrassment by cracking a joke. 'I have only just met you' I said. 'You are a bit forward considering you haven't even asked me out for a drink yet.'

'You'll live,' she said without a flicker. 'Take it easy for a few days, and incidentally, I don't drink, now get dressed.' She smiled as she left the room with me standing there with my pants around my ankles. Those were the days. These days comedy has gone, sacrificed as it has been at the altar of liberalism and political correctness. I rail against it at every opportunity.

I thought that I would still play sport, but out of the blue, disaster struck and this time it was life-changing. I was dancing at a wedding when my heart suddenly raced into overdrive at what must have been over 200 beats per minute. I thought I would die. It continued for about ten minutes and I almost passed out, but I did not tell anyone. I just made my excuses and left. I shrugged it off, but it kept on happening suddenly, even when I was sleeping. I expected every day to die, and just drop dead. It happened again during a badminton match, going off like a jack-hammer and at that point I had to seek medical help.

I knew that something was very wrong and that hospital was inevitable. I was experiencing bouts of tachycardia, and I was soon diagnosed with Arrhythmogenic right ventricular dysplasia. This is a rare disorder that is characterized by structural and functional abnormalities of the right ventricle and a propensity for ventricular arrhythmias and sudden death.

It meant that sudden death was a real possibility, and it scared the hell out of me. In short, my right ventricle is damaged, and the electrolyte levels need to be kept in check otherwise the normal heart rhythm gets *hijacked* and my heart beats at dangerous levels.

I had a spell in hospital in Telford for quite a while. I was getting seriously worse, and I had to be flown by air ambulance to St. Bartholomew's hospital in London. I recall being semi-conscious but looking out of the chopper as we flew over Wembley Stadium. I was really excited, and my heart raced even faster so I got a rollicking from the doctor looking after me.

After staying for a couple of weeks in St. Barts in London undergoing all sorts of tests including the treadmill, one genius of a doctor managed to find a concoction of beta blockers that actually managed to control my ticker. To this day, I still take that magic mix although I have had many more episodes and every day I experience ectopic beats – or palpitations. I have lived with the condition for many years and have been seriously ill many times. On a couple of occasions, I have just wanted the lights to go out.

I have had the electric shock treatment and it isn't nice. My wife was there when I had a really horrific episode and I had to go to a hospital urgently. The team were not cardiologists but had to shock me to get my heart back into rhythm.

At that point, it was so bad I actually said goodbye to Susan. I thought I would die and that wasn't the first time. Then the medical team (who were doing their best!) set the machine at the wrong level. They were not cardio experts after all. They were faffing around talking about what level to set the shock at whilst I was in tachycardia. 'For God's sake, just blast me,' I said, and they did.

Oops.

They certainly had set it too high. I might as well have been tasered. A blue arc flashed up as my body literally rose above the bed. I bit my lip hard and as I came down the leading nurse said, 'I think we set that a bit high.'

Well it did the trick. As I sat up I vomited and that, mixed with the blood pouring from my lip spewed out onto my burning chest. My tachycardia settled after they had to put me out for a while. I had been given an anaesthetic but it missed the vein and my arm swelled up to twice the size. It was excruciating.

Susan tells me that I was struggling to come round from the said anaesthetic and the doctor was slapping my face saying, 'Craig, CRAIG, wake up!' and he tried to tell Sue that I was coming round, but I wasn't.

Susan said to him, 'Two things doc; first of all his name isn't Craig, it is Carl, and the second is that he hates being slapped or hit on the head and if he was awake he would have punched you as a reflex action.' It took a couple more hours for me to come round, I am told. I am not sure what dose I had but it was big.

Sue was really upset about all of this, but I am still here to tell the tale, so there we are. By and large NHS staff have been awesome. There have been exceptions of course but that is normal for any huge organisation.

My poor health affected my chess greatly. Non-chess players fail to appreciate just how stressful competitive chess is. Imagine playing in a crucial game in the final round of a three day – or even seven day – competition. You are close to winning a prize, but you only have seconds left on your clock to finish the game. You have to find the correct moves or at least find any move.

There is a crowd of people watching and there are only forty seconds left, now twenty… now only five seconds remain and there are still three moves to make. The tension can be unbearable, and at that time it sent my heart into tachycardia a few times. I would go to a tournament but end up in hospital. I remember being blue-lighted from Nuneaton once when such a thing occurred. Still, at least I had a pocket set whenever I went into hospital and the doctors used to love talking about the game.

Sadly, it affected me so much that I had to retire from playing chess. This made headlines in the local chess column in the *Shropshire Star* newspaper which read: *Shropshire chess has suffered a blow with the enforced retirement on doctor's orders at the age of just thirty-two.*

Looking through my old scorebooks I note that on 8th May 1996 I had tachycardia during a game against Steve Tarr and I had tachycardia again, twice during a game against Klaus Wasmuht on 30th May. Clearly this just could not continue. I had to stop playing. I was literally killing myself. Each bout of tachycardia was doing damage.

Yet how was I supposed to stay away? Chess was my passion, an immutable aspect of my everyday life. I could not bear the idea of not playing again but what could I do? At one stage I had a discussion about a heart transplant and read somewhere that they were even using pigs' hearts! I was not so keen on that idea. I joked that after such an operation I would suddenly have a yearning to sleep on straw.

I tried self-help and I began to learn to control my emotions. This revolved around trying to put a game of chess in perspective. I cannot emphasise enough how difficult it is to try to be calm at the board whilst being as competitive as you possibly can. It is a distinct discipline.

My life was miserable without *proper* competitive chess and against doctor's orders I returned to the board. I figured that if I was going to die, I should rather do so at the chessboard than in some rain-sodden shopping precinct, or in an armchair covered in biscuit crumbs. I still play competitively of course and most of my opponents have no idea that I am really fighting two battles, one against them at the board and another against my heart, trying to suppress my emotions and stop the thing from going crazy.

There is a little more to this story. I began to manage my condition with fantastic medical support and almost two years after retiring I bagged the Shropshire county champion title and on June 30th 1998 the local newspaper reported as follows:

Champion Carl gets to the heart of the matter. Carl Portman has scored a sensational success by winning the Shropshire championship for the first time. Not only has he struck a blow for the 'average' player but it is a tremendous personal triumph as Portman has overcome a heart problem which forced him to retire from the game.

This was another significant milestone in my amateur chess career and my life in general. It shows that with determination and a mindset that says, *don't give up*, great things can be achieved.

In 2009 whilst living in Oxfordshire I had a new cardiologist called Tim Betts. He is an incredible man and a true inspiration. Not only is he the most engaging cardiologist that I have ever met, but he is also the most professional. His bedside manner is second to none and everything he does says: be positive, this is what you can do – do not focus so much on what you cannot. He was once chosen to carry the Olympic torch through part of Oxford – an honour befitting such an Olympian in the medical world.

In 2012 I played a 24 hour chessathon to raise money for my local heart unit. I am here with my cardiologist Dr Timothy Betts.

Up until 2009 I had refused to have an implanted defibrillator. I considered that having a relatively large and ugly titanium box implanted into my chest would turn me into some kind of Frankenstein's monster. I am very slim so it would have been obvious, not to mention painful. Besides, the unit is not to be confused with a pacemaker – it delivers electric shocks at some 840 volts at a time.

Dr. Tim was the only cardiologist who could convince me to have the procedure. He said, 'Carl you enjoy life, don't you?' and I replied in the affirmative. 'You want to play more chess, don't you?' he added. He knew what that meant to me and in September 2009 I became 'Iron Man' as my wife calls me. It was life-changing.

I have had three shocks from the devices (I had a replacement unit in 2014), including one on a fishing boat in the Arctic Ocean off the Norwegian coast. That night I really thought I might die after being blown across my cabin by a sudden and powerful shock, but I staggered on deck to photograph *Aurora borealis*. It truly was heaven and hell that night, and my old pal Jeremy Smith, who was my travelling companion witnessed the only time I ever shed a tear in front of him.

That shock probably saved my life incidentally. I had a sudden and extremely aggressive tachycardia attack. The defibrillator basically has three settings when my heart gets to a dangerous level. It will first try to ascertain why my heart is going fast – is it normal exercise or an abnormal occurrence? Then it will try to pace the heart back to normal rhythm, which is the pacemaker bit. If that fails it will charge up and administer a shock – a bit like you see in the films with the paddles. One two three and stand back! Ouch.

Initially I played my chess games with the haunting fear that the device would go off without warning and give me what they call an *inappropriate shock*, that is to say one that was not medically required. I had heard stories of people whose defibrillator unit fired up to thirty times in one continuous run almost killing the patient, or burning their heart out. I had seen a picture of an exploded battery in someone's chest and it looked like a scene from the film *The Thing*. It was dreadful but I had to suppress all these thoughts. You simply have to believe that these things are not going to happen to you, otherwise it might literally drive you mad. Psychology in chess and psychology in life. Both are critical factors to moving forward in my view.

The defibrillator does not prevent tachycardia, but it delivers a shock meant to get the heart back into sinus rhythm. Think of it like fire sprinklers, they don't prevent a fire, but they fulfil their role when one occurs. I still have to control my emotions during every game – especially when I have that one-minute remaining on the clock to make several moves. Tick, tick, tick, tick – find the best move, forty seconds, twenty seconds, ten seconds, three, two - FIND THE DAMNED MOVE AND KEEP CALM. I should stop playing Blitz chess online really but it is a drug that I cannot and will not give up. It isn't like alcoholism, where you can go to an AA class is it?

I will set the scene. Several *addicts* are sitting in a semi-circle in a cold village hall on a Tuesday evening. You decide to go first. You stand up and say, 'Hello everyone, my name is Carl and I have not played blitz chess for three months.' Cue a round of applause and a *well done* from the facilitator. Former footballer George Best said, 'once an alcoholic, always an alcoholic.' The same goes for Blitz chess players.

I should say that defibrillators save many lives and they are remarkable things. I essentially have a mini-computer in my chest. I can even download the heart rhythm information to a monitor in my bedroom which is then transferred to the hospital. Just try to imagine this. You are standing at one end of a room and a nurse can press a button at her/his end of the room which controls your heart rate. They can put you into tachycardia if they so wish. It's weird and initially very frightening but as an alternative to death I will take it. That's my life.

I do have to have the unit replaced every few years and I was due one such change at the same time as I was due to meet my music hero Ozzy Osbourne at a VIP meet and greet in Birmingham. It was a dilemma; have the heart procedure and risk not being well enough to meet the man a few days later or postpone it (which is a bit rude, actually) and meet him. The answer was clear – and Ozzy won, and I should comment that my brilliant cardiologist supported me saying that life is meant to be about fun, right? It was great to meet the Black Sabbath frontman. Susan could see that I was like a little kid all day in anticipation of the moment and I did manage a few words with Ozzy.

Sue laughs now when she recalls me telling him to sign my memorabilia 'with love' since I had put off a heart procedure just to see him.

Ozzy was flabbergasted, 'Really? Wow. You've put off a heart op just to meet me, thank you.'

He was genuinely incredulous. He was so lovely and we have a great photograph. They call him the Prince of Darkness but any real Ozzy fan knows that he is far from it. He may shuffle around these days due to a combination of cocaine, alcohol and Parkinson's disease but the man will always be an absolute legend. Forget the shell that is his body, the spirit and aura of the man is a wonder to behold. I have never seen anyone command an audience like Ozzy does and never seen anyone so adored by those very people. It is a very special relationship. Not everybody will understand, but then they don't have to. Ozzy fans are not seeking approval.

Meeting my hero Ozzy Osbourne in Birmingham in 2013. I put off a heart operation to do so – much to his amazement.

He will always be my *Metal God* but closely following in his hallowed footsteps are the likes of Lemmy Kilmister, Rob Halford and Ronnie James Dio. They are all frontmen I note, so if we are going for guitarists I will go for Steve Howe, Tony Iommi and Dave Gilmour. Go on then, I will throw in just two drummers. How about Ian Paice and Neil Peart? Finally, in the interests of equality my favourite female singer is Veronica Freeman from Benedictum followed by Doro Pesch. Okay, you are pushing me now, let us have Chris Squire on bass and Jon Lord on keyboards. Done! Don't ask me to pick a bloody road crew.

Hard hitting Lemmy was the one for quotes. He once said that there are two kinds of people in life, those you can trust and those you can't so be sure to learn which are which. Very profound I thought.

Back to the chessboard. The simple fact is, you need to be fit and healthy to play your best chess. To really do justice to your potential, you must feel good physically and mentally. You cannot achieve what you are capable of if you are ill, and sadly I am ill a lot. My mate Ray calls me AMBA. It means, *A Man Barely Alive*.

It is also one reason why I have so much respect for former world chess champion, Mikhail Tal. He suffered from terrible illness throughout his life, including the removal of a kidney, but he kept on playing – and smoking and drinking – until the very end. He was a blazing meteor that burned out too quickly, passing away at the age of fifty-five.

Elite chess players these days are super fit. The likes of Magnus Carlsen, the current world champion from Norway plays a great deal of sport to stay in shape, especially football. Mind you back in 1972, Bobby Fischer and Boris Spassky enjoyed swimming and tennis and Victor Korchnoi even took up skiing. Players can lose significant units of weight during a tense game and need to be body ready for it.

In the end I do the best I can with the health I have. I have had heart ablation procedures to keep me going, and it all digs into your resources of energy and stamina but I repeat that just because I am an amateur chess player, it does not mean I am not serious about my chess. Does the amateur naturalist not love butterflies as much as the full-time lepidopterist? Does the boy in the park not love football as much as Lionel Messi?

I love my chess as much as the next man or woman. Before a tournament my preparation is confined to the chessboard. I change my diet a few days before a competition, eating more *brain food* such as vegetables and bananas even though I am not keen on either. I will walk more and build up some stamina. It is not always easy (especially with the health issues) but my commitment to the task is unwavering. At least my approach gives the coming battle the respect it deserves, and I have a fighting chance.

My health has always influenced my chess activities but there are many ways to enjoy the game – not just playing but writing, coaching, organising, lecturing and simply reading about it. Caissa has come to my aid many a time in hospital. I do not think I could have endured some of the nights if I did not have a chess set and chess books.

On one occasion the poor chap in a bed opposite was in a really bad way. He had Tourette's Syndrome and he was cursing everyone. I just carried on reading my book on chess endings. Mind you it was funny when a doctor came in and said, 'Good morning Mr Davies' to be greeted with, 'Morning wanker; scratch my balls.' Yep, that happened. I was used to the chap by then and knew what was coming any time that someone went near him.

A young nurse came to see him and he sang, *I'll be up your flue in a minute or two*. Then he burst into more song,

One black sheep, one white one
And one with a bit of shite on.

It made no sense, but there were a few red faces I can tell you.

On another occasion an elderly man in the bed next to mine had a terrible rasping cough. I was talking to him a little over a couple of days and he was in a state of semi-consciousness, but the nursing staff could see that I was keeping an eye on him. My heart was playing up but I was very much *compos mentis*. The man had worked down the mines and his chesty cough was the net result. Around 2am he spluttered and shouted for a drink but there was no nurse around, so I got out of my bed and gave him a glass of water. It turns out that was his last ever drink. He died an hour later. The nurse woke me to tell me and I was terribly sad for him. Oddly, she asked if I wanted to see him, as he had no family. I did not think it was appropriate to be honest, so I declined.

Again, I lost myself in chess books to stop being depressed at my situation. What a relief it was - and is - to immerse myself in the history of the game and exercise my mind with chess puzzles and problems. I will confess to one naughty thing here. One of the patients in our eight-bed ward was a really gobby Londoner. He saw me playing chess on my pocket set. 'I am a chess player. I will give you a thrashing,' he said. He had been really annoying on the ward, loud and arrogant so I said, 'Yes, okay what about a pound a game?' He quickly agreed, so I took the set over to his bed and we began to play.

One can quickly deduce if someone really is a chess player or not by their first few moves. He was not. In fact, he was all mouth and trousers. I decided to teach motormouth a lesson because everyone was fed up with him, moaning and saying *me, me, me* all the time. I deliberately lost the game – the only time that I have ever done so in my life. He was full of himself.

I sighed and went back to my bedside locker, coming back with a crisp ten-pound note. 'How about a tenner on the next game?' I ventured. In an instant he agreed. Surely, he would have smelled a rat but not him. His ego was too big.

I proceeded to smash him and in fairness he handed over his ten pounds saying, (London accent please): 'I've been fakkin' done haven't I?'

'Like a kipper,' I replied.

I offered to play him again but he was having none of it. Still, it shut him up for the rest of the day as he sat incandescent in his bed brooding over the loss of the game and his cash. Thank you Caissa you little beauty.

Fast forward to 2012. I used chess as the vehicle to raise cash for my local heart unit at the John Radcliffe hospital in Oxford. I organised a twenty-four-hour *chessathon* at Banbury shopping centre. My pal, Richard Beckett would spend the biggest portion of the time with me, but other lads from Banbury Chess Club would come and give me a few games throughout the day and night. One of our lads, Chris Evans, is married to a wonderful Spanish lady called Irene, and she cooked up some tremendous Spanish cuisine to eat throughout the night.

I was delighted to receive the support of the then local MP Tony Baldry as he liked chess. We played a game and I offered my queen as a sacrifice. He looked at me quizzically and took it. He wondered why I would give away my queen for free. I joked that being a politician I knew that he would be unable to resist a free lunch so I knew he would take it – I then followed up with a neat checkmate. He took it all in his stride and fair play to him. We raised a few hundred quid and also the profile of chess in Banbury. At one point two policemen passing by stopped for a game – proving once again that chess is a game for all.

One of my discussion points with passers-by was the fact that people who may have had a stroke or heart attack can still use their brain despite diminished physical capacity and chess is perfect for stretching that very important muscle.

Health has therefore unfortunately held me back yet I do not lament what I have not had, I remain ever grateful for what I have enjoyed. Even though I am unable to remember a day when I felt *perfectly* fine, I still have good days where I feel like I could take on the emperors of the world. Those are the days when I submerge myself into the warm and comforting waters of chess.

It is true that through chess events and motivational talks in UK, Italy and the Czech Republic, I have raised a few pounds for the NHS and a local hospice but of course one does such things because one is motivated to do so. Reward or recognition are neither asked for or requested. However, I was stunned to be presented with an award by the British Heart Foundation in 2019 at a splendid gala in London. I had been nominated by my wife, Susan for the BHF Heart Heroes Inspirational Award for that year. No one knew who the winners were until the evening, and there were several other candidates. Initially I refused to go – I am actually not good at accepting gifts – and that was if I even won the thing. Sue gently persuaded me to go 'for her' and off we went for an evening out. I was therefore stunned when the celebrity Penny Lancaster (married to Rod Stewart) announced my name and I went up on stage to meet her and accept the award. Wow! The Duchess of York, Sarah Ferguson was sat at the table in front of me, and I smiled to see royalty applauding me. Nan would have loved it. I have to say with sincere conviction that it was the other award winners who inspired me. There was a heart surgeon who gave up his free time to fly abroad and save children's lives. Then there were children who saved all their pocket money or sold their toys to raise money for another kid with heart problems. I mean come on – it is fantastic. I was truly humbled. Why can't we have more of this in the news instead of the diet of negative, miserable crap that the mainstream media tosses to us daily?

The retired footballer Glenn Hoddle was a guest speaker, talking emotionally about his own experiences when he almost died from a heart attack. Susan and I had a chat and a lovely photograph taken with him, and the evening will live long in our memories.

The best tonic for my health has never been found on a prescription sheet, in a bottle, a pill or a blood transfusion. It has always been found on the sixty-four squares of a chessboard. I cannot live without it. If I cannot play over the board, I will play online. If that is not possible I can play by snail mail, or standard post as it used to be called.

After all, it would not be the first time.

Correspondence chess

*True words are often not beautiful,
just as beautiful words are often not true*

Japanese Proverb

THE GATEWAY CITY · ST. LOUIS, MISSOURI · The Gateway Arch symbolizing the opening of the West is the central feature of the Jefferson National Expansion Memorial, above the historic Mississippi Levee. Our tallest National Monument, the arch is in the shape of an inverted catenary curve, 630 feet high, designed by the late Eero Saarinen. The Admiral excursion steamer is shown in midstream, the world's largest inland excursion vessel. It is now being refurbished as a floating complex of shops, offices, restaurants, theatres, and museum.

post card

RF Stefans
PO Box 12613
GB WI 54307 USA

R: 4/09
S: 4/10 MT: 1

A) 8. 6151 8. 4837
   9. 5354!?

Carl Portman
41 Broadway Ketley, Telford
Shropshire TF1 4AS
ENGLAND

Hi Carl! Glad you
liked the coin! Looking forward to the English crown!!
But I'm in no rush. How are your games coming along?
         I feel I have Vanfcek in a small bind, but
it's still early. Hear from you soon!

62126-C © Art Grossmann Photo   BestQ

A correspondence chess card.
This game was played against an engaging American in 1997.

Some 45,000 years ago people painted on cave walls. The ability to communicate by writing something down has been an invaluable facet of human development. When you paint or write, you want to say something, to express yourself. It is just the same for chess.

141

Correspondence chess is perfect for those who cannot get out and about to engage in the game for whatever reason, be it health or age etc. Before the development of chess programs and computers, correspondence chess, sometimes known as postal chess was extremely popular. This was a form of the game where people played by post – the now *old-fashioned* snail mail.

Here is how it works. The players send the moves back and forth to one another on a specially designed card with a chess board and co-ordinates so that the protagonists are clear where the pieces are moving from and to. Each move is recorded on the card in an internationally recognised format, the purpose of which is to avoid confusion between languages.

There are different rules regarding the time allowed for making a move. This might be a move every three days maximum, or seven days and more. It is quite true that this process is slow, but then that is the very essence of correspondence chess. One has several days to contemplate a move which allows more time to delve into the very heart of the position. A player should then be able to look much deeper than he/she would in a couple of hours.

The Oxford Companion to chess notes that one Thomas Hyde refers to games being played in the 1600s between Venetian and Croatian merchants but they found the transmission of moves to be expensive. However, the golden age of correspondence chess was in the first half of the nineteenth century. Edinburgh and London played a match and letters were carried about 400 miles by mail coach travelling day and night. In January 1840 Britain introduced the penny post which led to an increase in correspondence chess.

I have played opponents from Russia, France, Germany,

America and the Czech Republic. I enjoyed exchanging thoughts and cultural snippets with everyone except the Russian who refused to engage in conversation – sending only his moves and signing his name. That was perfectly acceptable, and I bore him no malice but to my mind it sort of pushed against the concept of correspondence chess where the idea is to learn something more than just the chess moves. Each to their own.

I kept all of my correspondence cards from decades ago, and reading through them again pricks at the memory. *The American* wrote about my trip to the Soviet Union, whilst another player congratulated me on my 'success at Blackpool' which I don't even remember now as I have played there more than once.

Above all, I had the most interesting dialogue with the Frenchman, Marc Doudon. We exchanged not just cards, but letters and they were tremendous fun. I would write in French, and ask him to correct me, sending back his comments so that I might learn. Therefore, I managed to play chess and enjoy a free language course.

I believe that he was quite elderly at the time (in 1997) and he lived in Dijon, famous of course for its mustard. He was a good player. At some point, he offered me my weight in cheese if I beat him. I wrote back immediately offering a draw! There was no way I wanted so much cheese, thank you very much. This was just one of several comedic exchanges. He had a most excellent sense of humour. Yes, we drew, and he kept his cheese.

I note from reading the cards that we had several exchanges about the Euro which was obviously being introduced into the

European Union at the time. He asked how England would fare by *giving away* the pound, and I said at the time that we had no intention of doing so. We exchanged views about sovereignty and trade, and I asked if he would use the Channel Tunnel, so I was dealing with Brexit issues in a way long before the issue came up in the UK.

Marc was adamant that his beloved France should not lose its identity. I felt the same about England. There's nothing wrong with national pride which too many people now stupidly call extremism or xenophobia. Countries are analogous to people; we all have our own identity but also try to do well in our dealings with other humans. The idea that we would lose the essence of who we are by doing this is absurd. We can work individually and together but I believe every country should retain the inalienable right to govern itself. Others disagree and that is up to them. My philosophy on such matters is that I may not agree with your opinion, but I will fight for your right to hold it.

My American opponent lived in Wisconsin and he was a good sport. We swapped national coins and spoke about our civil wars. Robert E. Lee v Oliver Cromwell would have been an interesting discussion. There was so much more to our correspondence than the chess games. I learned geography, French and indeed history. Once again, chess sheds a positive light on all things.

I also played correspondence chess at home in the UK. I recall the 1994-95 Midland Counties Chess Union Correspondence Chess Championships. I think that is the first time I ever played. I had two games against one Les Cresswell, losing one game and drawing another. It was my fault for losing with white. At the time I insisted on my first five moves being: 1.d4 2.Nc3 3.Bg5 4.f3. 5.e4. I liked the weird stuff back then but they were sexy moves, not the best.

Correspondence chess still exists, but of course most people use their incredibly strong computer programs to help them make their moves. It is essentially two computer engines playing one another with humans facilitating. That might be fine for some, but it is not for me. I do understand that a computer program is an indispensable resource just as books are, but back then we humans decided on the move whereas the chess engines just list possibilities in order of strength based on cold calculation alone. Many people make a move just because the computer says so with no real understanding of why.

There are huge databases of correspondence chess games now and they include the pre-computer era as well as the present. Such games are tremendously useful to interrogate to see if one can find little opening nuances or uncork some fresh novelty here and there. The players will have invested days into studying various lines and trying them out. Even the top players consult correspondence games from the past as a matter of course. It is possible after all to find new ideas from days gone by. Old ideas in new settings they call it.

I talk a lot about the benefits of chess. In the case of correspondence chess, it clearly brings people together, not just from the next town, city or even country but across the world. From Costa Rica to Costa Blanca, we can all enjoy the richness and diversity of the game.

We still paint on walls of course, but nowadays we call it graffiti. The kids that do it are not the cool mavericks that they think they are. It's all been done before, thousands of years ago.

Maybe we will get fed up with computers. There are people today who literally cannot write with a pen and paper. They never had the ability to in the first place, as everything is done at a keyboard. Perhaps those heady days will return. Perhaps a virus will shut down all computers forever and then we will be forced to communicate as we once did, by correspondence… snail mail!

Now it is time to pack your bags and walk with me much closer to home as we step over the stile and into the hauntingly beautiful and ancient county of Shropshire. It is the birthplace of naturalist Charles Darwin, poet Wilfred Owen, industrialist Abraham Derby, author Mary Webb and footballer Billy Wright amongst many more.

It is also the county where so many of my chess memories lie. Tears of joy and despair resulting from battles at the chessboard stain the pathways and leafy country lanes where I have trodden as a youth.

That is the land of lost content,
I see it shining plain,
The happy highways where I went
And cannot come again

A. E.Houseman, A Shropshire Lad.

Floreat Salopia

Holy angel lift me from this burning hell
Resurrection make me whole
Son of Judas bring the saints to my revenge
Resurrection bring me home

Rob Halford - Resurrection

Floreat Salopia is Shropshire's county motto and it means *May Shropshire Flourish*. The chess community was doing just that, and I returned to the board again enjoying a feast of chess from 1983 to 2000. One night, Caissa appeared in my sleep and gave me a team talk. She urged me to give myself to her once again and continue my chess journey. My life was more settled, and I had time and energy to spare. Why not?

Thus, from 1983 until the end of the century (Gosh, that sounds old) I played and organized lots of chess. I enjoyed playing for the sheer fun of it, not worrying about grades or prizes. There were lots of weekend tournaments to participate in, such as the Shropshire congress (my local), Crewe, Sandwell, Chester, Birmingham, Goodyear (at Wolverhampton), Rhyl and many more. There were county and club matches and of course, correspondence chess.

It would be remiss of me not to mention Jeff and Nancy Cox. These were John Cox's parents and they both sadly passed away in the last couple of years. They founded the Shropshire congress in the 1970s and ran it for many years under their leadership. It still runs today with a different and proficient organisational team. Jeff and Nancy made a huge contribution to chess in the county and were as good as any parents could have been to me and I spent a great deal of my time at their house in Kynnersley. I miss them so much.

In terms of club chess, the GKN Sankey 'A' team had last won the Shropshire chess league title in 1980, and the club folded a few years later. I believe that a toxic combination of business and politics put the club to the sword. All I know is that it was the end of an epoch and a new home was required as soon as possible, and I was the one who found it.

This is where working in the MoD paid off again. I was at Central Ordnance Depot (COD) in Donnington. There was a top-notch Civil Service Sports Council club nearby and I was friends with the committee members, which helped to grease the wheels for me to find a new chess club called Coddon. Those letters were the COD of Central Ordnance Depot and the DON of Donnington.

Money was no problem as I could secure grants from the sports council, and this resulted in a rapid growth in club membership. I look back almost with incredulity to think that in those days on a club night during our matches, we actually stopped the clocks and temporarily postponed play for a short time half-way through the evening.

The opposition were delighted about this because they knew what was coming. We would produce trays of delicious sandwiches accompanied by tea and coffee. It was a veritable feast, and we were the only chess club to do this in the league. The downside was that the away team was almost always at their strongest because they all wanted to play at our club and get the free grub. The salubrious surroundings seemed to stimulate our chess development.

We had a first team consisting of Trevor Brotherton, me, Richard Archer, Alan Knight, Glyn Pugh, Phil Cameron, Ian Gilbert and a chap called Kiddy Makwaya from Zambia all at various stages, and we won the league first in 1989 and then for six consecutive years from 1992 to 1997 after which I left for Shrewsbury Chess Club and we won the league in the first year in 1998, putting the brakes on my old club. I admit to having mixed feelings about that. Then I moved to a new house and with it joined a new chess club in Newport – where we won the league in 1999. I hold the record for winning eight consecutive league wins with three different clubs. Heady days indeed.

Let's bring Richard Archer back centre stage again. I always refer to him as my little brother although the cheeky sod called me pops even when I was in my thirties. He flew as close to the sun as he could in his younger days. He could drink like a fish – but hold it too. It was like going out with electricity with Richard, you never knew what would happen. One Baltic winter's evening there was a knock on my door. I was living with Gill at the time and I answered to find a shivering, half-naked, blood-spattered Richard blinking at me.

He had downed a few beers in Telford and the story went that someone (a girl, I think) had thrown him out of the car onto the M54 motorway. Richie had managed to stagger to my place where he stayed overnight. There is a bit more to this tale. He was steaming drunk and barely coherent, but the truth is – so was I. Back then I could neck a few beers too and I had downed a few lagers at home followed by a couple of large

Pernod and cokes. I was hammered. Next morning, I awoke to find that I too was half-naked and lying in the bath. I tried to picture what the hell had happened. I still don't know. I managed to extricate myself from the confines of the bathtub as I heard moaning emanating from my girlfriend's bedroom. Where the hell was Richard?

I stumbled into the room to find my girlfriend sleeping soundly but there was no sign of little Richard. I opened the door to the spare bedroom to find a crumpled heap of flesh, dead to the world. He recovered much quicker than I did, and you would not believe the size of the roasting I got for the whole unseemly event from the other half. Those were the days. We both look back on this eventful evening, and laugh, but I didn't then. Not long after I stopped getting drunk and have not done so for decades, partly due to my heart problems but also because I just do not like being so unpredictable and out of control.

Going back to my flat for a moment, Richard would aim for my refrigerator on any visit and sniff out a pizza or any edible item contained therein. He could eat me out of house and home whilst listening to Venom, Wasp and Anthrax which I willingly planted on the turntable. His mother admonished me for 'introducing him to devil music.' I have no idea what Richard had told her, but I was innocent of such a charge and remonstrated that heavy metal was not devil music and if he liked it he could make his own choices. Sometimes I long to have those days back – carefree chess and good laughs. Where did it go?

I am proud that my chess CV states that I was a county chess champion, which I won in 1998. I will elaborate more on this achievement later in this chapter. One of the nice games I played as champion the following year was against the Shropshire Star newspaper chess correspondent Toby Neal. I hope he will forgive me for including the game at chapter sixteen.

Chess took me away from Shropshire of course. Working for the MoD meant that I could wangle special paid leave to play chess. It doesn't get much better than that. I played in local qualifiers in Telford to try to reach the national Civil Service finals that were usually held in Devonshire Hall at Leeds University. Most often Richard and I both qualified from the midlands region (two were allowed) and off we would jolly well go for chess, beers and the great camaraderie that existed between the players who gathered from all over the UK.

Those finals were great fun. There were some epic battles at the chessboard and although I found the going difficult initially, after a few attempts my confidence grew and I was content in my own mind that I deserved to be there. I relaxed a bit more away from the board and this reflected in some of my games.

There were always familiar faces at the finals, having repeatedly qualified from their own regional competitions. There was Kevin Thurlow, also known as the Redhill Ripper. He is a stronger player than me, but we have enjoyed some good chess fights, and I have at least drawn against him – but he plays a mean English opening and knows all of the wrinkles. You cannot catch him out. He is also a qualified arbiter and extremely proficient at the role. You don't mess with Kevin when he is in charge. It was years before I found out that he was also an expert on owls and a Leeds United fan. Sheffield

Wednesday football club are called *The Owls* so I wondered why he never supported that club and got a two for one bargain. Kev loves his cricket too and is the go-to man for any updates during a test match.

Another character was Tony Ashby who is well-known on the chess circuit. If I may say so, he was always the good-looking gentleman with the chiselled jaw. A kind of James Bond figure if you will. He has an acerbic wit and he played interesting, combative and creative chess. The man had the temerity to play a Wing Gambit against me when I essayed my favourite French Defence. It would be nigh on impossible to meet a more courteous human being and the world needs more people like Tony.

I recall a Scotsman – I shall call him McJack – who had a red face and a fiery temper. After becoming more incandescent by the minute during one game, he suddenly lost, and picked up the thick wooden board, lifting it above his terrified opponent's head as if he were going to smash it down on his cranium. Luckily he composed himself and smiled and walked away without a word, but he was seething.

Then there was another lad called Ian who was, to put it kindly, rather morose. He eyes were surrounded by dark circles and he had the look of a man who had just stepped out of a coffin. In one game, in an upstairs room he was the last player to finish. We were all downstairs gathered around an old piano, analysing our own games. We heard the creak of the door open and a rather sorry figure descended. He stopped in front of us all, looked around and said, 'Three hours for fuck all.'

Each and every one of us wanted to laugh but we managed to contain ourselves. The lad then went to the piano and played a morbid death march spouting that his opponent was lucky to win. This is a clear example of what losing at chess can do to a person. I take some losses desperately badly myself sometimes, but I will say this, I never blame my opponent. Never. Their job is to stop me doing what I want to do. That is chess. If you cannot handle it, don't play it.

Personally, I refuse to use the word *lucky* in chess, but I am happy to employ the term *fortunate*. When the game starts one is not given to chance, as one is with rolling a dice or dealing a card from a shuffled pack. You alone are responsible for the moves, ergo you have only yourself to admonish or pat on the back. When the clocks begin you are on your own.

Another plus for the Devonshire Hall venue was the fact that there was a snooker room upstairs. Kevin Thurlow and I had a competition which is still going on – something like the best of seventy-five frames and over the years we have managed to squeeze a few in on our travels. The score is currently 9-7 to me but I know the shark will be back at me next time around.

Sadly, my Civil Service chess-playing days are gone, but I cherish the time I had. I feel privileged to have been part of something so enjoyable. Representing the Civil Service was and always will be an honour.

I have always derived as much pleasure from organising chess events as playing in them. Over the years I have managed to persuade some phenomenal players to give simultaneous displays and lectures in Shropshire and Oxfordshire. These include Nigel Davies, John Speelman, Daniel King (twice), Nigel Short, John Nunn, Matthew Sadler, Natasha Regan, Tania Sachdev and Lev Polugayevsky.

For the uninitiated, a simultaneous display is one where the strong player – usually a master – plays multiple players at once.

They usually have the white pieces on every board and therefore make the first move. The contest is essentially the strength and skill of the master against weight of numbers for the opposition. The master does not usually incur many losses but there have been a few notable exceptions throughout chess history.

I cannot recall at what point I decided to invite the legend that is Lev Polgayevsky to Shropshire, but he was to be delivered to my house by one Arthur Mushens – himself an excellent chess player and former Combined Services and Shropshire champion – on Saturday 12th September 1992. Lev stayed at my home for the Saturday and Sunday evenings. He gave his thirty-board simultaneous match against selected Shropshire players on Sunday 13th at the Buckatree Hall Hotel in Wellington, which was itself a very salubrious venue. My recollections of that weekend are as follows. Lev was a warm, generous, and interesting man. Born in Mogilev (now Belarus) in 1934 he was a World Championship contender and one of the world's top players from the 1960s to the 1980s.

When I welcomed him to my home, I just wanted him to relax and I told him that we did not have to talk about chess. I showed him where the fridge and his room were, and insisted that he made himself at home. He was having none of it, and he wanted to talk about chess. At the time Bobby Fischer was playing Boris Spassky in their World Chess Championship rematch in Yugoslavia. That day was game seven and the moves were being shown live on Ceefax[2] so Lev wanted to get the chess set out and follow the match with him.

---

2   Ceefax was the world's first teletext information service and a forerunner to the current BBC Red Button service. It was started by the BBC in 1974 and ended in 2012 in line with the digital switchover.

As you can imagine, I was thrilled to be analysing the game with such a legend, right there in my own living room. He was unhappy with some of the moves. My girlfriend wanted to take a photograph at some point and the one in this book shows Lev and I analysing the position after Fischer had just played 41.g5 and he went on to win. I have included the game in chapter sixteen.

Studying with chess legend Lev Polugayevsky at my house in Telford in 1992. We are analysing a Fischer-Spassky game 'live'.

After that game, Fischer commented that 16...d5 was a bad move. Boris Spassky sort of concurred. Meanwhile back at the ranch (my house) Lev was chuntering away under his breath, shaking his head at the way Spassky was playing. He did not think he had to lose the game and we had fun looking at possibilities. Even though he knew that I was a mere amateur he kept asking for my opinions, what moves would I play and why? It was very instructive.

I made some loose notes on one page of A4 paper at the time, and I am glad I did. Referring to it now, I see that we talked until 1.45am and the conversation was mostly about Bobby Fischer. Lev wanted to talk about him.

He wanted to stay up late and talk. He said about Fischer that, 'He should be stopped and taken to an asylum.' He added that, 'He is a crazy man, but he is ill – schizophrenic.' We also discussed politics in both the Soviet Union and the UK. This was interesting considering the fact that Polugayevsky along with many other Soviet GM's of the day worked *with* the KGB if not actually for them. Like being a police officer – you are never off-duty really.

Lev wanted to talk about chess computers and what did I think about them? He asked if I enjoyed his book *Grandmaster Preparation* which he signed for me and spoke about several new ideas he had in chess but I did not note what these were. I was honoured that he was so interested in and respectful of my opinions.

There were a couple of other comical moments. Before we retired, I asked Lev if he wanted a tea or coffee before bed. He was incredulous. 'You don't drink tea before bed-time do you?' he asked and was really quite shocked when I said of course I did. I also asked if there was anything else he wanted just as he was about to go up.

In his lovely Russian accent he said, 'Yes, can you tell what is your country's Gross Domestic Product?' Hilarious. That's what you get when a Russian stays with you.

On the Sunday morning after a full English breakfast which Lev wolfed down, he insisted on setting the chess board up again. This time he wanted to go through some chess problems and puzzles with me. He gave me a task. We analysed a king and two knights versus king and pawn endgame. For non-chess players this is basically a very difficult part of the game to win if you don't know what you are doing. First I would play one side, then another. I had to find patterns to get the solutions and I was finding it difficult. He was really pushing me saying, 'Come on, you can do it – you just have to concentrate and keep working at it.' I reminded him that I was just a club player, but he didn't care less – he said that I would find the path if I kept working hard. This was my one and only introduction to the world of Russian chess training. Work hard and keep working until you succeed.

For the record, Lev's simultaneous result was as follows:

Lev Polugayevsky 27½-2½ Shropshire Select

Only one Shropshire player – Norman Andrews – won. I have more about that man in a moment. There were three draws made by David Everington, Trevor Brotherton and Carl Portman. Yes, I actually managed to get a draw but even here I have to burn the candle of truth. As the organiser of the event part of my focus was diverted from my game to the people, the venue, the facilities etc. Was it going okay? Did anyone need anything? Did I forget something? I wanted to ask if Lev was okay so on move twenty-nine as Lev came round to my board I simply asked, 'Is everything okay Lev?'

I have no idea if he construed this as, 'Would you like a draw?'

He looked at the position for a moment or two – extended his arm to me, smiled and said 'Yes… draw!' You can judge the game for yourself if it was – as Polugayevsky-Portman appears in Chapter sixteen. Incidentally, today's strong chess engines do have it as pretty much level, so I am relieved.

The one winner, Norman Andrews was one hell of a character.

He was Irish and he smoked like a steam train, having as he did mustard-coloured fingers through smoking. In fact, he smoked so much that it was said that every time he went to the toilet, he had a fall of soot! He had this beautiful Irish accent, bottle jar spectacles and a nicotine-stained beard. Norman had teeth like a row of condemned houses, and he wore an anorak that he had not washed for so long that it could stand up by itself – but everyone loved that man.

In some ways he was rather frightening, but Norman had a heart of gold, and he was madly passionate about chess. He was a very unpredictable and aggressive player, and he played an offbeat opening - The Budapest Gambit – to overcome Lev.

The single most memorable thing about Norman Andrews was without doubt his seismic cough. It was raucous, deep and coarse. It was phlegm-fuelled and deeply disturbing. The man must have had rusty lungs. He coughed all the time, right throughout every game, all day every day. It used to drive me and doubtless other Shropshire players mental. Lord knows what it did to the opposition. He would never be embarrassed; indeed he was oblivious to his own condition. The man had a good heart and I miss him. Bless you Norman Andrews – I hope wherever you are there is a little shop selling industrial cough mixture – not that it would do you any good at all.

David Everington was the person I looked up to most of all in Shropshire chess. The man is a legend and he sadly passed away at the end of 2020 which deeply upset me. You think that some people will live forever. I was in awe of David, and what he knew about chess. He could prepare his openings most creatively and then sprinkle some of his magic faery dust over known theory to add something of his own.

His knowledge of the history of the game was second to none. He was Shropshire County Champion on nine occasions. David was the man I chose to give the opening and closing remarks for Lev's visit, and he was up to the task. He gave our distinguished Russian guest a copy of Rupert Brooke's poetry which was eagerly received. David wrote a lot about chess and I have a copy of his 'D is for Dummkopf' booklet written in 1984 about Shropshire Chess. I was honoured to play for a short time in the same Shrewsbury team as him.

After the simultaneous event David, Lev and I took a short drive to visit Coalbrookdale. Polu insisted on having a photograph taken on the world's first bridge of iron made here in 1779. Whilst Mozart was over in Vienna composing, England was also constructing something rather special itself. We enjoyed an agreeable evening meal and then returned home where we watched tennis; it was Edberg v Sampras in the US Open. Lev liked his tennis apparently. Then it was time for bed without the tea!

As David drove Lev to London on the Monday morning I felt very sad that it was all over, but we kept in touch for a little while afterwards exchanging Christmas cards and other lively correspondence. Lev was living in Paris and he died of a brain tumour in 1995 at the age of sixty. I am still heartbroken about that. I remember him not just as one of the world's best chess players and inventor of a system in chess named after him but also as a friend, albeit a distant and temporary one.

With regard to simultaneous exhibitions in Shropshire, I should remark that before my own efforts, Telford had managed to attract the likes of Tony Miles and Victor Korchnoi. Sadly,

I never played in any of these events, but I did play Korchnoi in 2010 in London at the Chess Classic. I lost that game but it was a really good fight.

After 1992

The chess kept on coming. I was still working with the MoD in Shropshire and I had met my girlfriend at my workplace. Apparently many couples do meet initially at their place of work. Su (that is Su without an 'e') and I got on famously and we lived together for a while before getting married in Kynnersley in 1993. We lived in Telford and Newport respectively, very happily for many years. Indeed, Su was keen to learn chess and it was not long before she got hooked and started playing in the Shropshire league and then in tournaments.

Many people would think I had it easy having a chess-playing wife, but far from it. I was never able to fully concentrate on my own games in tournaments because my nervous energy was being used worrying how Su was doing. She beat a few men and yes the excuses were pathetic. 'I have a headache' and 'I lost because I have never played a woman before,' really do get used as reasons for losing to a woman.

She used to love beating the men.

It was also very amusing at tournaments to observe some chess players trying to chat up my wife. Chess is a male-dominated sport and Su might be one of just a handful of women playing in a tournament of up to 130 men. Now then; chess players are a very strange breed as I will elaborate upon in chapter six, and some of the unique methods for chatting her up were hilarious. One man kept trying to force a cheese sandwich into her hand saying how beautiful she was.

Another would *accidentally* touch her legs under the table with his foot and another fellow kept on wanting to give her his (egg-stained) cardigan as a gift. It was water off a duck's back for Su – she never ever let these things distract her and once the clocks had started she was in full focus. Heaven knows what stories other chess-playing women could tell. It makes me cringe really, how sad and inadequate we males of the species can be, but there you go.

I played at Goodyear, Morecambe and Birmingham then off to the Civil Service national finals again in Leeds in April 1993 which was fun, but my chess was less than impressive. I played Grandmaster David Norwood in a simultaneous exhibition at Dillon's bookshop in Birmingham in September. I lost playing another wonky opening (Owen's Defence) which should never be played in a simul as it is just too timid. Back then I played not to lose but nowadays I accept that losing is part of the process when playing to win.

It would be remiss of me not to briefly tell you what a chess tournament feels like. Usually we call them *Weekenders* or weekend congresses. Traditionally they occur over a Friday evening plus all day Saturday and Sunday. That's three days of hard concentration. When was the last time you did that dear reader? No wonder you have to be physically fit to sit there for so long. One slip and you've lost. This is the arena – this is Christians v lions scenario. We play five or six games against different opponents. It is not a knockout, so you can play all of the games. The system allows that you will play someone on the same score as you throughout, or as near to it so you will be playing someone who is performing the same as you in the competition. There are no rules about who you play in terms of age or gender so be prepared to play a seven-year-old kid barely out of nappies, or a nonagenarian.

There is tension before every round as the players scrutinise the *pairing board* to see who they will play. Then they find their board and the battle will soon begin. When it does, complete silence descends and even with a hall full of people you can literally hear a pin drop – it is bliss. The tension of the game can last for hours. You have butterflies deep in the pit of your stomach at times and you experience a range of emotions as you see good moves and wonderful combinations or feel despair when you stupidly lose a piece or get checkmated.

Sitting on an awful position for hour upon hour, fighting for your life is a thoroughly miserable and most depressing affair. However, delivering checkmate after outplaying an opponent - especially a stronger one - is joyous in the extreme. That is what you are in this for! Meanwhile the clocks are ticking, and your time is running down like a sandglass. You have less time to complete your task. Second by second, the conclusion of the game is drawing ever closer.

In essence I feel as if I am playing chess against three opponents. Myself, the person opposite and the clock. There is nothing like it and even as I write this paragraph I have butterflies thinking about it. I crave it even more.

Playing against someone who is partially sighted is one thing but playing opponents who are totally blind brings another dynamic to the game. Obviously, you have to announce your moves (such as bishop to bishop four) because they cannot be *seen* but the blind player will have his or her own board with raised squares and sharp points on certain pieces so they can literally feel their way around the board whilst memorizing the position. I have witnessed this many times over the years and I am in awe of how blind players play. Some are very strong players indeed and once again it is testimony to chess that it is a game for all.

In 1994 I played the Shropshire open and began messing around with the Blackmar Diemar Gambit (BDG), which is a rather wild chess opening. I actually obtained some decent results. I have an old friend in Trevor Brotherton to thank for showing me the BDG and it is certainly fun to play, though perhaps not in very serious competitions. Trevor is a good friend and a most excellent chess player. We used to exchange postcards with stupid poetry, not unlike Edward Lear.

Here's a fine example (yes I still have the cards)

Four and twenty rooks pawns, baked in a pie
If the pie was opened you'd find a little moat
Or perhaps a small stoat's egg lying in the gravy.
(I hope you like my poem. I composed it after 2 bottles of soy sauce)

Neither of us truly know why or how this started but we have never felt the need to defend our actions or explain them to anyone. It's just something we did and we still do occasionally.

I had beaten almost everyone at some point in Shropshire chess but not Trevor. I never could outwit him. We had a game published in an American chess book called *The Dogs of War* and it was a fine example from Trevor about how not to accept a draw in a drawn position. Just be patient, move a few pieces around and wait for the inevitable mistake. He was so adept at doing this against me, knowing how much I wanted to beat him.

I had another game printed in that book, which I won against another Telford stalwart, Richard Thomson. I always liked Richard though many didn't. He was sarcastic and arrogant but never obnoxious. Richard might insult you, but never in a nasty way, and he invariably did so with a smile and a twinkle in his eye. Some people didn't get him, but I did, and beneath all of the snobbish exterior beats a good heart. I think he was a solicitor which is another good reason not to like him, but we need characters like Richard to keep life interesting.

At the Rolls Royce Crewe congress in February1994 I essayed that Blackmar-Diemer Gambit against Mandy Haslinger and won with it. She was a very good player with lots of promise and I often wonder what happened to her. There followed the Blackpool congress which is a favourite of amateur and professional players alike, and I played some confrontational openings such as the Veresov, the BDG and the Morra Gambit. Is that enough blood and guts for you?

As Black I played this weird opening called the Grivas Sicilian. Alas, I did not get good results and gave up on it calling it Grivas bodily harm.

This was one of the busiest times of my life playing weekend congresses as an amateur player. I was thoroughly enjoying the cut and thrust, the tension, the competition and even the peace and quiet away from the madness of the world outside. I played in the Rhyl weekender in May where I note in one of my annotations that, 'I played a chap that continually chewed gum and looked like Bob Hoskins' and someone called Williams played the *Clemenz Opening* against me. That is 1.h3 and it is named after Hermann Clemenz (1846–1908), an Estonian player. I won – so I had the last laugh. Served him right for playing such rubbish, and he fidgeted a lot, too.

I packed my bags for the Warley Major congress and suffered a first-round defeat. I have a poor record of performing well in the first round. It takes a couple of games to warm up but by that time the prize winners are ahead of me. I must admit, in more recent times I have made it my business to do much better in the first round and the results have improved. I was in the best of company however, as former world champion Mikhail Tal had first round inertia as well.

I am a chess player and as such I do not like to lose. Back then I found excuses easy to come by, but I am much more gracious now. I wrote in my footnote at the end of that first round loss that, 'my excuse is that after a fifty-hour working week and a long drive to the tournament I was knackered.' I did not mention that my opponent may have done something similar or that he simply played better moves.

I lost my final round in that tournament when I needed to win. I used to say that I would rather have a bad weekend at the chessboard than a good day at the office, but I did not think so after this debacle.

I then played at the British Chess Championships in Norwich and blew a decent result in the last round. I was having a bad run. It happens, and you have to dig in and fight on. At one stage, years later when married to my second wife, Sue – I could not win in ten games but she walked past the board one day at home she casually commented, 'your problem is, you study too much and you should just play chess. Just play your natural game.' I thought that this was a revelation and I took her sound advice.

Incredibly, I then went a full seventeen games undefeated. I was simply thinking too much. Too many ideas, too many variations. Keep it simple, stupid! It's the same in any sport – you have to keep walking through the fire when your feet are burning. Success has many fathers, whilst failure is an orphan.

Back then, there were some enjoyable county games as well. Shropshire is a very small county in chess terms so we were up against it no matter who the opposition was. For example, Greater Manchester could out-grade Shropshire on every board if they wanted to. I managed a draw in one match, playing the Cozio Defence in the Ruy Lopez as Black. I hope it can be seen that my choice of openings was very diverse back then. Perhaps too diverse. It begs the age-old question, 'is it better to have a narrow repertoire or a wider one?'

I played in another simultaneous exhibition in something called the Batsford Chess Roadshow. It was at the Chester Booklands and Murray Chandler was the master player. We had a good long game where, as Black I played a Caro-Kann and I resigned on the fifty-ninth move. I wrote in my notes that, 'Murray said afterwards that if I had played 46...a5 he would have been without a plan.'

Oh well. I was always fascinated with Chandler. Not only did he play creative chess, but he also had this shock of long blonde hair and I always wondered if he had a bit of the rocker in him.

With the honour of being the Shropshire Champion I qualified to play board one for the county in the following season. Therefore, on 5th December 1998 I was paired to play against FM Lawrence Cooper in the Staffordshire V Shropshire match. I was white and played a solid Colle system but lost an enjoyable game in thirty-four moves. I have always been lucky to count Lawrence and his wonderful mum and dad as friends. You just could not find a more loving and lovable family, anywhere.

Loz and I both worked for the MoD at RAF Stafford at one point and looking back I am a bit annoyed with myself for not asking him to give me some coaching whilst I had the opportunity. It would be too late now; he would struggle to iron out my many bad habits. Loz is another person who has done fantastic work with chess, helping juniors, female players and others right up to international level. He holds a birthday bash where invited folks enjoy a feast of chess. I would take it seriously but with Loz playing and invariably Grandmaster Keith Arkell, I end up doing more of the photography – but I do enjoy playing Keith at that bash as such an opportunity to play a GM for free does not arise every day. Here's to Loz, his mum and dad and his favourite football team – Arsenal.

Pictured with Dr Hugh Gemmill (left) and Andrew Footner in 1998.
My county championship trophy (left) and league winner's trophy

with Shrewsbury chess club are on display.

The headlines in the Shropshire Star from when I was forced to 'retire' from chess in 1996 – and then my stunning comeback in 1998.

On the way to winning the Shropshire championship I played against great friends who were best of enemies on the chessboard. Such people included Colin Roberts, Glyn Pugh, Toby Neal and Richard Archer. I had to get at least a draw in the final round – against Richard – which I succeeded in doing but the opening was very lively after he played 1.b4, which was typically antagonistic of him. I played solidly and did not panic, and we agreed a draw in a slightly better position for me. I was happy to take it and be champ.

Colin Roberts is yet another of my friends who passed away at a ridiculously young age, and he left this world in 2018. We grew up together on the Shropshire chess circuit. He was a very happy-go-lucky character and nothing fazed him. We once raised money for a local hospice by playing chess for twenty-four hours non-stop at the Telford shopping centre. At around 2am, we could hear the wailing of sirens outside but couldn't actually see what was happening. The security guard told us not to worry, it was the Fire Brigade putting out a car that was ablaze.

The next day when the twenty-four hours was up, Colin and I packed up and walked to the car park for him to give me a lift home. What we saw before us will remain with me forever. What used to be Colin's car the day before was now a twisted burned-out shell. The vehicle that had been set ablaze the evening before was his! Some arsonists had paid it a visit. I was horrified and turned to Col. He looked at me and burst out laughing. I asked him if he was angry and he said 'Certainly not, I never really liked that car anyway. We'll get the bus home, and I will soon find another car.' That was Colin. I miss him greatly. I attended his funeral and gave a eulogy which was appreciated by his family.

In July 1999 I managed to play in the Civil Service finals in Leeds again, and then moved on to the British Championships in Scarborough playing in the under 175 event just a week or so later making a 50% score, which I was very unhappy about.

I did not know it at the time, but I would be moving to Germany in March 2000. One of the great things about chess is the fact that games can be recorded. They are written down so that the moves can be replayed again at a later date. Today, we can play back a game from as far back as 1475 move by move. Imagine that. It is effectively bringing history back to life. I write all of my games down in scorebooks and my 'big blue book' shows that my last game in Shropshire was for

Newport Chess Club against an old friend from the Coddon days – William Bates. I won that particular battle, so I left the Shropshire Chess scene on a good note.

Thus it was in the year 2000, at the turn of the century that I applied for a job with the Ministry of Defence in British Forces Germany (BFG). I was delighted to be selected and before long Su and I were off to Hohne which lies in Niedersachsen, between Hannover and Hamburg. I was running a stand-alone distribution outlet supporting my military customers. Logistics is key to everything we do. The bread that feeds our families does not jump onto a supermarket shelf on its own. The bricks required to build our houses don't magically arrive in the yard and so it was that Challenger 2 tank track did not appear on a firing range unless it came through me first. Logistics is a fascinating subject and has been an integral player in the successes and failures of many battles throughout history.

I wanted to improve my game but how would I be able to with the *distraction* of a real job (my profession) out in Lower Saxony?

Übung macht den Meister as they say in Deutschland.

Germany

You English are so funny – you all wash your hair in the sink

(Klaus – member of Carl Portman's staff.)

Moving to Germany was a rather scary but exciting chapter in my life and I was really looking forward to the challenge. Working in British Forces Germany was something I had wanted to do for some time and now I was driving down the autobahn on the *wrong* side of the road, towards my new home on Ginsterstrasse (Broom Street) with no idea what to expect. Su would be joining me in a week or so after I had settled in.

I can confirm that winters were very cold out there because of the incoming icy blasts from Siberia. For three consecutive Christmases we had snow and plenty of it. Summers were hot and there was little variation in the weather as we have in the United Kingdom where we might experience all of the seasons in one day.

My boss was a Lieutenant Colonel living several hours' drive away in Dülmen, near the Dutch border, but my agency had several satellite Distribution Outlets spread around Germany. Mine was the furthest east at Bergen-Hohne Garrison which was a major British garrison in the post-Cold War period. It had facilities located close to Bergen at Fallingbostel and Celle.

It was still home to 7th Armoured Brigade (The Desert Rats) when I was there, and other subordinate units. It formed a major part of British Forces Germany. Some 4,000 - 5,000 British soldiers occupied the garrison until it closed in 2015. Facilities under the garrison's control included the Bergen-Hohne Training Area which I supported logistically.

What used to be the infamous Bergen-Belsen concentration camp was still located nearby as a memorial site. My office actually sat a couple of metres from the railway tracks used bringing goods (and who knows what else) to and from Belsen and the storage barns were the original warehouses used for storing anything from hay to prisoners' clothing. It was an eerie place and I used to visit Bergen-Belson a lot on Sunday mornings where unmarked graves remind us of the atrocities that occurred there.

I say graves; many were simply large pits filled with corpses that could never be identified. I stood by Anne Frank's memorial countless times. No one knows where her actual grave is. What an amazing woman she was though, finding beauty in life in such a degrading and desperate situation. How dare we complain about some of things we do today, which pale into insignificance by comparison.

It is thought that some 70,000 people perished at Belsen, including 20,000 Russians and there is a memorial to them as well. Many thousands died after the liberation by the British on 15th April 1945. The perpetrators of these hideous crimes will forever be damned, but for the sake of all those who died, humanity has to learn and do better.

They say that the birds do not sing at Belsen. Well this is largely true, but this has more to do with the habitat than anything. There are a lot of pine trees and many birds don't use them for nesting etc. It was a place for quiet and deep reflection, and I ended up taking visitors around since I became so familiar with the camp. It certainly put life into perspective, that is for sure.

It was strange to think that after all that horror I was working in an organisation that was essentially about conflict and death, even though the military motto is *a force for good*. I sometimes wonder about humanity – do we ever learn? If all of the war dead could return and speak, would there ever be another war again? The reality for me is that military hardware such as the nuclear deterrent has to be in place as just that, a deterrent. World nuclear disarmament is not something that everyone wants, and that must be kept in mind. If I tell you there is a Doberman in my back garden you'll be less likely to burgle my house, I guarantee it.

Do I want peace on earth? Of course I do. That is but a naïve dream I fear. The reality is, we humans simply cannot be trusted. We have proved this time and again. Paradoxically, a military deterrent is arguably necessary to prevent war - although in one example, this would all change in a relatively short time after 9/11 terrorist attacks in September 2001.

My staff, with the exception of one were all German. My agency employed local staff, which was a sign of international unity. I had only one female member on the team and she became my interpreter in the early days. Frau Sieglinde Tierney or Ziggy as she preferred was a godsend to me. I spoke no German when I arrived but with the help of the Ziggy, the locals and by taking intense lessons I soon embraced the language and loved speaking it at every opportunity. I passed a military German language course with distinction. That was one of my proudest moments. My teacher was a very demure but rather scary German lady. I called her Frau Lehrerin which basically means female teacher. I think she took to me because of the humour I injected into the class.

We were trying to learn the articles *der*, *die* or *das* for vegetables. For some unknown reason a turnip is female, being known as *die* Rübe. I purchased a huge turnip from the local market before lessons one day and plonked it on the teacher's desk before she came into class. I wrote on it with a marker pen, 'I am a girl.' and drew a sexy dress too. The class were giggling away. Suddenly the door opened and she approached the desk, spotting the offending root vegetable. Frau Lehrerin picked it up and with her back to the class shouted 'Herrrrrr Porrrrrttmannnnnnn.'

Then she turned around with a serious expression and stared at us. Suddenly she burst out laughing, uncontrollably. I mean she belly laughed. She realised that it was a great way to learn. She then proceeded to give me a nickname. Herr Zwiebelmännchen which means *little onion man*. It stuck, and that was my name in class for the remainder of the course. I had to drive several hours to Joint Military Headquarters (JHQ) in Rheindahlen for my exam and it was a tough one.

In essence you had to listen to an announcement, which was only in German. It was a scenario – it could be any scenario, but it would be military related. The only way to get a distinction was to have just one listen and then answer a series of questions and hope that reached the required mark. If you had a second listen you would not be able to get a distinction but you could still pass. I felt confident enough to have one go. I wanted the top prize. Just like in chess! I interpreted that there had been a helicopter crash and there was fuel and debris all over the autobahn. I had to deal with the scene and keep the public safe. It was actually fun to work it all out and I managed to pass with flying colours to receive the coveted prize.

I was so pleased, mostly because my teacher had put her faith in me. When I got back to Bergen I was eager to tell her and we embraced in a bear hug. She had a good grip for a little old lady I can tell you. She had promised to buy me coffee and cake if I could get a distinction, and we went into town to celebrate. She was so lovely and I owe 'Frau Lehrerin' a great deal. It is funny isn't it that if you have an inspiring teacher you want to do well as much for them as yourself. I keep on asserting that the student is a reflection of the teacher – and this applies to coaching chess as well. On that subject, chess again helped me because I was so used to being able to prepare for something, to study and memorise and deal with pressure.

Back at the workplace, before I had learned any German, one of the lads on my team had a decent sense of humour and could speak a little English. On my first day at the office he came to see me and said:

'Boss, there are only three words you need to learn first and they are:

Wochenende (Weekend)

Urlaub (Holiday)

Feuerabend (work is over)

If you become friends with those words, we will all get on fine.'

Two months before I moved to Deutschland, the MoD flew me out for a recce of the unit and I found three of the staff asleep on the job, nestled warm and cosy against the winter Saxony chill in the open barn and another in the rest room, totally out for the count. With this in mind and after what Klaus had told me about the first words I should learn, I thought, you have got another thing coming sunshine.

It was game on.

They definitely saw me as the enemy at first, the invader come to eat their children and give them a hard time. Their former boss was a British Warrant Officer and way too soft. He used to bugger off and play golf, leaving them to it. Not me, that's not my style. I always had my own values and standards as a manager. Some I would happily compromise on but others, absolutely not.

Despite all of the management and leadership soundbites in books and training courses I already saw the customer as king. I did not need telling. If it wasn't for George coming into the DIY shop when I was a youth, I would have no job. He, the customer was my boss. I really nurtured this view, and I still do.

I tell everyone that we are all accountable for our actions, all of the time. We should give of our best on the job, and help each other out if we need to. I had to learn about their culture, fair enough but they had to learn about mine and why they were being paid to do a job there. It was a military camp not a holiday camp and one or two of the team were in for a shock. There had to be a revolution, not an evolution. I had a lot of experience of warehousing and distribution in the UK, and now that I was front-facing the customer I could see things from their perspective.

I needed the team. I may have been the conductor, but they were the orchestra and if I wanted them to play I had to speak their language, literally. I would practice my German without fear of making a fool of myself, which I did often. The best game I played was this. I used to go to the supermarket every Sunday to buy cheese, but the woman behind the counter insisted that I spoke English because she wanted to learn. I politely refused saying that since I lived in her country it was my responsibility – and privilege – to speak German. She said (jokingly but meant it) that unless I spoke in English she would not serve me, so I said that I would not budge from my own position. It was light-hearted fun but neither of us would acquiesce. Another member of counter staff would have to serve me.

Each Sunday I would go in and the following exchange would occur

'Guten Morgen Herr Portman'

'Guten Morgen'

'Kann ich ihnen hilfen?'

'Ja, natürlich. Darf ich Funf hundert grammes kase haben, geschnitten bitte'

'Auf English bitte'

'Nein, auf Deutch'

'Leider, nicht'

'Okay, bis zum nachsten mal'

'Tschus'

'Tschus'

It was hilarious. Every week was the same. However, a few years later, on the weekend before I was due to return to England I relented and gave her what she had wanted for so long. I approached the counter and asked her in English,

'Good morning, could I have 500 grams of sliced cheese please?'

She was stunned and deliriously happy! I received my cheese with, 'no charge Herr Portman' and I gave her a little thank you card saying how much she had contributed to my stay in Deutschland. It was a really lovely moment between us.

Whilst on the subject of language, I want to share a few of my favourite German words. The longest word I ever came across was:

Donaudampfschiffahrtselektrizitätenhauptbetriebswerkbauunterbeamtengesellschaft (Association for Subordinate Officials of the Main Maintenance Building of the Danube Steam Shipping Electrical Services).

Then there was the word I saw often for a women's chess weekend which was *frauenbundesligawochenende*.

What about a multiple pile up on the autobahn then? That was called a *massenkarambolage*. A couple more that tickled me were *flitterwochen* (honeymoon) and *schmetterling* (butterfly).

Best of all was the nickname that my chess mates gave me for my fighting spirit at the chessboard. They called me the *Kampfdackel*, which really means a fighting Dachsund. At first I was a bit put out. I mean, I would have preferred a fighting bear, or a tiger, or an eagle but a sodding dachshund? A sausage dog? Really? Apparently it was a compliment, and besides it was terribly funny, so it stuck and I accepted it with good grace. It's not the size of the dog in the fight, right?

Bergen, where I lived was a lovely little town and I quickly became known in the bank, opticians and supermarket etc. It was quiet and orderly. One day I opened the local newspaper to read the shocking headline that there had been a break-in at the big TV and radio shop in town. Apparently the criminals were pissed up local German boys, but the hilarious part was this. They had thrown some huge rock through the shop window and broken in. What did they steal? A television? hi-fi equipment or computers? Answer, none of them. Not a single item was missing except for one, a massive pink elephant that was always in the window! You couldn't make it up.

Initially some British soldiers were blamed for the break-in but they couldn't have done it. They were confined to barracks at the time. Some days prior, a few German lads had set about their colleagues in a pub. Big mistake. The regiment had just returned from an Ops tour. They were in fighting mood and needed an excuse to blow off steam. A few of them returned to the said pub and beat the crap out of the local boys. Primal instincts in a modern setting indeed.

I knew that my day job was going to be busy and I wondered what time I would have to play chess. As it happens the German structure of society suited me perfectly. They like to relax on Sundays and enjoy family time. The shops were closed for part of the weekend back then, and people did not feel the urge to be *doing something* all the time.

The Germans appreciate the land, having a distinct love of mushrooms and a special fondness for asparagus during *Spargelzeit* or Asparagus season. Also we finished at lunch-time on a Friday, so it was easy to throw some kit in the boot of the car (my banana yellow VW Beetle) and disappear for the weekend. The Harz mountains were great, and we would go to Wernigerode to relax and recharge.

Downtime was fun but there was a job of work to do. I still had to work on the *customer first* mantra with my staff. They needed to be clear that we were all only there because the British military were, and they were our customers. We had to look after them – after all, lives could depend on it. It took time but we got there eventually.

They affectionately called me the Island Ape (someone from the UK) which I found amusing. They were a good group with only one or two bad apples. It is almost impossible to sack a locally engaged employee because the German Works Council is so strong in law, but I did try to remove one man who was a nice enough individual but terribly indolent and inefficient. Dieter was also an alcoholic and I genuinely wanted to help him, because I remembered how my mum was in that situation.

One day he staggered into my office. His face was purple, and a pus-filled open sore was bleeding. He just broke down, sobbing. I immediately sought medical help and began drawing up plans with the authorities for his medical and social care, but Dieter suddenly died all alone at home before it could be implemented.

When we began to clear his desk, we found countless empty vodka bottles. It was terribly sad really. Was life really that bad that he had to find solace at the bottom of a bottle? Apparently so. To be honest, it was so damned rural out there that there was little else to do. I thought a lot about my mother and how she died – alcohol is a killer addiction for millions.

When those aeroplanes slammed into the Twin Towers on September 11th 2001, I was standing in one of my storage barns inspecting ammunition boxes when a visiting soldier from 7th Armoured Brigade ran in and told me there had been a terrorist attack on America. I went home to watch it on the TV and was as shocked as the rest of the world.

I wondered what the ramifications would be and knew that

the ripple effect would be huge. It would doubtless reach my own workplace. With the invasion of Iraq in March 2003 we were frantic, and we had to supply equipment to UK troops training out on the tank ranges. We also had to deal with ammunition containers, returning them to UK so there was a lot of work on.

At the time we provided logistical support for the 7th Armoured Brigade as well as the 9th/12th Royal Lancers, 3rd Regiment Royal Horse Artillery, 32 Engineer Regiment, Royal Engineers and the Queens Royal Lancers, known as the Death or Glory Boys. They would come out east and engage in battle tank training just over the Polish border and we supported them sending out equipment. I used to have weekly meetings with Quartermasters to decide what kit they wanted and where and when it should be delivered. I learned a lot about the Army from the QM's. Most of all I learned that my priority was not necessarily their priority. They were the customer after all. I wanted to do whatever I could for them.

I made friends with several of the soldiers. One or two were badly injured in conflict and a couple were killed. Some were deeply affected, both physically and mentally by their experiences in battle not just in Afghanistan or Iraq but in the Falklands and Northern Ireland too. People forget that terrorism is not new and the Irish Republican Army (IRA) saw soldiers and us civilians as fair game to murder.

At one point we had to take different routes to work and our vehicles were inspected for bombs every day. We had to be careful if we even heard an Irish accent when out and about and not talk about our jobs at all – fairly obvious stuff really but you'll be surprised how lax some people are with their security. I will always feel a great debt of gratitude to our military personnel who put their lives on the line on behalf of the country.

We worked our arses off at the start of Operation Telic, which was the codename under which all of the United Kingdom's military operations in Iraq were conducted. It began in March 2003, and I am fiercely proud of my team for stepping up to the plate to deal with all of the work we had in those initial few weeks to support the military. They had never seen anything like it in their lives.

We were swarming with military units desperate to pick up their supplies twenty-four hours a day. I had experienced this before with the Falklands conflict and knew we would be stretched to breaking point, at least for a time. Yet they were outstanding to a man – and one woman!

We were awarded a certificate of achievement which I copied to every staff member and put the original up in their canteen… it was well earned. Some of the staff had 'evolved' from working at the local market selling vegetables (nothing wrong with that, mind you) to being recognised by *front-line* military units preparing for a major conflict.

I took the whole team out to a local restaurant by way of saying thank you and they tucked into Bison steaks and Dunkel Bier (dark beer) with gusto. Ziggy necked a few wines and attempted to tell me some saucy jokes, but her German jokes were just not funny, so we ended up laughing at that fact. The beer flowed and we let our hair down and deservedly so. It was a job well done. The Brigadier commanding Hohne Garrison visited, and gave us his personal thanks, so I had a photograph taken and gave it to everyone to put on their wall at home. Sometimes, it's just the little things.

Certificate
of
Achievement

Awarded to

Staff of
Distribution Outlet
Hohne

The team running DO Hohne were required to work long and arduous hours to achieve the output to meet the tight targets in support of Operation TELIC.

The workload increased five fold during a five-week period and staff stayed determined and resolute in their task. It was a team effort underlined by high morale and the will to get the job done. Problems were identified and solved with a logical step approach. What is more, the activity resulted in unqualified praise from front line customers in their preparations for movement to the Gulf region.

There can be little doubt that the success has enhanced the reputation of DSDA(G) throughout it's dependency, and is fully deserving of this recognition.

Mr P D Foxton CBE
Chief Executive DSDA

Lt Col M D Ingram OBE
Director DSDA (Germany)

2nd April 2003

Recognition for the work that me and my team put in at the beginning of the Gulf war in 2003.

I can never forget the day when an exasperated soldier came into my office. He was having an issue with one of my lads – another chap called Klaus. I should explain that in the early days Klaus had no idea about customer service, but over time he really got into it with gusto. He liked the soldiers and they liked him. He was near retirement age and stuck in his ways but every day a small van would arrive from one of the Regiments to pick up some boxes of stores. I had always told Klaus to be as efficient with packing the boxes in the van as he could so that the driver might make only one trip instead of two, thereby saving time and fuel. He took this to extremes one day, bless him. He had packed the van but had one big box left and the only space left was the driver's seat. Yes, good old Klaus pushed and pushed and squeezed that box right in, despite protestations from the soldier. The van was quite literally packed full.

I went outside to look. The three of us stood and peered into the van. I said to Klaus that it was commendable that he was doing his best for his customer, but I asked him if he could see what the problem was. Honestly, he just could not figure out that the driver had to actually occupy the seat in order to take the stores away.

'Klaus… was ist los?' I said pointing to the seat. Suddenly it dawned on him and he smacked his forehead with his hand in true Homer Simpson style. We all burst out laughing and retrieved the box from the van – with some effort. The other lads were ripping the piss out of poor Klaus so I decided to give him a reward next day. I took him into the Garrison and bought him coffee and cake as a well done for doing his best. He was smiling all week. I also had a certificate made for him and he displayed it in the staff room for all to see. We should never punish people for trying.

For my final day in office the staff had arranged a surprise, comprising of three things for me. First of all, they put on a huge buffet, having made all the food at their homes which included a range of fine German meats, cake and bread. Yes there was some alcohol there but this was one occasion where I was happy to allow a beer or two at the workplace.

Secondly Ziggy revealed what her hobby was. For some months she had been learning belly dancing and she appeared in full dress and began to dance. The lads knew about it, but it was one of the few times in my life when I was quite shocked. She was often shy and reserved was Ziggy, but here she was thrusting herself rather suggestively in front of me and loving it. She lived alone, but I don't know why. She was an attractive woman and clearly a good mover too. I truly hope that today she has found a partner. She very much wanted to. Sadly, we never stayed in touch.

'Ziggy' performing her surprise belly dance for me at my farewell party at work in Germany.

The third and final arrangement was a gift. The team knew that I enjoyed writing. After Ziggy's dance they gave me a wrapped box about fifteen inches long and six inches wide. I opened it and inside lay a beautiful long white goose feather, especially cut at the quill to use as a fountain pen. It was gorgeous and very quaint. I thanked them and they all began to laugh.

On behalf of the team Klaus the forklift truck driver presented me with another box. He made a very short speech saying that the team would miss me and thanked me for working with them. I had a lump in my throat I can tell you.

Anyway, I opened the box and to my astonishment the team had purchased a Montblanc Bohème fountain pen. It must have cost a fortune. It had a 14-carat white gold nib and an inlaid synthetic sapphire gem on the clip. This sparse team had donated money from their own pockets to buy that pen and now I was choked. In one final slice of British humour I played one last joke on them.

In an instant I commented, 'it is very nice but if you don't mind, I will take the goose feather.' You should have seen their faces. I could not hold the tension lest someone burst into tears and my joke was revealed. Thankfully, everyone laughed. That pen is in use today after seventeen years and each time I pick it up I remember my team, or rather my friends. You can't do that with a keyboard. Several quartermasters gave me gifts too by way of regimental wall plaques and I also received a lovely medal from Head Office in Dülmen as someone who served in a civilian capacity in British Forces Germany.

This memoir is primarily about chess, not my working career so we shall now train the spotlight on my chess experiences in Germany. Su and I had barely settled in before I began searching for a chess club. I found one in a nearby village/town in Hermannsburg. Unsurprisingly the club was called SK Hermannsburg. It seemed to me that there were strong players in almost every little village in northern Germany, unlike back in the UK where you were more likely to find clubs only in towns and cities.

My first game for SK Hermannsburg was played on 15th October 2000. It was a Sunday and play was due to begin in the morning. I approved of the idea of playing on Sundays as opposed to weeknights, which we do in the UK. You don't have to play chess after a long day at work for one thing, and you can use Saturday to prepare for the game. On that first match it so happened that the SK Hermannsburg first team were playing the second team. I was in the first and on board one at that. When I arrived there was a huge pitcher of strong German beer next to my board. It was 10 am. The boys said it was for me to drink, and a special welcome treat, it being my first game for the club.

This was a cultural dilemma. It was customary for the lads to offer the beer, but I did not drink much and certainly not in the mornings or before a serious game of chess. Remember, I may be an amateur but I take my preparation seriously. I managed to get out of it somehow by having a sip and leaving it on the table for the rest of the game. No worries – the boys soon drank it when they worked out that I wasn't going to. I was fortunate to win as Black in some strange line of the French Defence where White played his queen to d3 on the fourth move!

I was quickly accepted by the team and other club members. It is fair to say that a couple of the lads were suspicious of the

Ausländer but they came around eventually. There was only ever one unsavoury incident at the bar in the venue where we played. One day I was ordering a beer and this German lad waded into me verbally about 'the fucking English, and why not go back home?' It was fair enough. I mean plenty of foreigners get stick in the UK so I should expect some when I live abroad. I had expected it much sooner to be honest.

This chap had not reckoned on the Wolf – or Wolfgang as he was better known. He was ever so slightly mad. I mean, he was bonkers. He carried a large knife (he loved hunting) and was prone to sporadic vitriolic outbursts, chuntering away in German about something or other. Anything could set him off. He absolutely loved me and Su and he felt in some way that he was our minder. Wolfgang was standing nearby when this lad had a go at me. Thus, before I could respond to him and stand my own ground he was marched out of the guest house by Wolfie and another couple of lads from the club, one of whom I would not mess with even if I were armed.

A few minutes later the lad came in with a puffy eye that was already becoming bruised. He sheepishly came up to me and apologised for his rudeness. I said it was okay and not to worry at all. Sticks and stones would never hurt me. When the lad left I asked Wolfie what had happened. He informed me that I was a guest in his country and also one of the chess team. No-one messes with the chess team. He was embarrassed on behalf of his country and he would not stand for it. He was most disappointed when I told him off! I said that his heart was in the right place but his fists were not. I would fight my own battles and I usually did this with words which can be more powerful than steel.

I said that if he were to have a fight with everyone who said bad things to me he would have a full-time job on his hands. I bought him a beer and he calmed down, but he was really upset. I loved that man – even with his crazy temper.

I should mention one other incident where my British humour got me into a bit of a fix. I usually played board one at least initially because I was the strongest player, and the teams are meant to play in board order of strength. But one day I looked at the team card and I appeared on board two.

Now I am not an egotist as anyone who knows me will tell you, but I sort of slipped into a Basil Fawlty sketch which went something like this.

'Board two. BOARD TWO? What is this lads? Am I not good enough for board one now? Have I not won enough games for the team? Have I travelled all the way from the UK to play on board two?'

Without further ado, I played the game on board two and quickly won. Indeed, we won the match, no problem. I thought they had understood my humour. Later that evening back at my apartment there was a knock on the door – around 7pm I think. I answered it and the whole of the chess team stood before me. The 'elected spokesman' had a big bouquet of flowers for Su and another lad held a large box of chocolates for me.

'We are so sorry to have offended you today. We are very upset about it. Please accept these by way of an apology' said the Wolf(ie) at the door. Everyone else was looking ashamed. We felt deeply embarrassed and ushered them inside. It was time to break open some beers and explain a bit more about British humour. They struggled with the difference between the humour of Mr. Bean, who they love in Germany, and Basil Fawlty, but after a few examples, carefully omitting the goose-step scene in Fawlty Towers, we soon ironed it out and no more was said – but they insisted that we kept the flowers and choccies.

That is how easy it can be to make cultural slips, but to be fair it is all part of the learning experience. If we become afraid to make mistakes or never challenge things we shall never learn. The Niedersachsen league became another chess sanctuary for me and I plied my trade in the Kreisliga Ost section. Teams soon sussed out that an Englishman was playing and quite enjoyed playing me so as to exchange information about chess in our countries. I was a novelty for some.

One of the best events was when I played in Dresden in July 2001. It was a very hot summer and the venue was the salubrious Schloss Albrechtsberg (Castle Albrechtsberg) which is actually a Neoclassical stately home situated above the Elbe river. It was erected in 1854 according to plans designed by the Prussian court and landscaping architect Adolf Lohse (1807–1867) at the behest of Prince Albert, younger brother of the Prussian king Frederick William IV.

It was certainly one of the grandest places (or should that be palaces) I have ever played chess in. I won my first game against Herr Keeve and had another fascinating battle several days later in round 8 against Herr Oliver Klewin.

I was very lucky that world-class grandmasters Alexei Suetin and Wolfgang Uhlmann were playing. At one stage I sat back-to-back with Suetin, but he wasn't at the board half the time. He was a chain smoker on an industrial scale and would have to keep rushing out for a fag between moves. I took a photograph of him sitting on a bench, puffing away completely alone in the world. There was something markedly sad about it.

Uhlmann was well-known to me and a hero because he played my favourite French Defence which many leading players would not do. I learned so much from his book *Französisch - Richtig Gespielt*.

This was a tournament where a young Jan Gustaffson played – and he later went on to great things with the online platform Chess24. There were 190 contestants playing over a couple of weeks. Of course, Dresden and the British (not to mention the USA) have a lot of history because of the dreadful events in WWII, and in some ways I wondered if I should play. I was the only Englishman and memories are long on all sides. The truth is, one has to rebuild bridges when they are burned down, and chess is a unifying force that helps to do it. Time and again I have found this to be true in life – especially in prisons, which I will discuss later.

My next tournament came in February 2002 in Hannover which was nearer to home. It was a qualifying tournament for the Deutsche amateur championships.

This was The Ramada Treff cup, a well organised and well attended tournament where the organisers ensured that the theme tune from the musical *Chess* was played through the loudspeakers at the beginning of every round, just to get us in the mood. Further, any females that played found a bouquet of flowers on their table at the beginning of the first round. Now that is what I call a nice touch.

We rightly discuss equality for females in chess but let me be clear. Equality does not mean 'the same.' I will repeat that. Treating people equally does not mean treating people the same. The knights of old would joust on horseback, risking their very lives in order to try to win the ladies' handkerchief. In my book nothing has changed. The ladies are still well worth getting on that horse for. So help me, women in chess are hugely outnumbered by their male counterparts and they deserve a medal for putting up with all the madness that comes with that.

Chess players *are* weird, especially around women. There, I have said it. Men are not as mentally strong as women in my view and we prefer safety in numbers. What I would like to see is a handful of men playing in a tournament consisting of 150 females. I wonder how they would cope. Would it influence their play? Would they feel uncomfortable? Probably.

That aside, if you remember, I was born a Knight and as far as I am concerned chivalry must never die. If you saw how much pleasure those flowers gave to the female players, you might arrive at the same conclusion. To all those who complain about sexism - get off the cross, we need the wood.

Curiously, I remember one of my opponents having a distinctive hair style called a mullet. I wrote at the time that it was so large, it seemed to be holding his head in place, taking it over like some parasitic alien. It didn't move – it was lacquered into place and had clearly set. At the rear, his 'neck blanket' was so long and thick I wondered if at any moment he might have to be sheared.

I must end the Hannover tournament with this anecdote. The venue was the Ramada hotel. Before the start of the tournament a senior member of staff found me and welcomed me to Hannover. I don't think he realised that I actually lived in Germany. Before the first round he took me to see two scale plastic models of the city of Hannover set behind glass and said 'Zis was Hannover before you bombed it' then pointed to the other one saying 'And zis is Hannover after we rebuilt it.'

I just looked him in the eye and said *'Du hast angefangen.'* (You started it). I also asked if he had ever visited Coventry, London or Birmingham. He knew what I meant, and it wiped the smile off his face. I marched off to begin my first game which I drew. I was living in Deutschland and would of course respect the country, but I was not going to take any sarcastic sermons from a sour kraut who thought he was being clever. This island ape has fangs and bites back. Annoyingly, I drew four games and lost the last one so it was an altogether forgettable event.

I lined up more tournaments in the next year or so including Freudenstadt in July 2002 where I played Grandmaster Mark Taimanov in a simultaneous exhibition. I really should have drawn but made an error at the end when he was arriving at the board quickly (there's my excuse, right there). It is quite amusing to note that I also played someone called Gerhard Christ in that tournament and the result was 1-0 to me. Now, when it comes to asking if I am a good chess player or not, I have actually beaten Christ. Enough said, right?

I played Halle an der Saale in April 2003. It is the largest city of the German state of Saxony-Anhalt, and the fifth most populous city in the area of former East Germany. Baroque composer Georg Friedrich Händel (later George Frideric Handel) was born in Halle in 1685 and spent the first 17 years of his life in the city. It's a very interesting place but of course I was there for chess, not sightseeing so I must return one day for a holiday.

With bags duly packed I travelled to Bad Breisig in July 2003 to enjoy a lovely little chess holiday on the Rhine. Obviously the air agreed with me. I had an excellent tournament and even beat Ukrainian Grandmaster Arkadij Rotstein in a small simultaneous exhibition. I should be perfectly fair. I did not outplay him and he did not outplay me. We were dead level when he blundered late on. I was pleased to win of course but disappointed about how it happened.

I particularly enjoyed playing in Spa towns but in some ways it was a bit too relaxing. To win tournaments or just get amongst the prizes you have to be ruthless. There's no time for distractions, you've got to play your best move in every game and keep your focus. Good rooms, nice food, river cruises etc. are all there to relax you when actually you've got to sacrifice all of that to win at the board and stay in fight mode.

What a great place to study. In this case the pool was on holiday in Spain, not at my mate's house in Germany

We arrive at the endgame of this chapter, and I shall say a few words about my club – SK Hermannsburg. We actually had a very cosmopolitan team comprising of German, English and Croatian players. We had black and white players, men and women, young and old. It was marvellous.

The lads loved their chess of course. One man, Sven was fairly rich and had a big house in the forest with an outdoor swimming pool. In the summer we would play chess in the pool. We used a floating chess board and people would pass us beer and BBQ sausages (cooked with great gusto by Wolfgang) as we played well into the night. Sven had a big swing set up between two trees about 30 metres apart. You climbed up a ladder, sat on the swing and went for it. It was such fun, and just like being a kid again. If on the way past at great speed, one could grab a sausage out of Wolfie's hand you were an honourable guest!

In keeping with Wolfie's crazy character, if you had the balls to sneak up and steal one of the sausages off the BBQ when he was making them, he would go berserk. I mean, ape-shit. His eyes would roll around in their sockets, and he would come after you, hand on his knife sheath. The BBQ was his domain alone. I can declare with some authority that there is nothing funnier than observing a petrified German in swimming trunks running around a garden with a hot sausage in his hand, chased by another (crazed) German brandishing a hunting knife, desirous of the return of the said food item. He would disappear down the garden shouting 'Give me my fucking sausage back' in a thick German accent and if you were lucky you might see two men rolling around in the bushes fighting over a now flaccid banger.

One of the men would be paralysed with laughter, the other would be spitting with rage. The madder he got, the more his adversary laughed. Wolfie would not be seen again until he had calmed down, when he would return to the BBQ to find not a single sausage left. We scoffed the lot. At this point the already incandescent madman would almost literally spontaneously combust. Man, I just loved it. It was the best of times, it was the 'Wurst' of times (Groan).

I was deeply saddened to say goodbye to the chess club and my crazy friends. They honoured me by creating an annual club tournament in my name called the Portman Pokal (The Portman cup) and the winner receives a rather nice trophy. It's nice to think that in some way I am still part of the chess club.

Anyway, as with all things good or bad, nothing lasts forever, and the wind of change was blowing in. I set my sails bound for England once again.

Hello, this is England calling

There'll always be an England
While there's a country lane
Wherever there's a cottage small
Beside a field of grain

Parker & Charles

Whilst sitting at my desk in Germany attempting to resolve a heated exchange between a British soldier and a local German about the 1966 World Cup Final, I received a telephone call from a pal in the MoD. 'Hello, this is England calling,' he said, as he often did. The purpose of the call was to tell me about a promotional job being advertised and that I might be interested in it. I certainly was.

I felt that whilst I enjoyed Germany and all it had to offer, I had done what I had set out to do with the team in Hohne. I did not want to stand still, or mark time like some did just to stay out there. I returned to the UK later in 2004 after securing promotion and a new job in Oxfordshire at the Defence Storage and Distribution Agency (DSDA) at Bicester.

Once settled into my new house I joined Bicester Chess Club in Oxfordshire which was founded in September 1988. It wasn't a big club *per se*, but the people were friendly and welcoming (just as a chess club ought to be) and as ever there were several colourful characters. The secretary was one Colin

Cheesman, a lovely chap. He was ex-forces I believe, and also a staunch Brighton and Hove Albion football fan. He was a much weaker player than me yet whenever we played friendlies, he totally upped his game and I always found it difficult to put him to the sword.

Chess games are not just about grades, but a playing style. It can be much harder to play against certain people and Colin was definitely in that category. We shared some helter-skelter games over many a pint of beer. The general idea seemed to be, sacrifice something – anything – and go for it. At the time I joined, the venue was Rodney House – another Civil Service club, but sadly that closed down and we found a bowls club. Even though we were chess players, most of us still did not consider ourselves old enough to join a bowls team yet, but the venue for chess was acceptable. Chess players can seldom be choosy.

Ian Moreton was a fiery Scot, sporting snow-white hair and possessing a gaze that could turn you to stone. He appeared fearsome and argumentative but if you peeled back a layer or two you would find a soft underbelly, and when he laughed there was a twinkle in his eye. To get that far though you might have to have a few disagreements with him. He was definitely old school and he told it just like it was, which was one of the things I liked about him. If seven people voted one way, he would vote another, but he always stood by his principles. A contrarian then, but a stout fellow and a man that you could rely on.

Then there was Richard Beckett. As a chess fan, a football fan, a lover of rock and metal music armed with a quick wit we were destined to be an instant hit, and so it proved. We have stayed pals ever since and he often comes round to my house for an evening of chess, Chinese food, a few beers and plenty of music. There is no Mozart when we get together - we prefer the jackhammer, table-thumping, head spinning bass of Lemmy Kilmister and Motörhead thank you very much. His favourite band is Marillion so we do tone it down now and again for a bit of prog.

I read that the five-time world chess champion Vishy Anand once listened to Rammstein, that wonderful German industrial metal band during training sessions. If this is true, then massive kudos to Vishy. I would love to know if it really happened.

I was Bicester chess club champion in 2005, 2006 and 2007 and top of the tree until along came Marcus Harvey and another strong player, Simon Lazarus. They were better players than me and that's that. Marcus was advancing so quickly that I knew that the opportunity to beat him would be fleeting. Richard and I still joke that we taught him everything he knows but we didn't teach him everything that *we* know!

I became club chairman from 2006-2008 so I played my part and thoroughly enjoyed it. I actually quite liked the venue. I require three things to keep me happy at a chess club. It must be quiet, well-lit, and warm. Take any one of those factors away and I am likely to want to leave.

I should explain that chess players are hardy characters. They have to be. All too often throughout my life I have played in freezing cold church halls, working men's clubs, broom cupboards (it seemed) and village halls. It was so Baltic at one venue, that I literally dressed up in ski clothing. I wore a duck down coat, gloves and a bobble hat, and even then I only just coped with the freezing temperatures in the room.

Before I left the house my wife would say for a laugh, 'are you going mountaineering love, or are you just off to chess club?' It is a sedentary pastime, which makes it even more difficult to warm up. I certainly do not go to chess club to get ill, but it has happened a few times. Is it too much to ask to just be warm? Playing chess in some god forsaken shit-hole on a freezing winter's night is no fun and I have had enough of it to be honest. Chess players in general deserve better but many won't pay for it and would rather *endure*. It is my honest experience that chess players want something for free or as little money as possible, never mind comfort. Honestly, some would play in an igloo if they only paid ten pounds a year. That is not for me thank you. Let's at least try to be civilised.

Of course, it helps if you get on well with other club members. Chess clubs are no different to any other enterprise, be it golf, bridge or model railway. There are always the supportive, helpful generous types and there is always at least one troglodyte who spoils it for everyone else. I am sure that at some point I have been considered to be both!

The troglodytes distinguish themselves easily and readily. They believe that they are much better chess players than they actually are, rudely interrupting games with *advice* and suggestions. These people are called *kibitzers* in the chess world. The word emanates from Yiddish, meaning, *to watch*. Even when you disprove their *wise* suggestions with hard evidence, troglodytes won't accept it and still cling on to the idea that their view is best. I believe this is called cognitive dissonance and many people suffer from this disease.

In chess you should not interrupt other people's games. Just play your own game. Watch another game by all means, but keep your mouth shut and say nothing. That includes grimacing, twitching, tutting, coughing, laughing or swaying near the board.

Incidentally, Richard Beckett has been the club captain at Bicester since its inception which is truly remarkable. He is another one of the unsung heroes around the country who donates his own time and resources to helping junior players to improve, holding as he does a junior class one night a week in peak periods. I want to pay tribute to him for that right now.

Marcus Harvey is now a FIDE Master, but he was just a nipper at the club when I was there, and I used to walk in the club and tweak his ear. He would snap around like a viper and chastise me, but we would both fall about laughing. He knew I was going to do it – every time. His dad, Rob is a right joker of the Paul Gascoigne mould, and he would laugh his head off too. He has a joke for every occasion. Sadly, he sometimes carries that into his chess games, but we can forgive him that. I can say that I beat Marcus in a *proper* game but not long after that he just became too good and he left me and everyone else eating dust. If I played him twenty times at blitz (five-minute chess), now it is very unlikely that I would even get a single draw.

Marcus was obsessed with chess, but he was also lazy. He was not bothered at all with studying – he would do things his own way. It transpires that this was just fine for him. I do not think I have ever known a chess player who has studied so little become such a creative, intelligent and strong player. There is so much natural chess talent in Marcus's brain that it has to be a gift from an unseen force. If you ever have the privilege to analyse a game with him, he will happily show you some magic at the chessboard. He always makes me feel that where I think I can *see* good moves I am actually half blind. Unfortunately for chess, Marcus has a *proper* job so he too must be considered an amateur, yet this serves only to prove what a silly title *amateur* actually is. It's such a shame, Marcus could be a Grandmaster one day if he had the time to devote to getting there, I would stake my house on it. He was blessed with a supportive family who I still see occasionally. They are amongst life's very best, for sure.

Away from chess, my marriage to Su ended – very amicably. I cannot blame anyone but myself, but cold, hard and honest reflection tells me that coming back from Germany in 2004 (I got two promotions in quick succession in the MoD and equated in civilian terms to a lieutenant colonel, so my responsibilities were varied and many) changed our dynamic quite

a bit. Su was also very busy working at an American military base. I was pre-occupied in Bicester, but also travelled away with work commitments. I think we spent a bit too much time apart, but I won't hide from this one – I was definitely responsible for us splitting up. I took my eye off the ball. We were very happily married for fourteen years and nothing can change that.

On a working visit to Washington D.C to exchange best practice ideas with the American military.

It is true to say that during this marital metamorphosis, Susan Watson suddenly appeared from nowhere back into my life. That same wonderful girl who visited my flat in Telford and blew me away had returned. My feelings for her had never changed. How could they? When someone makes such an initial impact upon you, you retain those feelings for life.

Sue (we have now moved on to a new Sue with an 'e' not the previous Su without an 'e'. Try to keep up) was working in Paris and she could not get her old mate Carl (that's me!) out of her mind. Back then there was a website called Friends Reunited which used to, well, reunite friends. She contacted me on that platform, and it was as if she had never been away for all those years. The hand grenade that was Susan Watson simply blew up in my heart and that was that.

We both knew where this was going and if fate was playing a game then it seems that we were destined to be together in the end. Susan also had a long-term relationship of some seventeen years, so her own parting would be difficult but we both agreed to leave everything behind and start anew together. It felt so right.

We were content to leave all of the material stuff behind. The houses and their contents did not feature for us and at least our former partners had property and some money which they both seemed happy about. It was still heart-wrenching for me and Sue but we did what we both believed in and wanted to do, so that's just that. The only thing I ever regret in life is hurting good people. A marriage is sacred, I still hold that cherished view, but marriage is also a contract, and ours had become one we signed many years ago. We did part amicably. There were no children involved which was another bonus.

We concentrated on moving forward and set about building a new life together. We felt just like we did from those early days in our youth – and we picked up where we left off. No one gave us anything, and we stood together looking only to the future. We knew that the heartache of break-ups would be worth it and that we would be settled and happy together. Some fifteen years on, that has proven to be the case.

I am pleased to say that Su is now happily married (to an American – but I have no idea if they met at the air base) and living in the United States of America. It has all ended well and there are absolutely no hard feelings. We can even still say Happy Christmas every year and be civilised.

Susan (Watson!) and I rented a house in the middle of nowhere, but it was not to our liking and we decided to make the huge commitment to buy a house together. That happened in 2007 and it was our biggest financial commitment to one another. The second and infinitely more pleasurable commitment was our marriage in June 2012 at Summer Solstice time, and I am still pinching myself here in 2021 to have finally *landed* the girl I first asked out. With our three dogs and a few tarantulas and scorpions we have a mixed and happy household. I am lucky and grateful that life has treated me so well.

Marrying Susan on 22 June 2012. She has brought laughter and colour to my life since the very first moment that I met her as a youngster.

Chess continues to occupy much of my life, and Susan has her own passion – showing our dogs, Darwin, Dickens and maybe in the future, Raven, who you will read about in a moment. They are border collies and in 2015 Dickens was actually on TV, as he won *Best of Breed* at Crufts. This was an amazing feat for a lad who as a puppy seemed to have no hope, eating two of my Christmas hats, a chair, half of the kitchen and a string of fairy lights.

He is effectively grey and white rather than black and white – although the technical term is a *blue* collie. This particular colour form of dog does not seem to be as successful as he has been in competitions, so I was immensely proud of Susan for taking him that far. It requires great patience, commitment and passion. Actually, Darwin was the first dog to win an award at Crufts – it was best in his class in 2010. They have since won countless championship tickets and best in shows but the bottom line is they are just our boys and we love 'em to bits.

I should confirm that in March 2021, Raven appeared in the Portman household. She is a female border collie and a gorgeous little thing she is too, coming from fantastic kennels. Like all puppies, she is a handful but dare I say that chess once again helps. I have learned when to stop, reflect, make a decision and act. A neighbour asked why we would call a dog Raven when a raven was a bird. I told her that a woman called Sandy isn't a beach. That shut her up.

We live a happy and peaceful life following our pursuits, whilst always supporting each other. Susan puts up with countless chess sets and books in almost every room and I endure the dog hairs and the walks in the pouring rain. Don't get me wrong, I love a walk in the rain but only when I feel like it, not necessarily when the canines do. We always plan things to do together such as museum visits, concerts, long walks or short break holidays usually in the UK so we can take the dogs and visit some remote place to re-energise. We could not live in each other's pockets 24/7 like some couples do. We require our own space, but when we do things together that is always quality time.

Getting away from it all and my idea of fun
– studying tarantulas in Belize.

We have had some marvellous trips with the emphasis on natural history. Our expeditions to the rainforests of Costa Rica, Guatemala, Belize and Australia (Queensland) have all been very special. Personally, I am never happier than when out in a rainforest at night hunting for spiders, snakes, scorpions and other assortments of arachnids. I love to be away from people, isolated from the everyday rat race. Nothing can beat standing in a rainforest alone, listening, smelling and seeing all around me heightens every bodily sense. It has an almost supernatural feel and is the very definition of magic for me.

It also allows me to put my utter insignificance on this planet into perspective. It reminds me that I am (and we are) merely part of a much bigger system. It is not my job to fit the world around me, I must fit into the world. We all must. These strange animals also reinforce my notion that humans are basically as ignorant as we are arrogant. If we don't understand something, we want to kill it or denounce it. I want humans to appreciate and accept that no animals are on this earth to be *useful* to us. 'What use are wasps?' people say. How arrogant. If wasps could speak they might well say, 'What use are humans?' Let us remember that humans are animals too. As naked and useless at birth as we are in our final hours we must hope that we can do something useful in between and leave something special behind. The purpose of life is surely to have a life of purpose.

Susan shares my feelings on this matter and despite initially being wary of my arachnid fascination, she has come to appreciate the fundamental role that spiders large and small play in the natural world. When I give lectures to schools and societies, Sue often answers the questions from the audience!

I share her passion for showing the dogs and gladly attend Crufts every year to give moral support. I even met Peter Purves which I had been determined to do for a while. He is a lovely man.

Susan and I share one motto, which is, 'We do it best, when we do it together.'

Life has a way of suddenly kicking us in the teeth and the news that we were about to receive would test our motto in the extreme.

In September 2020 Susan was given the devastating news that she had cancer. Initially it was diagnosed as being at stage two, but soon changed to stage four metastatic. We have since found out why the sudden change in diagnosis, but for legal reasons won't go into the detail here. Let's just say that two mammograms should have highlighted the issues but they were *overlooked* at the time. Sue and I both have to live with the consequences of this ineptitude. The cancer began in her breast then spread to her lymph, lungs and bones. There is no cure and it is not operable, but the plan is to see if it can be managed in some way. In the past, this situation would have centred around preparing for death, but nowadays there is much bigger focus on living by managing chronic illness.

You never think it will happen to you. Sitting in the hospital room and hearing those words, 'Mrs. Portman, we can confirm that you do have cancer.' In that single, terrifying and desperate moment, the world as we knew it changed forever. A hundred thoughts go through your head – how long does she have? Is there anything we can do? We won't get to grow old together after all. Most of all, since I was the one who has always been ill and Sue has been very fit, I wanted to transfer it all from her to me. I can bear a lot of pain; I am good at it. I am accustomed to it. But Susan is far too lovely a person to be the victim. The big questions that everyone asks is 'Why?'

Why Susan? Why now?

The simple fact is – because it is Susan and it is now. No-one ever said that life was fair, and as a Brigadier once said to me, 'That's why I have ginger hair and a small penis.' (Him, not me dear reader. I do not have ginger hair). Where is God when you need him? I often ask myself that question. Now is a good time for one of those miracles, if you don't mind. No? Going to stay dumb and mute? Well, okay then. You carry on getting all the credit and the kudos whilst good people suffer deplorably down here. What do you actually do anyway? Helping people recover isn't your kind of miracle, right? We gotta believe right, have faith, go to a better place. Heaven?

What is the *point* of God?

You see, it can get very testy in my head. Cancer creates such existential questions. Dare I say that once again chess had taught me something – to question everything, to work to find the truth at the board, and why not in life?

Luckily, Sue and I have always used laughter and comedy to get through life and cancer isn't going to stop that. Even at that initial low point we managed to find some hilarious moments. Here is but one.

Amongst the plethora of information given to a cancer patient is the advice about wigs because of the inevitable hair loss during chemotherapy. When this was given to Sue, I was still processing what she had just been told about the cancer so my brain was scrambled. Therefore, when the nurse told us about a company called Wills Wigs, all I heard (being a bloke and all) was Willy Wigs. I thought nothing more of it until I Googled it. You should try for yourself.

Bloody hell, I thought. She will do well to get that on her head. On closer inspection I realised that it wasn't the sort of wig you actually put on your head. They are penis rings with hair on! The thing is, who the hell would wear one of these and why? It would surely feel like having oral sex with someone watching.

The nurse did indeed say 'Wills Wigs.' I was still going to order a packet for a laugh but I thought better of it. I still might.

At the time of writing in April 2021 Sue has had ten chemo-therapy sessions and will continue for many months because the cancer is so aggressive. Who knows what the outcome will be or how long she has to live? The news was of course a life-changing moment but we draw on all our strength and love to stand together and fight. We are determined to let cancer know that it has picked on the wrong household. Susan has cancer, but cancer does not have Susan.

It was strange to shave all her hair off when it began falling out. She asked me to do it and no husband ever wants to do that for his wife but actually she looked quite cool. She will always be the Susan that stepped into my flat as a teenager, no matter what happens. I still see the beauty in her smile and her eyes. I am truly proud of her. She jokingly says that she cannot die yet, because she doesn't want to leave the dogs! I hope she is joking but I know my place in the hierarchy of this household.

I tell myself that I am being selfish when I think about her dying and *leaving me* behind. I don't want to be alone. I like the companionship, the love and the stability. I want to be the one to go first, because it is so utterly devastating for the people left behind after someone dies. No one else would have me now, not with chess sets in every room and tarantulas in the study. I will say this about cancer – it sure helps to put life into perspective. My top tip for anyone who has this or any illness physical or mental is this. Don't think of yourself as being chained to a wall – think of it as the wall being chained to you.

Cancer sufferers and their friends and families everywhere will be able to relate to all that I have said. Millions before us have succumbed to the disease and millions more will develop it. Watching the colours fade in the lives of those we love is the most heart-breaking challenge we can ever be faced with. But remember, death is part of life and if we can face it with dignity, fortitude and even acceptance at some point then we will have prevailed in our own way. It is not about the days in our life – it really is about the life in our days. Cancer does not define who you are. You do. *Nil desperandum* dear reader.

Back to the chess, and let me take you back to 2010 when Sue and I were living on the outskirts of Banbury. I was effectively *headhunted* by a tall, affable man with a Yorkshire accent and a twinkle in his eyes. His name was Neil Staples, a player at Banbury Chess Club. We knew one another from previous dealings with MoD Chess, and he had asked me about visiting the chess club, but it never happened. Neil is not a man to resign easily, either in life or on a chessboard and when he saw me again he reminded me that I would be most welcome at the club. I visited just to be polite in all honesty, but the rest is history. I still play for Banbury to this day. I also enjoy evenings playing chess with Neil who is a pugilist at the board, so we have lots of bloodthirsty games. We are roughly equal in play-ing strength which helps, so the evenings are never one-sided.

The club was founded in 1947 and has operated from numer-ous venues including the rather splendid, Ye Olde Reine Deer Inn, and parts of the building date way back as far as the medi-eval period with strong connections to the English Civil War. It has the renowned globe room where Cromwell visited, and some say made his headquarters during the English civil war.

This room has been attracting tourists for more than a century. Did Cromwell really plan the battle of Edge Hill from our chess club? Who knows, but it is certainly possible. The town of Banbury was inhabited by puritans at the time. Much has changed since then. According to satirist and journalist H.L. Mencken, puritanism is, 'the haunting fear that someone, somewhere, may be happy.' Banbury United Football Club still has the nickname *The Puritans*. The club crest has the figure of a puritan on it as well. I find this strange since puritans are nowadays largely looked upon in some quarters with derision.

Banbury chess club also has its share of characters and we share a common love of the game. Just before the coronavirus pandemic took hold, I managed to secure a local council grant to purchase several lovely wooden chess boards, and one of our own members, Gilbert Csecs, generously procured wooden pieces from the Chess and Bridge shop in London. We actually looked like a professional outfit, but this lasted only for a couple of weeks until we had to close the doors.

It is a great shame for our club that Gilbert has now moved to Devon so he will not enjoy those chess sets but his legacy remains, and we are grateful to him for his generosity. Hopefully, we will return to social chess again one day and when we do there will always be a chess board set up ready for Gilbert.

Of course, online chess is king nowadays, but I still prefer over the board chess where one can see the whites of the opponent's eyes and enjoy that tactile aspect of moving the pieces – just like I did at school. Give me 3D over 2D any day. There is something almost sensual about pushing those little chess pieces around a board. Their weight and shape along with the correct alignment all contribute to the aesthetic pleasure. The process is so familiar to me - concentrate, make a move, press the clock, write the move down… concentrate. Pens are an essential tool in the chess player's kit. Some people have *lucky pens* that they will use in every game. Others use a pen until they lose a game, then change it. Some prefer a click top, others a screw cap or a particular colour. You don't see anyone writing with a fountain pen these days, nor do people seem to keep a pen or two in the top of their blazer pocket. Not that people even wear blazers nowadays. Heathens! What is it they say, 'Times change, standards shouldn't.'

In addition to playing for Banbury I also play the occasional games for Solihull in the Birmingham League. Being a Brummie, it keeps me close to my roots. I enjoyed a season in the Four Nations Chess League (4NCL) with War and Piece which is made up of a team from the UK Armed Forces Chess Association. I also played a couple of games for Barbican Youth although youth was not something I brought to the team. This, along with the occasional game for the county of Oxfordshire and my own chess tournaments means that I have a bounty of chess options.

I was surprised and delighted to receive the English Chess Federation President's award for services to chess in 2015. Largely this was for my work in prisons, but also for much of the chess I had been involved in with schools and military chess over the years. It was a huge honour of course. I have been an ECF member since I was a youngster and been very proud to support the Federation.

I was a bit embarrassed, but very chuffed to be presented with the award just before a round of the 4NCL in view of all the players. ECF President Mike Truran did the honours. Mike is himself a tireless worker for chess and a heck of a good player too. He has been a guest at the Armed Forces chess finals where he was given a rare and special award himself by the Polish team.

In late 2006 I struck up an unlikely friendship with Sir Patrick Moore, the legendary amateur (there is that word again) astronomer who secured the title of presenter of the world's longest running television series for his work presenting the *The Sky at Night*. I read his autobiography one day and learned that he enjoyed chess, playing to county standard. It sounded like he was missing the game, so I wrote to him and he was very keen to play a correspondence game. I would receive a card with a message typed on his famous *Woodstock* typewriter.

Patrick had actually mapped the moon before man had even stepped on it. Do check out YouTube where Patrick talks about the importance of amateurs in astronomy, indeed some of them know more than the professionals!

He used to leave messages on our answer phone. Sue and I would arrive home from work, press play and hear in a loud booming voice, 'Hello Carl, Patrick here, give me a call for a chat.'

He invited Sue and I down to his house in Selsey in 2007 and we arrived in time for a stout luncheon of baked potato and tuna, followed by strawberries and cream. Patrick then produced his favourite chess set and insisted that we played. He described his own chess game as being a bit like leg spin in cricket and it is true that his moves were unorthodox, but he knew what he was doing. We drew the game having what I would call a gentlemanly draw, but I still have the note he sent me after saying I went too soft on him and he wanted me down to play again.

I recall one amusing occurrence that afternoon. Whilst Patrick and I were playing our game, he asked Sue over to the board. 'Would you refill my glass dear?' he said. Sue thought that the clear liquid was water and when she went to the tap he said, 'No no no dear, it's Gin – make it a big one and have one yourself too.' People of a certain age (me!) will recall that Patrick was famous for wearing a monocle and Sue had the unenviable task of being ushered to his monocle stand in the next room to select one for him to use. It was akin to William Shakespeare asking you to go and select a quill for him to write with.

In 2007 we received an invitation from Patrick to attend a celebration at his house celebrating fifty years of *The Sky at Night*. His friend Brian May, perhaps better known for being the guitarist in the rock supergroup Queen would be attending. Would we like to go? Would we? Yes indeed.

It is testament to my commitment to chess in general but Banbury chess club in particular, that I later decided not to go because I discovered that I had a league match on that same evening. Oh well – another one bites the dust.

What I loved about Patrick was his generosity. It is true that he was the least politically correct man that I ever knew (proclaiming that women had ruined the BBC, and that Germany should be dunked into the sea) but in a way it was just naïve. He was super intelligent of course, and I was so sad when he died in December 2012 with his beloved cats around him. I had been due to see him again. I miss him. He was a total one-off and we will definitely never see the like of him again. I hope that somewhere he has returned to the stardust which used to demand so much of his attention.

Playing chess my friend Sir Patrick Moore CBE at his home in Selsey in 2007. His style was as unorthodox as his personality.

Away from the board I was delighted to receive an invitation to attend Queen Elizabeth II's garden party at Buckingham Palace in 2009. The MoD had put my name forward in recognition (it said) for my public service over almost thirty years. I am not a royalist, but I have always admired and respected the Queen, I did see her when she visited our workplace in Shropshire in 1982 but this was different. It was an invitation to her house, so to speak, so it was quite exciting. Susan and I dressed up and the weather was thankfully fine. Some of the men totally overdid the dress and there's nothing worse than a chap who is not suited to wearing a top hat electing to wear one. One guest looked like Isambard Kingdom Brunel in some sort of stove pipe affair, and another looked for all the world like the Penguin out of Batman, but I shouldn't snipe – they were having a good time. They might well have thought that I looked out of place too.

At one point we all lined up in two rows and Her Majesty walked in between. She stopped a couple of metres in front of us and stared at Susan's dress. That was worrying. Our sovereign is small of stature but carries an extraordinary aura, and when she stares it is jolly unnerving. The Queen smiled at Susan and then gently walked on. It was a very pleasurable affair, and I have to say that the afternoon tea was splendid. The tea cakes had royal crowns on the top and of course the sandwiches appeared with crusts removed. An official DVD was taken on the day, so we have a nice memento.

The Lord Chamberlain is
commanded by Her Majesty to invite

Mr. Carl Portman
and Miss Susan Watson

to a Garden Party
at Buckingham Palace
on Tuesday, 14th July 2009 from 4 to 6 pm

A nice way to be temporarily detained at Her Majesty's pleasure.
The sandwiches were delicious.

Back to the chess. I will accept any opportunity to promote the game to the community. World Championship finalist and elite Grandmaster Nigel Short came to Banbury in September 2012 and he delivered a splendid simultaneous exhibition and lecture. He is always engaging, and he is an expert in the art of imparting knowledge from his level to our level (after all he was one of us once) which makes it easier to follow the games.

Of course, he is famous for being in the 1993 World Championship final against Garry Kasparov, but he would tell you that this wasn't the highlight of his career. Of greater significance was his defeat of former World Champion Anatoly Karpov in the candidates match to get to the final. I can see exactly what he means, as beating Karpov in a match (a series of games) as opposed to a one-off game is an extraordinary achievement.

Nigel stayed over at our house, and soon found my guitar. He began playing it and he is very proficient. He was also introduced to my collection of tarantulas and at one point I gently put one on the chessboard, but it did not faze him. We played some blitz games and I lost them all of course, although I was encouraged at one point when he said, 'Now *that* is a good move Carl.' I have some video footage of those games, but it is too risky to air it publicly as there was a bit of swearing!

Nigel and I are roughly the same age and he carries the torch for the *older* chess player, seeming not to lose his playing strength. That continues to inspire. He has other matters to attend to these days as a Vice President of FIDE – the world chess organisation. I can still vaguely remember him sporting long curly hair and an Afghan coat – I think that may have been at the Goodyear tournament in Wolverhampton. Any lad that featured in a band called Pelvic-Thrust (later renamed The Urge) was always going to be one to watch. He has had one hell of a chess career. I am sure he will come again to do another simul for me. Our political differences are as opposite as the black and white pieces, but it is chess that unites us, and long may that be so.

I was particularly pleased that International Master (and Woman Grandmaster) Tania Sachdev accepted an invite to Banbury to give a simultaneous exhibition. She is from Delhi originally and travels the planet commentating on chess. She is particularly adept at it too. It is a much harder job than she makes it look.

It was a lovely event, she played young and old, mother and daughter, male and female to show how diverse chess is, and it was a big success. Yet another incredible advantage of chess is the fact that it is possible for example for an eight-year-old to engage in battle against a ninety-year-old. Tell me, in how many other sports does that actually happen?

Tania stayed over at our house and she and Susan hit it off immediately. It's good that Sue does not play chess – it means that visiting players get to talk about other subjects. Tania was also a firm favourite with Darwin and Dickens. I was delighted to play some blitz games with her. It confirmed what I already knew - behind that engaging smile of hers is a killer of a player. She kept asking herself one question aloud – as if to give me (and indeed all chess players) a tip. 'Where is my counterplay?' We still plan for her to bring her parents round one day for an afternoon English tea if they ever visit the UK. Sue and I look forward to it very much.

The wheel of fun kept on turning. Another extremely pleasurable evening occurred when GM Matthew Sadler and WIM Natasha Regan, authors of a ground-breaking and award-winning book 'Game Changer' came to Banbury to deliver a lecture and joint simul. They were relaxed and approachable, not at all like some geeky chess players. Game Changer highlights the use of artificial intelligence in chess and in particular the incredible program called AlphaZero which taught itself chess and in a few hours beat the best computer programs available.

They also wrote another award-winning book called *Chess For Life* which revealed how chess understanding changes with the passage of time. We were lucky to have them with us. It is through chess that I have met such beautiful people like Natasha and Matthew. To my knowledge they are not together as *an item* so to speak but they complement each other perfectly, whatever they choose to do.

I do not want this to be a name-dropping exercise but the next event in my chess life cannot possibly be omitted. I mentioned that I have never had a coach. I spent a good deal of time being one for others, but what about me? I had this crazy idea one day. What if I approached elite chess Grandmaster Michael Adams and asked if he would give up a couple of full days to spend coaching me? Of course, it would come at a price. He was, I think, the fifteenth best player in the world at the time after all. But if you aim for the moon you might just reach the stars. My nan used to say 'if you don't ask you don't get' which I took as sound advice. Anyway, I deserved such a treat!

I got in touch and we agreed a fee and a date. I would go to his house and we would analyse some of my games and several other chess themes that I wanted to cover. At his request I sent him my last hundred games in advance, and he was able to quickly form some ideas about my play. We would have two days together.

Elite he may be but thankfully, Mickey, as he is better known is another down-to-earth chap. When I arrived at his house he answered the door in his *Guinness* slippers. I knew then that I could relax right away. We already had a passing acquaintance which made it easier to chill and get into the groove. We got stuck into plenty of chess work and he really tested me, which is just what I wanted. Mickey is patient and kind and of course a supremely talented chess player. To put it in perspective, it is a bit like someone spending a couple of days of private tuition with a top Premier League footballer. This is yet another wonderful thing about chess – accessibility to the stars.

I am not going to give much away (I paid for the privilege after all) but I will share one recommendation of his which all chess players might wish to consider. He said, 'Why don't you just play one whole season where you do not accept any draws?' Clearly this would not include forced draws and the like, but in essence, he had identified that I drew too many games when there was still play on the board.

He said if the game was theoretically drawn then what would I have to lose by playing on? He asserted that if my mindset at the beginning of a league season was not to play for or accept draw offers then my results would change significantly. This was of course excellent advice. I cannot honestly say that I executed it fully but I kept it at the forefront of my mind, and I did play on in some games where I would otherwise have split the point.

He tested me with lots of positions to solve and I was getting better as the hours progressed, tuning my mind in to what I was looking for. I was not nervous at all but I wanted to please him by finding the correct answers. I imagined what a month of coaching would have been like, but I was privileged that Mickey agreed to help me over the two days. He and his lovely wife Tara treated me to a curry at the local restaurant on the first evening and she also made a scrumptious Caesar salad the next day.

Away from chess I learned that he loves his cricket and quite likes Tottenham Hotspur. Such happy days are rare in life and have to be savoured. My thanks always to Mickey for his generosity. Even though he was being paid, you could see that he really wanted to help me improve. It wasn't just about money.

Enjoying a two-day private coaching session with elite grandmaster Michael Adams in 2014. He was fifteenth best in the world at that time.

I managed to play at the Gibraltar chess festival in January 2019. This is one of the best open tournaments in the world, without question. Run by the irrepressible Grandmaster Stuart Conquest it is a place where the amateur can freely mix with the world's elite and enjoy chess in a slightly warmer climate.

I got lucky with Chucky and managed to blag a brief interview with the great man. I am talking about Vassily Ivanchuk. He was the most difficult person I have ever interviewed because he has such a complex and unfathomable personality, but I will share (yet another) top tip with the reader of this memoir. I asked him what one thing he would recommend to an amateur player to improve their game. 'Get a good coach,' he said. 'Chess engines tell you the evaluations, but they don't explain the game.'

Stuart was kind enough to give me a place playing against elite Grandmaster Wesley So and Grandmaster Kateryna Lagno in a joint simultaneous exhibition. Kateryna earned the title of Woman's Grandmaster at the tender age of twelve. Wesley has been in the world's top ten for years now. I enjoyed a good game but went down, like everyone else.

Twelve years earlier in Gibraltar in 2007, I experienced one of my most embarrassing chess moments. I was sitting at the dinner table with my friends Kevin Thurlow and Tony Ashby, who were also playing. We chatted about various chess matters as you do. For some reason, the name of Grandmaster Tony Miles came up. He was one of my heroes, coming as he did from Birmingham, and having an uncompromising style both at the board and in life. I said quite loudly, 'Hey Kevin, do you remember when he reviewed Eric Schiller's book, *Unorthodox Chess Openings* which consisted of just two words: 'Utter crap?'

Kevin became rather flushed as he whispered across – 'Eric Schiller is sitting right behind you!'

Fuck me – he was!

What the hell were the chances of that happening? How embarrassing.

Schiller's table must have heard as they all went quiet. Of all the tables in all the tournaments in all the world – Schiller had to sit back-to-back with mine. Nobody said anything but I cringed. Maybe there is a God after all, and he played a nice little trick on me!

The Covid-19 pandemic robbed me and many others of a nice warm January in Gibraltar. It is a very special tournament as I say. I love to watch what I call *golden seagulls* flying by the Caleta Hotel. At night they are still on the wing, and the sodium exterior hotel lights catch them on the wing drifting around like little balls of fire. It is also an opportunity to see my first butterflies of the year and with it the promise of so much sunshine and beauty to come back in the UK. It is not just a great chess experience, it lifts the spirits, it really does.

Turning to the British Chess Championships in Llandudno in 2017, I bumped into International Master (and Woman Grandmaster) Jovanka Houska. She was trying to locate the playing room amongst the labyrinth of walkways at the venue. I tried to point her in the right direction but became unsure myself, so we spent some time opening various doors until we found the correct room. It was very amusing. I am not sure precisely how our friendship evolved after that, but she and her wonderful Norwegian husband Arne are now firm friends with me and Susan.

We have a great laugh and a catch up occasionally accompanied by good food and fine wine. Jovi has won the British Women's Championship an amazing nine times and I have said that if she can make it ten, I will supply the bottle of champagne. It is an offer I shall be delighted to deliver on, and I know it will happen. I wanted some more coaching at one point and Jovi spent a couple of days with me going through some interesting material. There were plenty of games and openings and she tested me with some tricky rook, pawn and king endgames. Many know that she is a lover of the Caro Kann opening and she has written a book on that very system.

Jovi was good enough to give me some insights into why she plays it. I am happy to share another couple of points, drawing from her chess wisdom. First of all look for good squares. It's not just about the squares that the pieces already occupy – look for optimum squares for where these pieces might best be placed. Secondly do not be so rigid about the values of the pieces. They are only static at the beginning of a game but during the game they become fluid. A rook might be less effective than a knight or bishop. It depends on the position. Chess is a game of exceptions.

A coach like Jovi makes chess come alive at the board. Oddly, I have not engaged her in a simultaneous exhibition yet, but that time will come. Jovi would tell you that I showed her a highly interesting line in the Alekhine's Defence for the player with the white pieces. I could not possibly reveal what it was, (or could I?) but she had not seen it before. You see, we amateurs can still throw gold nuggets at the kings and queens. Indeed, I was chuffed to read Savielly Tartakower write, 'A master can always learn something from amateurs!' He explained in his best games collection in his game against Marshall, in Liège, in 1930, that an idea was, 'due to that excellent British player Dr. Duncan.'

Jovi is one of those rare people who thinks before she speaks and what she has to say is especially interesting if her view is opposite to mine. I can hold a conversation with her with wildly opposing views without it getting personal. I went too far once and in her own inimitable way she told me off (understatement) so I behave much better now.

She wrote an excellent novel entitled *The Mating Game* which at the time of writing might be released as a movie – albeit in a radically different adaptation. If it is as sexy and racy as the book it will be a good watch! I wish her well and hope she gets rich on it. She and Arne are life's good guys.

Now for the realization of a dream.

I have already declared that my childhood hero was Anatoly Yevgenyevich Karpov. He was World Champion from 1975 to 1985, thus covered the period when I was at school. It wasn't his fault that Bobby Fischer refused to defend his title in 1975, and some have dismissed Karpov because of it. I have to say that is heresy. Karpov did the next best thing. He proved himself in multiple tournaments after that, winning most if not all of them, clearly demonstrating that he was the best, at least officially. A match between Fischer and Karpov would have been out of this world, but it did not happen so we will never know who would have been the victor. That's life. Move on.

But he would play Carl Portman! It so happened, thanks to efforts from both Grandmaster Raymond Keene and ace photographer David Llada that I learned that the twelfth World Champion would be giving a simultaneous exhibition in the beautiful city of Chartres, south west of Paris, as one of the main events at the French Chess Championships. This was August 2019. I contacted the organisers, told them about my dream and incredibly they agreed to me being one of the lucky fifteen players to face Karpov.

All I ever wanted was to meet him, but now I was actually going to play him. I was as excited as a silly teenager. I had waited for forty-three years for this moment, but I wasn't there yet. Anything could happen. I could become ill. He could become ill, there could be a meteor strike on Chartres. That would be just my luck.

I travelled to France in a state of contained excitement, still not quite believing that it would happen. The evening before the event I attended a masterclass by Karpov who went through one of his favourite games, and during his Q&A afterwards I plucked up the courage to ask him why he supported chess in prisons. He said, 'Chess gives prisoners the key to a free world.' Now that to me is a profound statement. He said that chess can help people to restore contacts on the outside in a free life, and that chess gives people a chance. However, 'second society' must also give support to inmates. It must 'give opportunities to prisoners.' I totally agree with that sentiment.

The momentous day arrived and I awoke to a sunny 20th August 2019. The simul was not until the evening so I had the day to prepare some chess. To be honest I already knew what I wanted to do so I went to the town square where some friendly chaps from the French Chess Federation had set up tables to play chess against locals and passers-by. I took a table and in the end helped to coach some young schoolchildren. It was fun. The language barrier was not too bad. My French is not great but we got by. It was lovely to sit in the sunshine and help the kids.

I met some very friendly people including a lady called Valentina who was a Russian, living in France. She knew Karpov and was going to get me to meet him personally, but events contrived against this happening due to a language misunderstanding. Valentina spoke no English, and I hardly any French. However, a friend of hers later translated a conversation for us and we agreed that maybe one day I would come back to Chartres and talk about chess in prisons. Chartres is such a beautiful city and I am definitely going back. Like the wolf, I shall return to the scene of the battle.

The hours ticked by and finally, evening came. I took my place at one of only fifteen chess boards. It was a beautiful balmy evening in the market square and I breathed in the moment, committing the sights and sounds to memory. The pink sunset reflected on the walls of the buildings, and there was the smell of coffee, bread and cigar smoke. The tension was palpable, and the square was jam-packed with spectators. I wanted to avoid getting smashed in a few moves, but I had done my homework and prepared something. I hoped that Karpov would go into the line I looked at and by a slight transposition he did.

Playing my hero Anatoly Karpov in Chartres, France at a simultaneous exhibition in 2019. I lost but I was the last player to finish.

I am incredibly proud to have been the very last player to finish, and at one point it was just Karpov and me, one to one in a rook and pawn endgame with the whole crowd watching.

One of the French organisers shouted, 'Zee Englishman is last to finish' and he burst into applause. I was losing but there was no time to even try to improve my position because I had to move pretty much instantly as we were the only two players. His technique as just too good, but then he is Anatoly Karpov, right? We made forty-two moves and I savour every one of them. We smiled and shook hands, and he signed my scoresheet as well as his own memoir book, *Karpov on Karpov*, which I treasure.

To be completely honest, Karpov will never win personality of the year, he is far too serious a person (a rich philatelist, businessman and a committed communist) but it was never about holding a meaningful conversation with him, I just wanted to meet him. Now that I have played him at chess, I can move on.

My final congress before the Covid-19 Pandemic was Kidlington in Oxfordshire in February 2020. I entered the open section (the top one). I played four games (excluding a half-point bye) and came out with a tournament grade of ECF 186 so I was delighted to still be able to play to a decent level despite my advancing years. Who knows when my next OTB tournament might be? Kidlington is organised by an old friend and strong chess player Gerard O'Reilly and he is a really genial character. I recommend participating in it to finish your winter off with a chess feast.

Talking of characters, it is time to take a closer look at the weird world of chess players in general. In particular what you can expect to face at the board. Some professionals tell us to play the board. Others say play the man. Some say play both. What you do is up to you but I guarantee that some behaviour will definitely demand your attention.

Are you ready?

Meeting World chess Champion Magnus Carlsen in London
in 2018 at an invitational event.

This is my game face. I am not sure who took the photograph or when.

Saints and sinners

Every saint has been a sinner and every sinner has been a saint

Anon

In my experience there are two types of opponents. Those that behave themselves and those that do not.

The people who belong in the former group just play chess. They are the saints who do not feel compelled to employ underhand tactics to influence the game. Let me be clear. The vast majority of chess players are saints. Good people.

However, the sinners are a different story. These miscreants employ gamesmanship in order to try to achieve their objective. I am not saying that they cheat but they will push the boundaries and test your resolve. One of the most responsible roles I ever had in life was to be the foreman on jury service. I was the one who had to stand up and deliver the verdict. If these people were in the dock – I would serve a *guilty* verdict on the lot of them.

I hold the immutable view that chess is sport, and sport is competitive by nature. Therefore, some people will not play by the rules. The sooner we accept that this happens the better. The saints are prompt to the board, shake you by the hand and play the game without trying to distract you. They might even analyse a game with you afterwards. The whole affair is an enjoyable experience for everyone. But you don't want to hear about that yet, do you dear reader? No – you want the sordid details. Oh, go on then.

The following question is very valid. What can you do when people behave improperly at the chessboard?

The best way of course is to win the game. These scoundrels will understand the language and pain of defeat. We all deal with poor behaviour in different ways. Me, I am old school. I remember a sign in my local fish and chip shop in the 1980s which said, *Please don't ask for credit, as a smack in the mouth often offends.*

I accept the abiding principle that we cannot all go around throwing punches, therefore the only advice I can give is to find your own way of dealing with it. You will have to put up with nefarious behaviour throughout your chess career, I guarantee it. Not so much at the higher levels (if you get there) but definitely at school, club, county and tournament level.

What I am about to reveal is the naked truth, taken directly from four decades of my own chess experiences. Remember that some people are deliberately provocative whilst others have no idea that they are annoying you – it is just the way they are and there is a big difference. Old sins cast long shadows and one day the sinners will have to answer for their naughty deeds.

I shall use some arbitrary headers to describe the sinners.

The starers

These blackguards cherish their deeply held belief that they can psych you out by staring at you. The worst group for doing this is juniors. Shock horror! I never used to stare at an adult when I was a kid, it is extremely rude. However a significant number of juniors deploy this tactic. Maybe they are coached to stare? The best thing to do is give as good as you get. These urchins will not be able to hold their gaze longer than you. Try it with your own kids at the breakfast table. If they beat you – send them to their room at once.

The clock bangers

After essaying their move these rogues will bang their clock in dramatic fashion as if to add emphasis. It isn't funny but it is annoying. Next time, shift the clock just after they make a move, then watch them fracture a finger as they bang the table. Failing that tell them to stop clock banging or you will let the tyres down on their car. Note: This won't work if they don't actually have a car. Therefore always do your preparation before a game.

The double handers

In chess, you are supposed to press your clock with the *same* hand that you have move your pieces. A few players cheat by using both hands – one finger already poised a centimetre above their clock so they can save milliseconds over a few moves. Condemn this practice immediately and tell them to refrain or you will claim the game or extra time on your own clock. Chess players should be familiar with the basic rules of the game.

The kickers

Many years ago, I played a tournament game in Birmingham against a well-known chess author. Up to that point I had respect for the man, but things quickly took a turn for the worst. This bounder tried every trick in the book to put me off. It began with him offering me an extra strong mint each time he played his move, just as I began concentrating on my reply. He did this several times and I said, 'I don't want a sweet, thank you, please don't offer me one again.'

A couple of moves later, I received an almighty whack on my shin. The cad kicked me under the table! He tried to make it look like he was simply crossing his legs, but he wasn't. After coughing, belching and offering me a sweet yet again he kicked me once more, really sharply. I snapped and said, 'If you kick me again under this table I am going to kick you back – really hard.' He never spoke. We played a few more moves then bang! It happened again. Certainly then, a declaration of war. His attempts to break my concentration worked. I focused less on the game and more on how to kick him back. I chose my strategy; I was going to pretend I was stretching my legs but oops – his shin would get in the way. I went for it. My foot shot out and made contact with his shin – and it was a kick that Bruce Lee would have been proud of. The man winced just a little but did not jump back. I wondered if he had a wooden leg.

I was still annoyed, after all he had kicked me more times. I doubled my determination to win – which I did, and he had to resign. I cannot begin to tell you how gratifying that felt. He never offered his hand and I never offered mine. It is the only time in my whole chess life that I gloated and said, 'I see you still lost', as I sarcastically smiled at him and left the board.

I would love to reveal who it was. All I can say is he co-wrote a very well-known book in the late 1980s but he died some time ago so he cannot defend himself. My advice to anyone who is kicked deliberately by an opponent is to kick 'em back! Then again, you'll probably get into trouble for it so just deliver a nice checkmate instead.

The food fiends

After shoving his (it is never her) fingers into a piece of cake this sinner will offer it to you. Such altruistic souls will offer you food only when it is your turn to move in a disgraceful attempt to break your concentration. Feel free to take the offering if you wish, but I have no idea where their fingers have been. If the cake is suitably stodgy it can be used to prop up wobbly tables. Cakes with marzipan are especially good for this. If the cake has whole brazil nuts in it, then you might accept a slice and use a couple of the nuts as pawns if circumstances dictate.

The sausage rockets

This porcine horror really happened. A rather unkempt gentleman sat opposite me having arrived very late at the board, but he did not apologise, which is just poor form. His hand was pregnant with a sausage and egg cob. These used to be surprisingly common at chess tournaments.

He mumbled something and offered me his fat, sweaty hand, smeared as it was in grease. How nice. He sat down and played a move instantly. As I was considering my reply, he took a gargantuan bite from the bread roll. The net result of this rather egregious act was that the sausage flew out like a rocket from underneath the egg and it landed with a dull thud, skidding along on the chess board. I wouldn't have minded, but it knocked my king over – and I certainly wasn't resigning to a sausage. The man scooped up the offending banger and shoved it into his mouth without even apologising. We drew the game, much to my annoyance. How dare you fire a sausage at me sir.

The slurpers

Slurpers seriously wind me up, especially if I am losing. They annoy me so much that I actually want to strike them. They sit there slurping their tea/coffee. It's absolutely vile. On one occasion I asked my opponent, 'Do you have to slurp?' He did not reply. Slurpers should be sent on some kind of correctional course to learn how to drink properly. Wildebeest slurp at watering holes but chess players should refrain from doing so.

The munchers

These wastrels should be locked up or banned from chess *sine die*. Eating at the board is vulgar and disrespectful. I occasionally endure opponents who open a packet of crisps and start eating them at the board, whilst I am thinking! You are not allowed to distract your opponent, so what do they think opening and munching crisps would do?

I have played opponents who ate sweets, crisps, sandwiches, bananas (a favourite), cake, soup, chips, chocolates and fruit. One madman once mutilated half a melon in front of me and he only had two teeth in his head. It was ghastly, and I had nightmares for weeks. Eat your food by all means, but away from the board – it is chess, not a bloody tea party.

The late arrivals

In competitive chess, players should be at the board at the same time to begin play. You know, like two football teams should actually be on the pitch when the referee blows his whistle. However, in chess the rules provide some dispensation. A player will have their clock started (and time being used) up to one hour before being defaulted. Some people are late for legitimate reasons such as oversleeping or illness etc. However, some arrive late deliberately to try to destabilise you. Some will even arrive just before they are about to default on time. By then, you have relaxed because you think he or she won't turn up and your chess brain has switched off.

This breed of opponent is happy to sacrifice their time and they will then play their moves super quickly in the time that they have remaining. It's a bit sad, really. I mean what other sport would allow this? Incidentally, it is not just amateurs that do this. Some professionals do it also – and at elite level too. I can name one Grandmaster who does this. David Howell. However, in his defence he is such a popular player (and lovely chap) that chess fans want to talk to him all the time. If he arrived at his board ten minutes before the game he would have to swat away all the annoying questions and autograph hunters etc. So instead he arrives just a bit late ready to play instantly – so there are no distractions, and he is in the zone for the battle ahead. I can accept this, and he is not being rude. Incidentally I have never known a female player arrive late to the board. They are far too organised. Take note lads and have a word with yourselves.

The gurners

Some chess players openly show their emotions at the board, whilst others never do. Of those that do, there are two types still. Those that genuinely cannot help it and it is part of their emotional make up, and those that do it as gamesmanship. Some people will gurn.

A gurn is an extremely distorted and particular facial expression and involves projecting the lower jaw as far forward and up as possible and covering the upper lip with the lower lip. Basically, just pulling funny faces. The best gurner in history was Garry Kasparov, followed in my view by USA Grandmaster Hikaru Nakamura. It is worth watching their games just for the expressions alone.

Personally, I don't mind players gurning at me, but I do mind spectators doing it. My recommendation if someone is watching your game and starts pulling faces is to simply stare at them. You could ask them if they are having some kind of stroke. If not then tell them to stop pulling faces as it is putting you off.

The laughers

Laughers make little sarcastic, dismissive laughing noises just after you have made a move. They might sneer, and that may develop into a little chuckle but very occasionally it might metamorphose into a full cachinnation. The only action to take against these individuals is to challenge them and ask what they are laughing at.

If their response is unacceptable, kick them hard, under the table and say, 'you are not laughing now, are you dick head?' Note: You cannot do this to juniors or women. It's just not cricket. You will have to devise your own strategy to tackle them. It won't be easy. The juniors will tell their parents and you'll be labelled as a beast and expelled from any future games.

The women will cry. Then you will have to apologise to them to bring them round. You might have to hold their head up before they faint, which means you will be labelled a pervert. All this and you have done nothing wrong in the first place. Note: if you don't want to be labelled a pervert, then do not attempt to kiss the lady gently on the cheek whilst trying to revive her.

The sneezers and coughers (Disease Carriers)

I cannot tell you how many colds I have caught from irresponsible opponents who played chess whilst they were poorly. One man was so ill at the board that he almost fainted. He looked as if he was two minutes away from the morgue. Some people cough all the way through the game whilst others spend all of their time clearing their throats.

Sneezing is another issue especially if – as happened to me several times – your opponent does so directly at you leaving small globules of snot on the board. That sounds repulsive doesn't it? Welcome to chess. Covid-19 might change the way chess is played in this respect, but I doubt it. We will all have to mask up now. We won't even be able to see our opponent's faces soon, so there may not be any proof as to who we are really playing.

The nose blowers

As above. You can do this discreetly. You do not have to sound like a sodding foghorn and then stare at the contents of your handkerchief afterwards, as some opponents have done. The most notorious nose blower at elite level was the late Grandmaster Tony Miles. He was always blowing his hooter. It was more from habit than medical necessity and it was gross. Move away from the board if you are going to blow your nose loudly, then return quietly to the board afterwards.

The newspaper readers

I once played a man who insisted on reading a newspaper during our game. I would make my move, he would respond immediately and continue reading. We drew that game. Had he not spent so much time being clearly bored with my standard of chess and instead concentrated more on his own game he might have beaten me. I should warn you that people also place books at the side of the board as if to say, *Look at me, this is what I am reading. I am way too clever for you to beat me.* The best way to deal with this is to *accidentally* spill your coffee (that you shouldn't be drinking at the board) over the book. Watch their smarmy faces then.

The Cloggies

I cannot tell you how angry I get at people who participate in chess tournaments whilst wearing noisy shoes that are inappropriate for the floor. These nitwits should be taken to one side, spoken to tersely and made to wear slippers for the rest of the tournament. Get the memo – when people are concentrating on their chess games they do not want to be distracted by you pacing up and down trying to be the centre of attention. Wearing shoes with segs on a wooden floor is phenomenally annoying and a totally unnecessary racket. You don't look cool, you're a first-class arsehole.

The 'check' shouters

These are the attention seekers who announce 'check' inappropriately loudly, thereby shattering the silence and breaking everyone's concentration in the playing hall.

Everyone then feels compelled to look at that person's board as if something mystical is happening. Usually, check shouters are just shite players who crave attention. You may announce check if you really must, but please do so *quietly*.

Juniors are particularly culpable here. I do not hold them

solely responsible. Some of the blame must be shared with whoever taught them chess. I played one junior who seemed to want to get as many checks in as she could just so that she could announce it loudly as if it were in some way improving her position. I checkmated her but refrained from standing up and shouting CHECKMATE! at the end. It is okay for her to do it, but not me I will wager.

Occasionally, fully grown adults shout 'check' but they are too thick to realise how ridiculous they sound. Most people in a competitive tournament don't say check – we just know we are in check, right? You are fully entitled under the rules to announce it but be mindful of the fact that if you insist on shouting it out you are disturbing others – which is illegal under chess rules. Players who shout 'check' should be treated as follows. Be sure always to have a megaphone with you, then when the opponent shouts check, turn it on and shout 'YES, I BLOODY KNOW.'

The extremists

These clowns are prepared to do something so extreme that you will barely believe your eyes. I actually had an opponent place an air gun by the side of my board before play started and mutter, 'I am gonna win today, aren't I?'

Luckily, I am not so easily intimidated. 'You'll need more than that,' was my rather game retort.

I do wish I could tell you who that was, but I have long since forgotten his name. He pulled it out of a bag, and it was probably a kid's toy, who knows? It certainly looked realistic. This was thirty years ago – and he lost. There was no silver bullet for his game, I am afraid. You couldn't do it nowadays – he would be arrested and if I had my way, the result would be the same.

The filthy germ-ridden handshake

This is a really bad and a really common one and all chess players are aware of it. Chess congresses can have upwards of one hundred males and only three little toilets to share. Some of those males will have the squits (diarrhoea) – due to nerves. Many do not wash their hands (or indeed any other part of their bodies) and the handshake before and after a game is most unpleasant. Incidentally, the toilets usually get blocked and cease to work so you then have a hundred men using two lavatories. I worked in a piggery for a while and it smelled more pleasant than some of the toilets I have to use at chess congresses. It's really, really miserable and a breeding ground for active bacteria. Hopefully the Covid-19 pandemic will improve hygiene behaviour amongst chess players, but I won't hold my breath. On second thoughts, I will.

The advantage for ladies here is clear. Whilst men are packing themselves like sardines into their piss-stained toilets, the very few women at tournaments have a nice fresh toilet of their own free to use at will. It must be heaven.

The odoriferous

I was that unfortunate manager who had to tell a member of staff that he had body odour issues. He was a lovely fellow, and he took it well. I even bought him soap and deodorant, so he used to wash in the toilets before other staff arrived. You cannot really do this with your chess opponent, so you will need a coping mechanism.

If you want to play chess – especially tournaments - you had better be mentally prepared to play against people who do not wash. I don't mean skipping the occasional splash, I am talking about not washing for days or weeks.

Some chess players will appear to have slept in a hedge, even if they are accommodated in a nice clean hotel for the week. I have known individuals to wear the same jacket or cardigan for many years. These are usually adorned with old food morsels, such as egg, grease and/or assorted breadcrumbs. It is a wonder that when they are outdoors they are not attacked by flocks of birds.

Beards are particularly useful for collecting remnants of food. Not washing hair is another old classic on the chess circuit. I once played on a board next to a man who had not washed his hair for so long that I could actually see nits jumping around on his head. In this matter I am totally serious and I have a witness!

The ladykillers (Feminists, charge your pens)

Let us not get too politically correct about this. Some women use their feminine charms – and assets – in a game of chess. There is the famous case of an Australian man who lost to a woman (shock, horror) and complained that he did so because her cleavage was too distracting. That was a poor excuse, of course.

However, I shall never forget one game I played against a woman who had particularly large and admittedly show-stopping breasts. She arrived at the board wearing a very low-cut top. Now, that is her business not mine, but what followed was just too much for a young lad – young and thrusting I was. She proceeded to lean over and place her ample bosom on the table just near her end of the board, making some pseudo-attempt to look calm. This was over the top, almost literally. Before I am accused of being a vile sexist I will absolutely stand by my conviction that this was gamesmanship, or should I say gameswomanship? I was there, you were not.

I did my best, I swear I did, I am a man after all. I tried not to look. 'Focus Carl' I kept telling myself. The trouble is she kept shuffling around and it was getting so bad that I actually did not want to exchange rooks – hers being right up the end of the board near her cleavage. What if I slipped? What if I knocked a rook down into her chesty abyss? At some point she offered me a draw. I should have put myself out of my torment, but I fancied I could win the game, so we were at it for another hour. She played very well to hold the rook endgame because I was definitely better, and we did indeed draw.

If we ever play again, I am going to wear green budgie smugglers, and see if she likes it. Mind you, by then everything will have gone south, and rook endgames will be the least of my worries.

The foot tappers and knee jerkers

I will concede on this one because I do it myself. During the heat of the battle at key moments or in time-trouble people will feverishly jerk their legs as if they have restless leg syndrome. You just have to be aware of it. Only if they knock the table – and therefore the pieces, should you take them to task. It's amusing walking into a room full of twitchers and jerkers. It's like a mass meeting of human jelly. Old and young people do it, and no-one is immune.

The popinjays

These narcissists are the epitome of the vain and conceited person. The one who dresses overtly extravagantly to impress in some way. Sometimes it may be an *I went to University* tee shirt (so what?) and on another occasion one might be faced with a sharp suit and mustard cravat.

Occasionally the popinjay will wear a hat. Now then, a Fedora is admittedly always going to be cool, especially a black one but if you insist on wearing a baseball cap with your suit (as some do) then I am afraid I am going to have to consign you to room 101.

I hasten to add that a chess-themed necktie is most acceptable but any kind of neckwear with flamingos or teddy bears on just screams 'I am a knob.' If you cannot live up to what your clothing says about you, then stop being pretentious and get a grip on reality.

The lazy piece placers

The correct way to move a chess piece is crisply and smartly, by placing it directly in the centre of a square. That way we can readily identify which pieces are on what squares. Yet some players insist on placing their chess pieces half on one square and half on another. Again, indolent juniors are the worst culprits in my experience. Once more, I should not be overly harsh on them. After all, someone presumably taught them how to play and they were clearly lacking in manners. Remember coaches – your juniors are in many ways a reflection of yourself. I always make it my job to politely remind people that their piece should sit within the square or I will ask, 'can you tell me what square that is on?' Do it enough times and they usually get the hint. Failing this, call the arbiter and ask him/her to stop the clock and remind your opponent of the rules.

The shushers

Chess is a quiet game, to be played in peaceful repose. Yet for any number of reasons our noise-free atmosphere can be shattered. Usually the culprit is someone talking – often at the entrance to a tournament room or at the refreshment bar where people forget that they can be heard.

The other great favourite is the post-mortem; in other words, the moment that the game finishes the players begin a conversation about how it went – thereby distracting the other players. When this occurs, the perpetrators are likely to fall victim to a shusher. Usually, it only takes one *shhhhhhhh* to do the job but chess players being what they are quite often ignore it and carry on.

On one occasion, and to my great amusement I witnessed a seasoned shusher who shushed so loudly that he invoked the anger of the gentleman on the board next to him, so he shushed the shusher. 'Don't you shush me,' the original shusher said most indignantly. Hilarious.

The knight adjusters

These sneaky villains are not to be trusted at the board, and therefore in life generally. We chess players set our pieces up the way we wish to, paying particular attention to our knights, of which we each have two. One sits on the king's side and the other on the queen's side. We position these either both facing left or right, facing together or facing forward, directly at the battlefield. Some deranged and quite frankly unstable people actually have them facing *backwards*. That is to say the knight's faces are pointed towards the player who will be commanding them.

I deem this to be heresy but they do have the right to do it. Occasionally, an opponent has the bare-faced audacity before the game even begins to reach across and adjust *my* knights to the direction that he or she prefers. What? Really? I don't think so. I give them a stare of incredulity, raise an eyebrow and instantly put my knights back to how I originally placed them.

This does not guarantee success because some deviants change them again when you have popped to the disease-ridden loo, or the tea bar. You return to the board to find your knights facing in a different direction. Let me be clear, this is scandalous behaviour and cannot be tolerated. Adjust your own knights as you wish but leave mine the hell alone or I will *adjust* you.

To all those people who suffer at the hands of the people described above, I have one piece of advice...

Illegitimi non carborundum

The Saints – they mean well

Now for the saints. These are the people who have suffered unforeseen occurrences during a game, or who behave in a way *not intended* to be gamesmanship, they just don't realise the error of their ways. If you are not a sinner then by definition you are a saint. These events all occurred. If you do not believe me, well you weren't there were you?

The limp wristers

A handshake should be a handshake! When you shake hands, you should do so smartly, precisely and with a good firm grip like we used to do before about 1990. Above all, it should be meaningful. Here is the process. Engage – grip – shake – release. Unfortunately, all too many people offer their hand as if it is a limp lettuce and even then they don't shake, they just barely touch. Listen ye well. Either offer a proper handshake or do not bother. Please refrain from any half-arsed attempts. Women are guilty of this. Juniors are guilty of this and at least 30% of men are guilty of it. If you offer me your hand to shake, mean it or I might accidentally fracture your wrist.

The fainters

I have had a couple of people faint at the board. Be mentally prepared because it can happen. I have already articulated how stressful chess can be at times. One day a man coughed so aggressively that he fainted and fell forward, face-planting the board. When he sat up, there was a pawn stuck in the corner of his eye! It fell out quickly, but it really hurt him. He carried on playing despite squinting at the board. I can declare that this was none other than Norman Andrews from Shropshire. Bless him.

The epileptics

The first time I knew about epileptic fits was when an opponent experienced one at the board. It shocked me and those around me. The shaking began and then the unfortunate lad fell off his chair, convulsing on the floor and began foaming at the mouth. I did not know at the time how to deal with it, but now I know what position to put people into and *not* to put fingers anywhere near the mouth. It was a very unfortunate event and actually quite frightening. The chap recovered and continued playing, thankfully.

The vomiters

If queasy, look away now. I have experienced the warm feeling of someone vomiting all over me and the board. The material was soup-like. I distinctly remember carrot and some puke-coloured mess all over my tee shirt. I believe the cad had been drinking before the game. No names, no pack drill. I won the game so I don't really care!

The tear jerkers

Bless them, I have had more than my fair share of juniors burst into tears – especially in school. It goes with the territory of a competitive pursuit like chess. In a way it is a rite of passage. Losing hurts and in many ways that is healthy. If winning feels good, then losing is meant to feel bad. That is unless you are in it just to make up the numbers and not worry about the result – which is also completely fine.

I had one junior in a class burst into tears when I checkmated him. He really sobbed. I comforted the lad and asked him why he was so upset. He was only ten years of age. What he said next haunts me still. He had a dream that once his king was killed, he would die in real life too. How do you process and deal with that? It's not in the textbooks is it?

I told him that my own king had been killed thousands of times in my life and I was still perfectly fine. Luckily, that did the trick, but we cannot presume to know what goes on in the minds of kids. Chess is very serious to some, especially if (like this lad) their parents are pressuring them to win every game.

The deaf aids

Aids for the deaf and hard of hearing have improved significantly over the years. Some chess players have to wear them of course, but back in the day some of the earpieces used to go berserk and activate with a strange, piercing, shrill sound. Nowadays it is much better, but I am amazed how often players don't alert their opponent to the fact that they are hard of hearing. Why do they need to do this, you might reasonably ask?

Well this is chess, and if your opponent offers a draw (this is mostly done verbally) you surely need to be able to hear that this has occurred. One of my friends has a hearing aid and occasionally misses draw offers. Also, with the advent of cheating in chess as a result of software developments people are very wary of anything stuck inside someone's ear, making a noise. It may not be politically correct but I do not care. I believe that the person with the aid, or the captain of the team should alert the opposition that there is a partially deaf or deaf person in the team and that if the aid does go off or someone wants to make a draw offer they can deal appropriately with both events to avoid embarrassment. This could be done discreetly.

The stomach rumblers

Do not underestimate this issue. It is the bane of my life. The trouble is, I wolf down food before an evening match at the club, but digestion begins from the moment I sit down in that silent room. It is very embarrassing and in a quiet room the sound is amplified. It sounds like an approaching thunderstorm with its rumble, rumble, rumble. Many other chess players suffer from this, and it is even more embarrassing when it is a woman. Don't ask me why, it just is.

The farters

I apologise. However embarrassing you might think this is – we have to cover the subject. There is a lot of farting in chess tournaments. Since the majority of a chess room consists mostly of males, it is the men who fart the most. However, on one single occasion I was playing a young lady who unfortunately let one go as she leaned across to exchange bishops. It wasn't silent. In fact it was a real fizzer, and it was deadly. If I recall we both soon agreed a draw and went our separate ways.

Chess coaches will be acutely aware that their young charges fart all the time, sometimes on a thermo-nuclear scale. At one of my weekly classes I could predict which boy was going to come in and deliver a raspberry to make the angels blush. Me? I try to hold it in, but that's not always easy is it? There have been a couple of occasions when I have had to let off a flutterblast. Who hasn't? Just stare at the board, *never* look up – and play on. Alternatively, if you really do have to let a noisy threep off, select someone close by, stare at them and then tut loudly - in that order. A good solid scowl might also help to pass the blame.

The wristwatch alarmers

Chess players are not allowed to have mobile phones or indeed any electronic device with them when they play. Apart from the cheating aspect, in the early days it was just about a phone going off – thereby disturbing and distracting the opponent, which is not permitted under the rules. Therefore, phones were removed from the playing area. If a phone went off – it was an instant loss of the game. Great – no noise distractions.

Why then are some people still allowed to set those ridiculous alarms on their wristwatches? You know, the alarm beep sounds on the hour every hour. Why? What the hell do these people have to do on the hour. Why do they have to be reminded that it is o'clock? Here's my advice to these people. Stop it. Stop it today. It's not the 1980s, and those alarms are stupid.

And now for my top three selected anecdotes…

The mobile phoners

I have already written about mobile phones, but it would be remiss of me not to articulate the following incident. I was playing in an Armed Forces chess tournament once when a mobile phone rang. I think the gentleman was from the navy. Anyway, he had inadvertently left it in his pocket and because it went off he incurred an immediate loss of his game before he had even pushed a pawn.

He was furious. He retrieved his phone and answered it – since he had already lost his game. After a pause he said, 'Thanks for nothing love, you've just cost me the fucking game.' He looked around and apologised to the group saying, 'That was the wife ringing to wish me good luck.' We struggled with all of our collective might to contain our laughter.

The mischievous reverends

Some years ago I played at the Morecambe Congress. In one round I was drawn against a reverend. He was a lovely man with a honey sweet Irish accent. Think Father Ted and you've got it. Before the game began we shook hands, as you do. Then he said:

'What is your name please?'

'Carl Portman'

'Caaaaarl Portman', he said writing it down carefully saying my name aloud. He continued 'And what is your grade?'

'135' (or whatever it was). He wrote it down and then he looked at me and said, 'And now, what opening will you be playing today?'

I laughed my head off.

A couple of rounds later that same rev was sitting on the board next to me playing a lugubrious gawky-looking individual. He asked him the same questions and on the final request to name his opening the man baulked and said, 'I am not telling you that, how rude.' The reverend smiled, looked at me and winked. What a great bloke.

Synchronised (pork) scratching (SPS)

This was something that I shamelessly orchestrated. It was in the Shropshire league and I was playing for my club – the Coddon. There was one member of the opposing team who was infamous for continually shushing people at the slightest noise. Sometimes I found it unnecessary because it used to break my own concentration, so I decided to turn the tables. I sold the idea to my mates without any trouble. At the given moment I would nod, and we would all pull out a bag of pork scratchings from our pockets and take a bite out of a nice big crispy one simultaneously. This we duly did, and we shattered the quiet with a symphony of pork. The chap went mental giving us an almighty shush accompanied by a face like thunder. We suppressed our laughter and even some of the opposition saw the joke. My behaviour was naughty but damn, it was fun.

Another time we all turned up dressed in clown wigs,

funny hats and even dyed hair when I played for Newport in Shropshire – and clinched the league title that night too – it's all in a day's work at the chessboard. Where has all the comedy gone? We are all so damned serious these days. So politically correct, so offended. Not me, I can take a good a joke as well as give it.

In fairness, I might have been annoying to people down the years. I mean, it's bound to have happened. I do like to think I am reasonable and fair but that's just my perception. When I was a kid I used to listen to my Sony Walkman at the board and bang my head to heavy metal so that must have annoyed people, but I was never taken to task as I should have been. Seriously though, it goes without saying that I do not condone bad behaviour at the board and I will call it out if I have to.

This comes with a warning - you have to be careful who you are messing with – there are trained killers out there in the chess world, as we are about to find out.

Armed Forces chess

Always remember to pillage before you burn

Viking proverb

I have been extremely lucky. I thoroughly enjoyed my career working with the Ministry of Defence alongside military and civilian staff across all three services in the Armed Forces.

During that time chess has featured prominently. Some may be surprised to know that there is a thriving chess community in the MoD and as a long-standing member of the United Kingdom Armed Forces Chess Association (UKAFCA) and indeed as editor of their chess magazine OPEN FILE, I am very proud to maintain my links with Service friends, past and present.

The UKAFCA was formerly known as the Combined Services Chess Association (CSCA) which began a long time ago in the 1980s but before that there was a separate RAF Chess Association. Indeed, the RAF had a magazine in the 1970s and probably even in the 1960s The three services united in chess several decades ago. It was not until more recently that the name changed to the UKAFCA to reflect the times and the way the MoD looks at sporting organisations, especially for funding.

I am hugely grateful to retired RAF Officer Paul Watson for providing me with the following information. The post - World

War II stirrings of chess in the Armed Forces seem to have occurred in the early 1960s. In September 1963, the following short notice appeared in 'Chess' magazine:

CHESS IN THE ARMY

Captain HT Walker, RE is busy trying to get in touch with Army chess players of reasonable standard anywhere in the world, with a view to putting Army chess on its feet. Any chess player, services or 'civvy', visiting Berlin, is welcome any Monday evening from 1945 hours at the club founded by Ian H Ross at Wesley House, Klosser Str. Spandau.

This was followed the following month by:

IN THE RAF TOO

'I read with interest your article on chess in the Army. Chess has made great strides in the RAF too this year. A club has been formed which is gaining strength slowly but surely. Postal chess has been used as the best method of getting all our far-flung players into a single club. At the time of writing over forty RAF players are participating in a handicap tournament. Events planned for the immediate future include an all-play-all and a postal match with our Army friends.'

This letter was signed off by Chief Technician Tom Harrison.

Postal chess certainly flourished in those far-off days but there was no substitute for over-the-board combat and on 14 Dec 1963 a match between the RAF and Army was played in London (won 9-3 by those in light blue). Thereafter, matches regularly took place involving players from all three Services.

That's a marvellous snippet of military chess history.

Whilst I have enjoyed a great many chess tournaments throughout my life, nothing really compares to this merry band of chess brothers and sisters. It is true that the military work to a command-and-control structure, and there are very obvious reasons for that, but when it comes to a Services chess, people leave their rank badge at the door. Everybody is in it for the game. This applies to civilian staff in the same way.

Every year there is a national chess competition, usually at a military base, and the members of the UKAFCA come together to try to win places to the annual NATO finals which are hosted each year by a different NATO country. I shall expand upon this scene shortly but first let me just take you to the UKAFCA finals.

It operates like any other tournament with games played over several days having either one or two rounds a day. There is an official arbiter (referee) and it is hugely competitive as there are prizes for being the champion of each of the Services and for the MoD. Imagine how proud one would be to be able to say, 'I was the RAF/NAVY/ARMY/MoD chess champion.' What a delight that would be to add to your CV. It is a significant achievement and something to tell your friends and family about.

As with most tournaments, there are the usual suspects for the prizes, because the strong players tend to stay in the services for a long time. It is true though that the finals cater for people of any strength, from beginner to very strong – we have even had FIDE Master level players participating before.

Whilst the chess is serious, the socializing is serious fun, as you might expect amongst a group of military staff. There is nothing more pleasurable at the designated evening in the middle of the tournament when we have a blitz chess competition (playing at five minutes each player for the game) and the drink flows. The more alcohol that is downed, the greater and more daring are some of the sacrifices at the board.

A few games of chess accompanied by a nice glass of red or a few beers is all that is required to while away a few pleasurable hours. The Gurkha boys play particularly uncompromising chess, and they don't like to take draws. What great lads they are and they absolutely love their chess.

Of course we have a referee (better known as an arbiter) for the proper chess. They know to cut a little slack to the group because the tournament is so unique. For example, in honour of one player, Jerry Hendy who became ill in Texas (read on later in the chapter) we had a round of chess where everyone had to wear an improbable hat. Jerry was a great wearer of strange and frankly ridiculous hats.

Chess has never been as much fun as this. Serious chess with a twist of comedy and strange hats all round in honour of a friend.

I mean, how many of you can say you have ever played an opponent with a penguin on his head? I have; and a Portuguese manowar, and a parrot, and a cardboard box! It wouldn't be allowed in a *normal tournament* under FIDE rules, but this is our tournament, and we do it our way. To be fair the likes of Kevin Thurlow and David Sedgwick possess an excellent sense of humour, in addition to being enviably proficient at the job so we are always in good hands.

In recent times we have been joined by Grandmaster Matthew Turner who kindly gives a simultaneous exhibition against us. He is a wonderful sport, and I can also reveal that when it comes to alcohol the man can hold his own with the military boys. His simuls are fun and engaging and the banter as he goes around is hilarious. He is what is known as a thoroughly good egg.

I have had some great games in the finals but also some scarring defeats. That's chess. My nemesis is one David Tucker. He is a retired civil servant and certainly a stronger player than me. He is a formidably clever man – the kind of chap you want to phone when you need a friend on a quiz show. Whilst it is true that I have beaten him in both blitz and correspondence chess, the real test as any chess player knows is beating him at classical chess where the time to play is several hours in total. We have played three or maybe even four times (he will tell you) and I have only managed one draw.

People always look forward to a Portman-Tucker clash because they know it is personal. I lost a game to Dave in the final game of the final round of one tournament getting checkmated with two bishops. To a degree I helped him by playing some inferior moves, but he finished it off nicely. The winner is the one who makes the next to last mistake as chess legend Savielly Tartakower once said.

That game still haunts me, and it always will. I think it is fair to say that Dave raises his game and makes an extra effort playing against me – after all he has everything to lose. If and when I do actually defeat him, I am going to buy a round of drinks for everyone in the room at the time. Don't worry – Dave wouldn't dare deliberately lose against *me* just to get a beer.

Mr. Tucker has some very amusing character traits. No matter how well I perform in my games, Dave will bring me down to earth. For example, playing in Texas in 2018 in the 29th NATO Chess Championship I played a good game to get a draw in a simul against former US Champion Alexander Onischuk. There were only 11 boards, so I had done extremely well, and several people congratulated me. Not Dave. In true Tucker fashion he strolled up and said, 'Hmmm, yes, okay but you could have played some stronger moves earlier on.' I laughed and told him never to change, except for his underpants.

I could beat Garry Kasparov himself, and Dave would find a fault somewhere. The reader must understand though that he does not mean any of it maliciously – it's just his way. If you receive an admonishing wagging finger you can take it as some sort of compliment.

The NATO chess competitions are splendid. There is a tradition that players of each country should exchange a little gift at the beginning of each game. This could be something as simple as chocolate, a fridge magnet, pen, badge, book, mug, cap or some sort. Some of the gifts are quite nice, such as the medal I received from the Canadians.

Then there are the Haribo sweets. Yes, Dave always seems to play someone who gives him Haribo candy as a gift. He invariably offers very nice gifts himself, but he gets the kiddies sweets or the maple syrup in return. Heaven knows how many bottles of the stuff he must have at his house. He must pray for pancake day.

Like all of us, Dave does not like to lose, and he does not hide it. He is not nasty, nor does he make excuses, but he is just so melancholy, as if he just lost a £50 note. He gets depressed but as soon as he wins again he flashes a cheeky smile that knocks twenty years off his age.

During the covid pandemic we made a point of engaging in a telephone call every week so as to stay in touch. He lives alone and it is no fun being shut away for months. We still make those calls today. I have a lot of time for Dave. Last time he stayed over at my house, Susan washed and ironed his shirt for him – the lucky lad. She likes him too. When the world starts to adjust itself back to some kind of normality I look forward to engaging in battle with him at the board.

There is another Dave who I am privileged to be friends with. Lt Cdr Dave Ross RN is Chairman of the UKAFCA and one hell of a nice bloke to boot. The Royal Navy is lucky to have such a man amongst its ranks. He originates from Newcastle upon Tyne and he married a Scottish girl. Helen and Dave are a force to be reckoned with. They are a perfect match and tremendous fun to be around. Dave loves his chess, and the occasional pint. He is generous, kind and very witty. Helen possesses an irrepressible sense of humour that would be perfect for stand-up comedy. Think female Billy Connolly (without the beard!) and you've got Helen.

Another fine fellow is RAF Officer Stephen O'Neill. He has been a member of the Armed Forces chess scene for more years than most, and he has been there, done it, got the tee shirt. In fact, Steve probably made the tee shirt. He tells us the following true story, which is taken (abridged) from his book *From Kosovo to Kandahar*:

Kolobrezeg, Poland in 2005. All of the NATO chess events are official and a grand opening parade, medal ceremony and closing banquet are always formal affairs. The Polish Chairman had managed to get a very senior Army General to open the tournament and speak at the grand parade. The General's English was not bad, better than my Polish. He did however have one flaw. He was unable to properly pronounce the word 'chess.'

The following is a snapshot of the General's welcome address:

'I warmly welcome you all to this very prestigious event, the annual NATO Cheese Championships. I myself love cheese, my children love cheese, and I hope that you also enjoy your cheese.'

Steve said that this went on for about five minutes and the Brits had tears streaming down their faces but the Germans attempted to rebuke the UK team, because they could not see the funny side of it all.

Who would have thought it? The Germans with no sense of humour? Surely not. I know for a fact they do.

There are too many friends to mention in the UKAFCA, but they all know who they are. I really do consider them to be my extended family. I will say this. Some folks tend to pigeon-hole military personnel as just being 'people who kill for a living.' The very nature of the job of course requires them to bear arms if they have to, and they put their own necks on the line as a result.

We should remember though that they *are* people. They have families, mortgages, and dreams of their own. They are the ones we call upon in this country when the chips are down. They are apolitical and do whatever the Government of the day asks of them. Personally speaking, I wouldn't rather put my life or this great nation in the hands of anyone else. Thank you all ladies and gentlemen.

My first NATO tournament as part of team UK was held in Brest, France in October 2012. Such occasions have a real sense of pomp at the opening and closing ceremonies, with the respective military personnel from each country wearing best dress uniform and the civilians in their best bib and tucker (in our case Dave Tucker) so to speak.

My mate Dave Tucker watches on, sharing the tension
as I wrestle with a losing endgame against Turkey.

Usually at the opening of the tournament a VIP of the rank of General is introduced to the teams. I remember arriving at the opening ceremony to be greeted by a group of bearded bagpipe players – not very French I thought. It was a good tournament and lodgings were very acceptable. I managed a fairly creditable 3/7 in France but the chess was very tough going, playing four opponents comfortably over 2000 FIDE which was stronger than my own rating.

With friends Commodore Laurie Brokenshire CBE (left) and GM Raymond Keene OBE at the NATO Chess Championships at MoD Shrivenham in 2016.

In 2016, it was the turn of the UK to hold the event, and we did so at the Defence Academy of the UK in Shrivenham. I did not play. Rather I was on the organising committee doing official photography, meetings, announcements, inputting games to the computer from scoresheets and generally helping the team to keep our NATO visitors happy.

There were day trips for the wives and girlfriends of the teams – to Windsor Castle and other notable places. Of course, I was but one member of a much wider team, all of whom stood up to the plate and delivered in spades. The lads who ferried people to and from the airports and the day trips deserve a special mention. Fantastic commitment to the cause.

The event was considered to be a raging success. The evening banquet on the final day was the high point and Dave Ross received an ovation the like of which I have never witnessed before at a NATO function. It was like Last Night of the Proms. The man is a rock, and it was very well deserved. Grandmaster Raymond Keene OBE gave a speech in several languages, and Commodore Laurie Brokenshire CBE, RN delivering a magic show to astound and amaze. Laurie was a member of the magic circle, fostered seventy children, and was a world class puzzle expert. He cycled the east coast of Australia and was awarded the CBE in 2003. With his splendid white beard and mastery of magic his grandchildren used to call him Grandalf and he loved that.

Tragically, Laurie passed away in 2017 and Dave Ross and I attended his funeral in Hampshire. A very religious man, I truly hope that Laurie is enjoying the promised land as his unwavering belief persuaded him he would. Maybe there is a God. If anyone would have first-hand knowledge it would be Laurie.

He loved 'How great thou art' by Carl Boberg. Apparently when he was out cycling with his wife Ethel they would sing it aloud. Here's a stanza just for you Laurie...

When through the woods and forest glades I wander
and hear the birds sing gently in the trees
when I look down from lofty mountain grandeur
and hear the brook, and feel the gentle breeze.

My own beliefs are more Pagan or even Humanist than Christian. If you call me a Heathen, I will take it as a compliment. I truly miss our theological discussions. I have kept some of our weighty email exchanges to remind me how incredibly special a man he was.

As for Ray Keene I will say this. It is true to say that he is a controversial figure in the chess world, but I form my own view of people directly through my own dealings with them. Ray has supported Services chess and my own requests for his help unstintingly for many years, giving of his time, money and expertise, asking nothing in return. This is much appreciated. He has given far more than he has ever taken from me. Let he or she who is without sin cast that first stone, I say.

At the end of the banquet, the final ceremony began - our official handover to the Hungarian team for them to host the NATO event in 2017. Finally, I should remark that the Polish team won *our* event and deserved winners they were too. As ever Germany were close. Denmark and Greece are also always strong contenders.

In March 2017 I was elected to be the captain of the UK team for Budapest. What a fantastic honour. I felt tremendous pride in being the captain, whose job it is to attend key meetings, keep the squad happy, and possibly even be part of any dispute's hearings. The way it goes in military barracks is that the rooms are often shared, in the way that footballers used to do in the old days. I twinned with Dave Ross. It's funny what you learn about people when you share a room with them. Dave is to a degree a creature of habit. I do not drink much but he, like most military chaps can certainly down a few and hold it perfectly well. He is younger and very fit so it is no problem at all. I would go out into town early evening with the lads and play chess in a local pub. After a couple of beers I would be ready to go back to my room, after all you never knew when the captain might be called upon to discuss some issue or other. The lads would carry on and enjoy themselves, which is fair enough.

The tournament hall in Budapest. These are the moments I dreamed about when I learned the game as a kid.

At some point in the early hours Dave would come into the room having had a few, do whatever he had to do in the bathroom then go to his bed. He would literally plonk himself face down under the covers and stay like that until morning. Then he would suddenly wake, rise and shine, take a vitamin tablet and be ready for the day. What a marvel! He would go out for a run as well. I felt like I should be in a care home. I was very fit once upon a time, but many harvests have been gathered since those days and poor health has not helped.

In addition to being the team captain, I participated in the tournament which added greatly to the pleasure. At some point, I realised that I had represented my school, my club, my county and my country. Not bad for an amateur after all. Thanks again Caissa for blessing me back in that hot summer of 1976.

My score was 3½ this time, and four of my opponents were rated over 2000 FIDE including a 2228. Going into the last round if I could have won and finished on 4½ it would have been absolutely brilliant for me, but I managed to screw up the final game in terrible time trouble when I should at least have held it. I was gutted. No one ever said that chess was easy.

There was a bit of a scandal here I am afraid, and it involved me, of course. In round two, I was paired to play against one of my own squad members, Andy Foulds. Now it is simply not in the *spirit* of the competition to pair two people from the same squad, even if it is within the rules. Okay. I was playing for NATO and he was UK (It is complicated, I am NATO and UK as Captain) but it was still the same squad.

That early on in the tournament the (rather officious) Hungarian arbiters could easily have paired us against someone else - there were 105 participants after all, but they left it to the computer. Andy and I decided to play *under protest* as this had never occurred before and no-one would listen to us. We would therefore make our statement at the board.

We agreed to a draw after only five moves. After a few minutes we agreed the draw, shook hands and signed our scoresheets 'under protest.' The organiser of the tournament was not amused, but you mess with the Brits at your peril. He said we should still have played the game and fought on. We told him as politely as we could where to get off and not make such a pairing again. We come to NATO to play other countries, not one another. Andy and I went off for a sight-seeing walk around Budapest which was most enjoyable. We did both feel bad about it because we are chess players and we enjoy the fight but I would do the same again and I have no regrets.

Imagine my utter disgust, not to mention incredulity when I was paired against another UK squad member Jake Thomas in the next round. What was I to do? I could be paired against *my boys* for the next three rounds so there was little sense in just agreeing protest draws and losing points, so I had to play. Jake wanted to play against me because I was a stronger player, and he was there for chess. That made my mind up. I would play, for Jake.

I took no pleasure in beating him. None at all. He actually played very well. I should have celebrated a win at a NATO final, but this was quite bitter to me. I wanted to play people from other NATO countries. That's what I was there for. I complained vociferously again and said that if I were paired against another Brit I would refuse to play. No more compromises.

The next draw saw two Germans paired together and they submitted a formal complaint - which was upheld! Funny then how the organisers ignored the UK protest but the Germans effected the change. The next morning at breakfast I just happened to be sitting with Andy Foulds when the organiser came across with a bottle of Palinka (a very strong fruit spirit) and his humble apologies. That was appreciated but it did not change what happened. I think I hold a record now in NATO Chess of playing two players from my own squad in the same tournament. I gave Andy the Palinka incidentally – what a marvellous sacrifice from the captain.

I should remark that a set of specially commissioned stamps was struck for the occasion. That is not something that happens very often (if ever) and it was a very nice touch from the organisers. I like to collect a few chess stamps myself, after all you know what they say – philately will get you everywhere.

Navy Command

NAVY OPERATIONS
NAVY OPS-SM COMMS
Building 86
Northwood Command Centre
JSU Northwood
Sandy Lane
Northwood
Middlesex
HA6 3HP

To Whom It May Concern: 26 February 2018

SELECTION OF MR CARL PORTMAN TO REPRESENT THE UK AT THE 29th NATO CHESS CHAMPIONSHIP: LUBBOCK, TEXAS 3 – 9 JUNE 2018

I am delighted to inform you that due to his outstanding contribution to UK Armed Forces Chess, Mr. Carl Portman has been selected to Captain the UK team at the 29th NATO Chess Championship[1]. Mr. Portman has been a long-term supporter of services chess, dating back to his time working in the Ministry of Defence. His guidance, leadership and experience of this role will be invaluable in steadying the team against some exceptionally talented chess players.

The NATO tournament[2], now in its 29th year, is an extremely prestigious event which attracts approximately 100 competitors from around 18 NATO nations; the standard of chess is extremely high with many international standard competitors. The Team Captain will be required not only to represent the UK at chess but also to attend several formal social events during the week which usually involves engagement with Senior Military Officers and civic dignitaries from the host nation. I have included the invitation from the United States for your information. Mr Portman's experience and diplomatic skills will significantly ease the burden for the remainder of the team.

Yours Aye,

D C Ross
Lieutenant Commander, Royal Navy
NAVY OPS-SM COMMS
Chairman of the Combined Services Chess Association

---

[1] The top 6 players from the Combined Services Championship go forward to represent the UK in the NATO tournament.
[2] The NATO Chess Championships and its history can be found at www.natochess.com

A letter to be proud of – the invitation to be captain of the UK team at the NATO chess championships in Texas, USA in 2018.

The next year the NATO final would be held in Texas, USA. The Americans had never held the championships before, so this was a long time coming. I wanted to be there. I look back with great appreciation and gratitude that the lads selected me again as playing captain for this tournament. Carrying the UK flag into (chess) battle will always be an honour.

Flag bearer for team UK in Texas. A moment to be proud and happy. I only wish my grandparents and Mum could have seen it.

I had organised this trip so that I would stay with a good friend in Arizona for a week, fly to Texas for the tournament for a week, fly back to Arizona for a few days and then fly back home to UK, so it was a tad exhausting. But I relished the opportunity to see more of the United States.

Arizona in June was of course scorching. At one point it hit 115°F or if you prefer 46°C. I love the warmth so it did not bother me too much. My good friend is Veronica Freeman who happens to front the rock band Benedictum. I was thrilled to be a guest at one of their rehearsals and to meet their phenomenal guitarist Pete Wells. Veronica and I had loads of fun, enjoying meals out (tasting Elk for the first time) and visiting local towns such as Sedona with its red rock mountains. It was gorgeous. As someone who has always loved reptiles and arachnids I greatly enjoyed inspecting the collections at the Phoenix Zoo.

Veronica is a free and lively spirit and one hell of a singer. She reminds me of a Navajo Indian. Her German husband, Irfan had died suddenly some months before, so she was glad of the company. She had previously stayed at my house with me and Sue back in the UK, so we all knew one another very well.

The chess tournament was held at the Texas Tech University in Lubbock. Whilst there, one of the organisers, Danielle Singleton looked after the UK team – as well as everyone else. It was a huge complex and she would turn up every day to give me and a fellow player Danny O'Byrne a lift to the venue to save walking in the scorching heat. She looked after our every detail and I promised that if she were to come to the UK I would reciprocate and look after her. Incidentally, Danny and I have a very curious habit. We will meet up at a tournament at random to find that we are wearing identical footwear. We have no idea why this happens but there you go. He is another first-class individual with a deep love of the game, and incidentally an elite wildlife photographer.

In 2019 Danielle left the USA for the first time in her life and stayed with me and Sue in Oxfordshire. I took her to London, where she wanted to visit Abbey Road – and that famous Beatles crossing. We also visited St Paul's Cathedral. I had visited neither attraction in my life, so it was a pleasure to share time with Danielle doing that. Once again, this was an example of chess bringing people together and creating new friendships. We call her our Texan gal, and she is a really bright spirit.

The tournament was uncompromising. I played four opponents graded over 2000 FIDE including FIDE Master Finn Pedersen from Denmark, and I had a great game playing an obscure line as White in the Caro Kann which went 1.e4 c6 2.Nc3 d5 3.Qf3. He congratulated me on playing well afterwards which was really sporting of him. I finished on 3/7 which was not too bad. That and my draw with Alexander Onischuk in the simultaneous exhibition made it a pleasurable trip.

I pride myself on being organised, able to mix with military and local dignitaries of all ranks and I perform my duties as best I can. Yet as with all of us, some things occur that are out of our control, that we cannot plan for. Sadly, and on my watch, a dreadful situation developed relating to one of our team.

Jerry Hendy – he who wears improbable hats - became ill. Very ill. He had done way too much in the Texan heat, visiting a lady friend the week preceding the tournament and generally letting his hair down. He was already in need of rest, but that's just not Jerry. One night, back with us in Lubbock he went out with the lads (I was back at the ranch) and was performing karaoke at some club. Ever the clown, and relishing the limelight, he went wild and the locals were loving him. Word has it that at some point he banged his head whilst headbanging or doing some kind of air guitar. Jerry became sick and unwell the next day with a pain in his head, neck and shoulders.

We told him to rest but he played his game with a wet towel around his neck. He became bed bound very quickly but still somehow managed to play again the next day and indeed he had a super result. Despite me getting one of the American military folks (thanks Chip!) who had some nursing skills to look at Jerry, nothing could be done. Jerry apparently had no travel insurance and it proved ridiculously difficult to get him any kind of medical assistance in the US. I have had more success in third world countries! Lord knows how Americans without much money are able to get treatment, but there we are. Jerry did somehow get home a few days later, but still experienced raging headaches and pains all over.

He saw his doctor and was told that he had done too much and to relax for a couple of weeks. It was not long before it was confirmed that he had an aneurysm. I was unable to confirm whether this was in the US or back home but in any event he was in an induced coma in Bristol. Dave Ross and I went to see him. He could not talk and was not responsive, so the road to recovery was and is long. It was heart-rending to see a man so full of life, laughter and mischief prostrate and paralysed. We can only hope that he recovers to some kind of normality. Time will tell. At the very least he might hopefully play some chess again, it is after all a game that he loves. As for Jerry and normality, that is an exquisite oxymoron.

At the next UKAFCA tournament at Kineton Station in Warwickshire we all wore fancy hats for one round in his honour. If Jerry applies his fighting spirit in chess to life he will make significant progress. The man is down, but he is far from out. I am still amazed that he got the results he did in Texas despite feeling like shit. It is testimony to a good and resilient man.

I should explain a little of the UK chess team psychology. First off, several teams prepare very seriously for the finals. They might organise official training sessions in the weeks and months leading up to it, and even have some kind of physical fitness regime. The UK team prepares by downing a few pints in a suitable ale house the night before the event. No team in NATO can compete with our lads when it comes to drinking. The Belgians have a good go, and the Germans are predictably adept, but we win this one hands down or should I say bottoms up.

The other thing we do in the UK team is have a system of fines over the week. All of the money goes into the pot for the final banquet when traditionally we spend the fines money on a bottle or two of decent red wine to complement our table. One example of the fines system is as follows: Today we might say that the rule is, 'If you say the word 'chess' you will be fined a dollar' or something like this. It can add up to a lot. Usually, the puppet master of this scheme is one Warrant Officer Dave Onley who is very proficient at tripping people up, thus securing funds for the final evening. You have to pay up without arguing – I wouldn't fight Dave Onley in a phone box. He is one of those quiet people that you desperately want on your side, because when it kicks off he is just not going to be found wanting!

The best is yet to come. Whoever has incurred the most in fines over the week must also pay a *forfeit*. Dave Ross was the recipient of this dubious award in Brest. We told him that his forfeit was to go over to the German table and tell them a joke to make them laugh. It doesn't get tougher than that. Dave, being the gentleman that he is duly accepted his punishment and began ruminating as to what joke he would tell them.

Meanwhile naughty Carl (that's me) had gone over to the German lads and told them the plan and they were *verboten* to laugh on any occasion. After another glass of red, Dave mustered the courage and sauntered over to the Germans.

'Hello lads, I have a joke for you.'

No response – the German lads just look at him.

'So, a man goes to the doctors and says doctor, doctor I've got a strawberry stuck up my bottom. The doctor says, 'Oh don't worry, I'll give you some cream for it.'

Silence.

Tumbleweed.

Dave returns. Cue fits of laughter on the UK and German tables. These are the golden days that we will all look back on.

Switch now to our stay in Budapest. It was the final banquet and once again an incident occurred which involved the Germans and the Brits. Picture the scene. Our tables were close. Wives and girlfriends had flown in and joined us for the final soirée. Sue was there, thus she can testify that this happened. The Hungarian organisers had done a splendid job (despite the balls up with my chess pairings) and I could have no complaints. They hired a pianist who played some mellifluous tunes in the background as we dined. After the speeches and awards it was time for a game.

The pianist would play some war songs and we all had to guess what they were. At one point the pianist played the British WW II wartime song originally written as 'Colonel Bogey' which became part of the British way of life when it was set to the tune: 'Hitler Has Only Got One Ball' (it was originally 'Göring Has Only Got One Ball' after the Luftwaffe leader suffered a grievous groin injury, but later reworded to suit the popular taste.

Oh dear, this could be embarrassing.

We all looked across at the German table. Suddenly their captain, the incomparable Karl Koopmeiners began to conduct his team, and the Germans sang it with us. What a relief! Nobody was offended. There were no lawsuits, no help-lines, and no bad feelings at all. It is called humour and the Germans, contrary to popular opinion have plenty of it. This was good-natured and very typical of the sort of camaraderie on display at a NATO event. We should really invite politicians to come along and take note.

Karl (him) and Carl (me) always have a photo taken together when we meet – it is sort of tradition. He and Susan get along famously, and she thinks he is a fine man. By the way, he can be a very dangerous chess player if he is in the right frame of mind. I look forward to more chess in the future and hopefully another NATO final or two. I would love to be captain for a third time, but we shall have to see. The finals in Belgium 2020 had to be cancelled because of the pandemic. I think that is the first time it has ever been cancelled.

Never mind Brexit and Europe, this NATO family sticks together. You pick on one, you pick on us all. The shared love of chess unites all NATO countries and has done so for decades. I should not declare favourites, but I have a particularly close relationship with members of the Polish and German teams. Possibly because I speak German for one, and also that I engage in the Polish tradition of Wigilia on Christmas eve occasionally. My friend Lt Col Sławomir Kędzierski always gives me a little gift on behalf of the Polish Land Army when I see him, as does Col Tomasz Malinowski, who is the Chairman of the International Military Chess Committee,

In March 2021, I was contacted by Slawomir and told that

I am going to be presented with an award by the Polish MoD Committee rewarding me with the medallion as a friend of NATO Chess. That is a huge honour, and I shall cherish it. Both Germany and Poland teams are super strong chess teams and they take their preparation seriously. This is a trait that I admire. NATO chess lives on and when the pandemic is over it will get back to normal, although what any new normal will be is anyone's guess.

But enough about the big soldiers. What about the little ones? I decided to enter the noisy and energetic world of junior chess coaching. Kids couldn't be more difficult to deal with than Belligerent Brigadiers or Garrulous Generals could they?

Well, could they?

Coaching

Work hard in silence. Let success be your noise

Frank Ocean

Let me get one thing straight. You do not have to be a grand-master to be a good chess coach in the same way that you don't have to be Pele to be a good football coach. Coaching has many facets, not just a knowledge of the subject matter but an ability to plan, deliver and connect with your students.

I have witnessed very strong chess players displaying lamen-table coaching technique, simply because they were unable to convey their thoughts into words and action plans. This is not a crime and the work is not for everyone. It is a distinct discipline in my view.

I am fortunate to possess good inter-personal skills. I can mix easily with people from all walks of life. My intellectual limitations aside, communicating and motivating is something I have done in the workplace for decades, and those same skills have enabled me to share the game I love with thousands of people over the years.

I left the MoD in December 2011 on a voluntary early release scheme and I was able to focus more on chess. Sometime in 2014 I decided to coach beginners and intermediate players, as well as taking on the voluntary work with chess in prisons. I began by advertising my chess CV and soon secured some work on a one-to-one basis, but later I struck lucky when upon a recommendation, I became the official chess coach for the Dragon School in Oxford.

The school was founded by a committee of Oxford dons, and teaching began in September 1877 at rooms in Balliol Hall, located in St Giles', central Oxford. The Dragon School is a highly renowned boarding and day school for boys and girls from four to thirteen years. It is a prestigious school, and the likes of poet Sir John Betjeman and actors Hugh Laurie and Tom Hiddleston attended, as did Tim Henman, the tennis player. There have been many more notable pupils.

The motto of the school is *Arduus ad solem* or '*reach for the sun*' which I brought into my chess sessions in class. I wanted the kids to aspire as high as they could at the chess board.

Stepping back into class, coaching juniors at the Gosford school in Oxfordshire. Passing the chess baton on is always a privilege.

In my humble opinion, one requires a certain mentality for coaching juniors at chess. You need patience, excellent preparation and delivery skills, an ability to deal with quickly changing scenarios and a clear appreciation of how children *tick*. Of course, a certain level of knowledge of your subject matter helps.

My age group were essentially eight to thirteen years of age and I had three separate groups over the course of a Monday afternoon and early evening to include beginner, intermediate and advanced classes. I am not a qualified schoolteacher and I must say that I developed a real appreciation for anyone who teaches full-time. I used to be one of the 'teachers have too many holidays' brigade but I tell you, they are welcome to them. I have no complaints. You have to recharge, re-energise and be continuously thinking about next steps. You need to be clear about what you want the children to have learned in the next term and how that will be delivered.

It is incredibly rewarding, but it takes a lot of energy and if you are not on top of your game right from the off – every week – the kids will quickly find you out. One-to-one chess coaching is fine, but when you have anything up to twenty-eight kids in your class at various playing proficiencies it is a different ball game.

You have to connect from the moment they step into your class. I remember when I was a kid that I learned the most when something was fun or quirky. Therefore, I introduced a big demonstration board which I hung up before the kids came into class. It would have a chess problem on it and I would write something on the blackboard (it is all electronic now, and the board isn't black, but it will always be a blackboard to me) to give them a clue about the position and they would all come in and gather round trying to be the first to solve it.

That kept them busy. They only got one try, so they could not blurt out the first thing that came into their head. If they shouted and got it wrong, they had to take their seat, leaving the others to have a go. It taught them to think before they spoke which is something I could take note of myself occasionally.

I would write something on the board like, 'Find the checkmate, it's very strange, finish the game from very long range' so it might be a distant checkmate with a queen or bishop or rook. That sort of thing. I also introduced Syd Bricknell's silly made up words from my own youth. I would say, 'who knows how to make an ostrobogulous move?'

They were smart kids and argued that there was no such word but before long they were all putting hands up saying, 'Sir, I just made an ostrobogulous move.' It was charming. After working in an adult environment it was a refreshing change working with kids. That said, they are just as direct as any army officer, I can tell you.

I maintain that chess does not develop character; it reveals it. Children are a young example of that.

The most difficult issue for me was that the pupils did not all arrive to class at the same time. Oh, what a dream that would have been. The school had a combination of day and boarding pupils, so some would have to eat, others would have to see the nurse etc. etc. Thus, they would arrive in dribs and drabs. Should I repeat the same thing from the beginning every time someone arrived? No, that was just not practical.

I therefore had to think of something that would encourage

them to be there as near to time as possible. But what? I could easily have brought a tub of sweets in to entice them but that meant a sugar rush and a more boisterous class when I needed them to sit and concentrate! It was also a kind of bribe and the children would probably only attend to get a sweet, rather than enjoy the chess. No, that was just no good. The only way was to make them *want* to come and play chess above all else.

I called our classroom 'the room of concentration' (a technique I picked up from the European Chess Union training course) and I made it clear that chess players were an elite unit. They would all be part of something if they worked together. If everyone had a good term then I would bring in a big tub of sweets on the final term day and I was always good to my word.

I guess that's the bribe right there but actually the kids never really mentioned it, they did come for the chess. I used to wear bits of battledress to reflect chess being a fight, which included a nice Viking helmet. The kids could wear it if they played a good move. I would do crazy things to get them to remember themes. Set yourself on fire with enthusiasm, and people will come from miles around to watch you burn, that's my view.

I would tell the kids that the chess pieces could talk, and that if the children listened very carefully they might hear what they were saying. I got them to imagine that every time they moved something that piece or pawn would ask them, 'why did you move me here?' and that the kids better have an answer otherwise they shouldn't be making the move. It was very funny to see some of the pupils occasionally leaning into the board – listening to the rook or the queen or the tiny pawn.

One might laugh but there is a serious point to this. We should not make a move without justifying it. 'Why did you do that?' is a question asked of all of us from time to time in our lives. Do we always have an answer other than, 'I dunno, I just did?' I use this technique in my own games, for sure. Listen to your pieces dear chess player – you might be surprised what they have to say.

There is a school of thought that asserts that we play chess according to our character. For example, a quiet, reflective person will play quiet positional chess, and an aggressive person will play gambits and swashbuckling chess. That is not my experience, or my view and we should be wary again of stereotyping. I have known quiet people play very aggressive chess (I am thinking of Glyn Pugh in Shropshire) and yet other aggressive people play very reserved chess. Kids have their own personalities, and their chess can be equally unpredictable but as long as they have fun and love to play, I am happy.

I can share a rib-tickling moment and a more serious one. In one lesson I had to show the kids what *en-passant* meant. It is a curious move allowable at certain points in a chess game and it is French for *in-passing*. I stood out front and said, 'Who knows what '*en-passant* means?' One hand shot up like a lightning rod.

'Yes?' I asked.

'It's a goldfish sir' the young lad exclaimed.

'A goldfish? How do you work that out?' I was confused.

'Well it's French sir.'

In a flash I got it. 'No, not Poisson – I said *en-passant*.'

I would not let the children call the pawns, *prawns* or the knights, *horses*. I would slip into this silly Russian accent (which they loved) and say, 'prawns are zee leetle creatures that walk on zee bottom of zee sea. We do not have sea creatures walking along zee board, we have zee pawns, not zee prawns.'

There were always arguments about someone allegedly cheating by touching a piece and not moving it etc. How to solve such arguments if you were not at the board and did not see anything? Taking sides would be unfair to one of the youngsters, even if deep down you knew who was fibbing. That was when I introduced my own method, which came to me whilst half asleep one night. The coin of truth.

I would tell them that I never saw the alleged incident but that *they* both did. They had sixty seconds to sort it out between themselves otherwise I would be back and flip the coin of truth, which would be the deciding factor. It would tell me who was fibbing and who was telling the truth. Honestly, I only ever had to flip it a couple of times. The kids would rather sort it out themselves than be *found out* by the magic coin, which never lied. I am not saying that it is in the coaching manuals but it worked for me, and I know that others have taken this idea into their own chess classes with success!

I always presented a *star of the week* certificate and often the winner would be the one who owned up to telling porkies. They learned that being honest was the best way. Once again, this is where chess helps to test and identify character and values, even at so young an age.

I move to a more serious state of affairs. One day the school asked me, 'would I have a child who suffers from RA in my beginner's chess class?' I had no idea at all what RA even was. They emailed me a risk assessment for the boy and I learned that his condition was rising anger. Apparently he would fly off the handle and either attack another pupil or try to break something in class. He did not like to be touched at all, especially by other children but if I accepted him into my class and there were any problems, I was given a number to call so that a teacher would come to the rescue.

Would I have him? To my knowledge I have never refused any child the opportunity to play chess. Of course I would accept him. I used to brief ministers so I was damned certain I could deal with an angry young whippersnapper.

The little fellow was duly brought to my class the following week, and he was left with me. I was given a card with three emoticon faces on it. One was happy, one was sad, and one was in between. He had to point to one to let me know how he felt at the beginning of the lesson. He stabbed a finger at the middle one, shrugged his shoulders and soon found another youngster to play chess with.

Now in my chess class, whilst I am of course cognisant of any medical or other conditions I just let the kids play chess. It is first and foremost a chess class, not a therapy group or counselling session. Chess does the talking. I do not have a child with dyslexia who plays chess. I have a child who plays chess who happens to have dyslexia.

Not long into the lesson he started to get agitated (he was losing his game) then he walked towards my desk and tried to pick up the computer keyboard to throw it. No way – not on my watch. I grabbed the keyboard off him, which really surprised him. I told him that I would not accept that behaviour in my class, that he was there for chess or he would not be welcome at all. If he wanted to play chess I would help him. I told him to decide – he could walk back to a chessboard or out of the door. In fairness I would of course never have let the boy just wander off but a bit of psychology is fair game in my book.

He never said a word – he just walked straight back to the

chessboard and the rest of the lesson was trouble-free. I did not think he would come back the next week, but he did. He walked in and produced the coloured card with the faces. Before he pointed to one I looked him in the eye and enquired, 'Do you like using this card?'

He replied instantly. 'No I don't.'

I said, 'Why don't we just rip it up and throw it in the bin and not bother again; you can just come in and play chess like everyone else?'

His eyes lit up like Christmas trees. 'Can I really rip it up?'

'Go for it,' I said.

He summarily ripped it and threw the pieces into the bin. We laughed. Honestly, I never had another issue with him. In fact about four weeks in he finally checkmated someone. He shouted, 'Sir – sir I just gave checkmate' and he came bounding over to me and gave me a high five! Considering he supposedly never actually liked physical contact with anyone, this was a colossal moment. I drove home that night with a broad smile, and I couldn't wait to tell Sue. Chess does remarkable things. It builds bridges. All that lad focused on was his chess and his sense of achievement, not any medical condition.

The thing is, children will test you. They are not so stupid as some people think. They will throw a hook into the water and see if you take the bait. Depending upon how you respond they will behave accordingly and trust will be built or not built after that initial test. It is classic child psychology and I am well aware of it – after all just like every reader, I was a kid myself once.

I have always loved chess because of its accessibility. The motto for the Federation of Chess is *gens una sumus* – we are one family. I would not argue with that. For me, coaching is about giving something back, planting that tree under which I am never going to enjoy the shade. I have coached children who had little confidence at all until chess brought them out of their shell. Planting that little seed of chess into the minds of the young, then watching it grow and blossom as part of their lives is a very special and rewarding thing. There are many far better chess tutors than me out there and they will be able to relate to what I am saying.

I cannot conclude this without putting *The Sniffer* into the spotlight. He was one very special student. Again, we are not supposed to have favourites, but it is surely inevitable that some people (children and adults) will shine a little bit brighter than others. Teaching at beginner and intermediate level did not improve my own chess strength, so it was an obvious delight when a student tested my own chess capabilities.

The student in question is Ben Aubury. He attended the beginner's class at the Dragon School and although I obviously knew every pupil individually, it can still be easy for a student to fade into a sea of faces – as my classes were more than double the size that a recommended chess class should be. Ben was tiny in frame and only nine years of age. I would give each child as much of my time on a one-to-one basis as I possibly could. One day I arrived at Ben's board. He started moving the chess pieces around and talking about Mikhail Botvinnik!

He showed me several moves from one of his games and asked some very pertinent chess questions like, 'why do think white made this move?' The penny dropped instantly. Here was a lad who wanted to play chess. No, this was a lad who loved chess. Whereas under normal circumstances, students would *graduate* as they progressed one class at a time, I hooked him straight out of beginners, bypassed intermediate and hurled him into advanced. I still remember driving home that day thinking, 'how on earth did I miss that?'

Unsurprisingly he improved rapidly with the combined efforts of myself, his brilliantly supportive parents and the school. Most of all it was his own voracious appetite for self-improvement, working autodidactically. Chess quickly became his all-consuming passion. He was soon too strong even for advanced class, often playing three or four of the group at once.

I had the classic dilemma here. Do I hold him back and wait for class to catch up or let him advance further and faster and ask everyone else to keep up. If this had been the USSR I would have recommended placing him in a young Pioneer's chess palace. His parents may or may not have liked that, but Ben would have loved it. His mum and I agreed for him to have some one-to-one coaching with me, and I would go to the school an hour early, before classes began and work with Ben on chess.

We quickly established a routine. Before he came into class, I would hide a packet of his favourite crisps (Quavers) somewhere in the school room. His job was to sniff it out. I cannot remember how that game ever started but *Sniffer* would soon find the food, and we would settle down to study with him munching away quite happily. He would eagerly show me what he had learned the previous week, moving the chess pieces around with a flurry at the board. He didn't like losing, and that is what spurred him on. Even at a young age he understood the meaning of the phrase 'get bitter or get better' and he continued to work at his game and improve. He had an insatiable thirst for new information, new ideas and more games. I had to work very hard in the week to prepare the right level material for him.

I made Ben a promise. When the day came that he exceeded my own chess grade (it was inevitable) I would purchase a very large cake. His grade eclipsed mine in 2020 on the English Chess Federation grading list, as he pipped me by three points. I am sure that he actually sent me a cake – but I owe him one, along with several packets of Quavers! The Covid-19 pandemic has prevented me from delivering on my promise, but I look forward to the day when we can meet up again.

He has since represented England at junior level, and I am extremely proud and privileged to have given him a foot up onto the chess ladder. He can go as far as he wants to – but schoolwork does and should occupy much of his time in these younger years.

I have my own personal views on what made Ben stand out from the other pupils. There are several attributes that led him from beginner class at the Dragon School to the ECF Junior England Squad.

A passion for the game of chess. (Not just moves but the history too)

A dedication to hard work (He always wanted more and more homework)

Always being curious (He never just accepted what I said)

A good spoonful of natural talent (a genuine feel for the game)

A desire to win and be the best (Success brought smiles)

A supportive environment. (School, coach, parents).

I could have included an inherent love of crisps, but that would be churlish. I am going to include a photograph of Ben in this memoir, which to me encapsulates everything about him. One Christmas at the school I was struck by a scene that reminded me of Charles Dickens's *A Christmas Carol* where Ebenezer Scrooge was the only little boy sitting in school in the holidays, reading *Robinson Crusoe*. Everyone else had gone home.

Ben Aubury studying in his favourite Christmas hat at the Dragon School in Oxford.

Ben was studying a position that was difficult to solve. He had his bright red Christmas hat on as he always did at Yule time. I turned around at one moment and saw this little figure, hunched all alone over the chessboard. He was truly quite lost in a world of rooks and pawns. Nothing else mattered. Not the other boys, not me, not food – not even Christmas. He just had to solve that problem, which of course he did. At the moment I saw him, I just knew I had to try to get a photo for posterity – he would look back on this moment one day. I retrieved my phone from my briefcase and quickly took the shot without him even knowing. I am so glad that I did. It freezes in time one defining moment in a young man's life. Incidentally, his mum loved it, as did Ben.

Chess is a seriously addictive game and it reveals how people behave at a basic level both in victory and defeat. I saw little difference between the eight-year-old girl in my class, jabbing her finger aggressively into the face of her stunned opponent and an adult inmate doing exactly the same thing in prison. It stirs emotion. It matters!

After several years working at the school, I did not renew the contract, purely for logistical reasons. The nightmare journey from Banbury to Oxford on the M40 and A34 used to take forever on a bad day, and the traffic was becoming too congested. I am forever grateful to The Dragon School for giving me the opportunity to work with such talented and enthusiastic children. It is my deeply held wish that they might transfer some of the skills they learned playing chess to whatever they choose to do in life. I reckon I will look at the TV one day and see a famous person and say 'I used to coach him/her at chess.'

I continue to visit schools and give lectures and simultaneous exhibitions to raise the profile of chess, (and rainforests, and arachnology) but it is mostly one to one now. It is easier on Skype although much less desirable than face-to-face.

I have worked with a few memorable students who were not juniors. I coached a then ninety-year-old Church of England Priest. The man in question is Father Michael Campling, and he is a member of Banbury Chess Club. He is the living embodiment of an extraordinary man. He arrived on this earth in 1927, the year that José Raúl Capablanca played Alexander

Alekhine for the World Chess Crown in Buenos Aires. Alekhine was the victor. Michael was ordained in 1953, the week before Her Majesty Queen Elizabeth II was crowned.

Even at ninety-two, he was playing tennis every week, chess matches at the club, practicing the viola and carrying out his religious duties. He is the only Priest I know who wears a motorcycle jacket at the chessboard! He retains possession of all his faculties and enjoys his chess, so it was a pleasure to try to help him with some studies.

I was delighted to have helped give him a special gift on his ninetieth birthday. He mentioned that he always wanted to meet Grandmaster Raymond Keene, as he had read his chess column in the Times since it began. As I mentioned earlier, I knew Ray reasonably well through the military chess association and I asked if he could help, and perhaps meet with Michael. He agreed immediately, not only sending Michael a couple of signed chess books, but he bought him (and me) lunch at Simpsons in the Strand in London. Now that is what I call going the extra mile.

I shall never forget observing Michael engaged in theological discussion with Ray, whilst playing chess against him at the table and eating the most delicious beef that he or I had ever had. The roast potatoes were super crisp, cooked as they had been in goose fat. It really made Michael's birthday, and it also demonstrated that it is never too late in life for surprises and new experiences. I am indebted to Ray for his time and generosity.

If there really is a god, I thank him for keeping Michael down here. He is an inspiration to so many and a real superhero, although even he does not go as far as to wear his underpants outside of his trousers, but with Michael nothing would surprise me.

On a different occasion one of my *students* was a genial retired gentleman who I shall call Artur (not his real name) and his son had paid for a few chess lessons with me. I shall never forget our first session. I asked Artur what he wanted to get out of our time together and he said he just wanted to win a game at his chess club. His grade was very low, but he was desperate just to experience the thrill of winning one game. Chess coaching means adapting to a student's needs, and it is not all about what the coach wants, so I thought about what I could do.

He wanted an opening as White, something solid so I thought I would show him the Colle opening. We played some moves on the board. 1.d4 d5 2.Nf3 e6 3.e3 Nf6 then I played 4.Bd3.

'I don't want to play that,' said Artur.

'What do you want to play?'

'I want to play 4.Bb5 check.'

'Well you can do that Artur, absolutely. However, I don't think it is a good move. Black has many ways to reply and in any case if he puts a pawn on c6 you have to move your bishop twice, which is not a good idea in the opening phase.'

'Oh, okay then,' he said.

We agreed that it should go on d3 if we are looking to play the Colle. There the bishop has one eye on the Black king side and the h7 square if and when Black castles. 'Aah righto, I've got it,' he murmured. I said that we would set the board up again and just go through those first four moves – because to be fair his game was very rudimentary. We set the pieces up again and Artur played white. 1.d4 d5 2.Nf3 e6 3.e3 Nf6 and 4.Bb5 check!

'Artur, what are you doing? Remember that we said the bishop was going on to d3 here?'

'Did we?' said Artur. 'Oh, I cannot remember that, I have dementia you know.'

At that moment I thought, how the hell am I going to get this man to remember an opening if he could not remember what happened a few minutes earlier? To cut a long story short, I found a way for him to at least try to recall what went where. I told him a little story as the pieces moved which helped him recall where they went.

It was tough going for those sessions, but one of the happiest days of my life arrived a few weeks later when the telephone rang. I answered it. 'Carl, it's Artur. I just wanted to tell you that I won a game at the club last night, and I used the Colle opening, I am so pleased. Thank you for everything.' He sounded like a little kid; he really did. Mission accomplished.

And finally for some long distance fun, I even got my great mate Ray Hale to play chess. He had a chess board set up in his office in Eastbourne and every couple of days he would make a move and relay it to me. It was a great way to stay in touch. He gave me some top tips himself, the best of which was (and has always been), 'get those horses out early.' Thanks Ray! He is an expert in arachnology, and an authority on the explorer Alfred Russel Wallace, so he will have to leave the chess to me. His wife Angela is also a spider expert and she is the driving force behind the man in her life.

I loved this period of my chess activity, but I had plenty of energy left for more. Most communities (schools, clubs and societies) can easily access chess but there was one community that could not, and it would benefit greatly from engaging with the royal game in my view. This community could not come to me, so I had to take the chess out on the road go to it.

My chess crusade had a new mission.

What I needed was some prison time.

Chess in prisons

People will forget what you said, people will forget what you did, but people will never forget how you made them feel

Maya Angelou

I once read a book entitled *The Grass Arena* written by former inmate John Healy. It is now a Penguin Classic, and for very good reason. It is the true story of a man who lived rough in London for many years surrounded by vagrants, prostitutes and winos. He was getting into trouble and drifting in and out of prison. It was whilst incarcerated that he was introduced to chess, and that changed his life for the better, forever.

Once released he never returned to prison, instead he spent his time playing and studying chess, even giving simultaneous exhibitions. His view was – and is – that chess is the opium of the mind and is liberating for prisoners. The book was made into a film – where John was brilliantly portrayed by actor Mark Rylance – and this story truly had a profound effect on me. I am proud to call John my friend nowadays. He is a complex and intelligent individual. I owe him a great debt of gratitude for sharing his views and insights on chess, and the relationship that it has with prisoners.

How did my chess in prisons journey begin? In March 2014 I applied for a position with the English Chess Federation (ECF). It was a voluntary post called *Manager of chess in prisons*. The role had appealed to me long before that time, but the post was already filled. For whatever reason the incumbent soon departed, and I took the opportunity to step in. The remit was very simple, yet far-reaching; to foster interest in chess in prisons.

There are a good many challenges in this area. First of all, I had to actually gain access to prisons. Unless you are a *guest* that is not so easy. One requires the blessing of the governor, but first off, I wrote to the Secretary of State for Justice. I wanted to garner support at the most senior levels which I hoped would make it easier for me to work around the prison estate. I also visited some key personnel in the Ministry of Justice to get them onside.

To some degree I was successful. Everyone was behind the initiative, but the one thing I sought from the government was hard cash to purchase equipment and books. Unsurprisingly, they all declared that there was no money in the pot. Strange really how in 2021 they found billions for the Covid pandemic. Were they just sitting on the cash back then? I am left wondering how badly did they really want to turn recidivism around?

I argued that the government was already spending millions of pounds of taxpayer's money on managing re-offenders, and that surely if chess could help reduce this they could make a saving. They agreed, yet they still could not – or would not – commit to releasing any funds. The most positive response I had was from MP Michael Gove who was then the Secretary of State for Justice. He wrote to me as follows:

Your analysis of the need for us to make prisons places of educa-
tion and constructive activity is entirely consistent with our future

policy direction for prisons in England and Wales. We are deter-
mined to make sure offenders are given the support they need to
redeem themselves and turn away from crime. I wish you well with
your continued work to help offenders and spread the benefits of
chess. The work of organisations like the English Chess Federation
is vitally important in helping turn around the lives of those who
need it most in our society.

I was particularly interested in one word in that letter. *Future.*
I wanted to know why education and constructive activity
was *future* policy and not already in place. I have since learned
through my own prison visits that whilst educational support
may be in place, access to it can be quite another matter. In
the years between 2014 and 2021 at the time of writing there
has been great turmoil in the prison system.

The turnover of Secretaries of State has not helped. There
have been six in total and I am not afraid to declare that when
I began, MP Chris Grayling was in charge (for almost three
years) and at that time had effectively banned books in prisons.
Grayling was in my view harming the prison system with his
atrocious policies. He is my nomination for the most ineffec-
tive politician of all time. As one prisoner said to me, Grayling
claimed expenses for his Pimlico flat close to the Houses of
Parliament despite having his constituency home less than
twenty miles away. How were prisoners supposed to have any
faith or trust in such a man or take any lectures from him
about playing fair?

I used to rage when I saw him on *Question Time*. He was
as slippery as an eel in a bucket of jelly. He never answered a
question directly, and he was about as popular as a dose of the

clap. I am sure his mother loved him though. I bet he would ban this book if he had the chance.

Since then, we have been blessed with Michael Gove (one year two months and five days) Liz Truss (ten months and twenty-eight days) David Lidington (six months and twenty-eight days) David Gauke (one year six months and sixteen days) and Robert Buckland who at the time of writing holds the post. If there is no stability at the top, or those at the top don't have a proper appreciation of the department they are running, it is no wonder that positive change occurs very slowly if at all.

Undeterred, I set about using various channels through the ECF and social media platforms to spread the word. The ECF kindly donated some chess sets and boards and before long people in their private capacity were offering to donate books and equipment. My faith in humanity was restored as I began to receive books from individual collections. Word gets around quickly in the modern age and I soon had enough kit to spread around several prisons. Each time I visited a prison, I donated several chess sets and boards, along with books and the occasional chess clock. I also put together a useful little guide for developing chess on the inside. As always, the London Chess Centre have been incredibly generous over the years, always giving me free chess magazines to take with me.

I can vividly recall my first prison visit. The foreboding tall fences, keys jangling and noisy inmates were an assault on the senses. There was lots of shouting on the wings but there were also quiet moments. I never cease to be amazed at how talented some prisoners are. Walls are often adorned with their art – some of it as good as anything I have ever seen. There are poets, writers, musicians and all sorts of creative people on the inside. Believe it or not at any one time there are hundreds if not thousands of people inside who have not yet had a trial – some of whom will undoubtedly be declared innocent. Think on.

I learned very quickly that people do not go to prison *for* punishment. They go *as* punishment. This is a fundamental point. The role of any prison is to rehabilitate. I mean, from the very moment an inmate walks through the prison door. My own view on this is that the purpose of prison is to have a prison of purpose. Some governors totally get this and they embrace chess as a positive and beneficial pursuit. Others either don't understand or simply aren't interested. Turning ignorance into enlightenment is a never-ending journey.

The costs of keeping people locked up, and subsequent reoffending rates runs into billions of pounds. It costs around £42,000 per year per prisoner, some £116 per day, as declared by the Ministry of Justice. We, the taxpayer, are footing the bill. Surely then, anything that can be done to reduce costs and help people turn their lives around is a force for good?

You would think so, but I was surprised at how many people were incredulous at the notion of me taking chess into prisons. 'You are just helping the scumbags to think more strategically so that they can commit more crime,' was one view. Another popular one is, 'They deserve to be locked up and the key thrown away.' So much then for trying to give someone hope in their darkest hour when the demons are dancing on the prison walls.

Whilst I can understand the emotion, I would ask one simple question. When a prisoner emerges from jail and he/she moves in next door to you, what kind of a person do you want to live alongside? Someone who is trying to build a better life or a bitter, angry and resentful individual, scarred by being locked up for twenty-three hours per day with no access to any kind of education? It's a no-brainer really.

Let me state unequivocally that I am a hard-liner by default. If you do the crime, then you do the time. I have no sympathy. Some people are evil to the core, and must be locked away for life to protect the public. I am fine with that, but if people want to shift their focus and move on to a more fulfilling life without crime I am willing to help. I would not wish my entire life to be judged on any one mistake and I am sure that no one else would. People are locked up for many reasons not just violence and murder. In fact I believe only 30% of prisoners are incarcerated for violence.

Nelson Mandela was in prison. So was the actor Ricky Tomlinson and plenty of others who are essentially *good people*. In 2000, old-aged pensioner Mary Rooney was dragged off to prison for not paying her council tax. She had her own principled reasons but the law meant that she had to be locked away but should they bang her up for twenty-three hours a day and throw away the key? Give her a good thrashing? What possible good would that have done? Would Mary have paid her council tax upon release? She would have been even more embittered and resolute. I can think of plenty of lads at school who had the slipper and the cane many times, but that physical violence never changed their thinking or their ways. It merely made them more determined not to get caught!

It reminds me very much of Charles Dickens's *A Christmas Carol*. There is a scene where Ebenezer Scrooge had spoken without thought about letting the poor people die if that was what they would *rather* do, instead of going to the poor house – thereby decreasing the surplus population. The ghost of Christmas present tells him that before he opens his mouth he should be clear who and what the surplus population is before he passes judgement so thoughtlessly. I feel that way about my work in prisons. Society is always quick to judge.

My relationship with prisoners is of course purely chess-related and the role covers all of the prisons in England of which there are 117 at the moment. Resources in terms of time and budget are clearly finite so I do what I can when I can.

Aside from my ECF work, I am the chess columnist for the Inside Time prison newspaper which reaches thousands of people, and each month I write a short chess article, providing a chess puzzle for prisoners to solve. I offer a prize of a chess magazine for the first correct entry drawn. These are worth their weight in gold on the inside and one prisoner told me that he wanted to win the magazine so he could put it down his shirt to offer protection in case he got stabbed. See, chess can even save lives!

The hundreds of letters I have received highlight how chess has improved mental health, thinking, decision making, social development, reading and writing and mathematical skills. It is true to say that it has on at least one occasion saved a life. One man felt suicidal, found chess, fell in love with the game and decided not to kill himself. Powerful stuff.

Chess has dissuaded some inmates from taking drugs again and I have several letters declaring the intention to turn away from crime. Instead of going out to commit robbery at 7pm, one man said he would go to a chess club instead. What governor would not welcome that? If prisoners are engaged in battle on a chess board they are not fighting on the wings with each other or prison officers.

Chess is the perfect opportunity after the madness and noise of a prison day to come together as a group in quiet contemplation with a cup of tea and a game at the prison chess club. I have personally witnessed how immensely beneficial this is and some chess clubs are reaching out to offer support.

I must say that I do love to give a simultaneous exhibition when I visit. I will play up to twenty people at once but sometimes it exceeds that amount. This kind of thing is usually reserved for Grandmasters, but I am very adept at this at a certain level and have my own technique. I seem to be able to focus better against multiple opponents than I do against one. I have no idea why that is.

Giving a simultaneous exhibition at Stafford prison in 2019.
I did six hours straight without a break or a drink!

You cannot be a wilting flower to do the job. Prison is a tough and sometimes unforgiving place (just like the chessboard) and depending on the type and category of prison you can expect different responses.

I recall giving a twenty-board exhibition in a Category A prison. These are the most dangerous prisoners and security is obviously very high. As I entered the hall and the men were sitting behind their boards, I had been told that there was a combination of murderers, terrorists, armed robbers and the like and that they did not like to lose at chess. I was undeterred and my tough upbringing has always helped me to stand up for myself. Yes, there is a lot of testosterone, plenty of trash talk and threats of, 'how I am gonna get my ass kicked' by a very tiny minority of prisoners but I just laugh it off. I tell them that I have seen it all at the chessboard (true) and no amount of trash talk will intimidate me.

There was one nationally well-known *celebrity* prisoner in the group and one officer approached me before the start and said, 'He is a cocky git, if you beat no one else, just beat him.' No pressure then. I allowed people to consult and this particular man had a friend with him, so I was effectively playing two people per board. We played through to an equal and very tricky rook and pawn endgame and most of the other games were finished, the prisoners were gathering around and the tension was palpable.

To be fair, neither of us offered a draw, and we played on. I was shuffling my rook back and forth, waiting for a tempo here or a small error there. It came! He missed a trick, and I pounced, winning the game. He shook my hand and stormed off without a word. Most opponents are very respectful, very courteous and simply glad to have a visitor and play some chess.

I have had a few interesting moments but only once ever

felt threatened. On one prison visit a player cheated and I held him to account. He didn't like it and asked if I was saying he was a cheat. I have already said that my policy is to stand up to bullies. I told him that when I left his board I knew what the position was and that I could set it up exactly. The position that stood before me when I returned was totally different.

I had sacrificed my queen for an imminent checkmate, which was not now possible because he had shifted a knight from its proper square to another where I could not deliver mate – therefore I was a queen down and lost if it stood. I told him that if he had put the knight on the square it currently occupied knowingly then *yes*, he was a cheat. He said he hadn't, but I stood my ground. 'I offer you a draw' said the man. I refused, now angry at his arrogant attitude. He stood up abruptly and rather menacingly but before he could do anything – if he was ever going to – a prison officer and another prisoner escorted him briskly through an exit door!

The chaps next to him knew what he had done, and I think they were pleased that I took the bloke to task. Chess is like life as I keep on saying. When you make your move you cannot take it back or as William Shakespeare so succinctly put it, 'what is done cannot be undone.'

I was particularly impressed when I visited HMP Buckley Hall. When I met the inmates as they arrived at the chess room, some were carrying printed games of mine from years back. They had taken the trouble to prepare against me. They had been to the prison library and officially obtained printouts (via library staff) of some of my games which appeared online. In the weeks prior to my visit they exchanged thoughts and ideas about how to beat me. I could not have been more impressed and I told them and the governor as much.

The inmates had been very positive, utilising resources (the library) and working as a team. In prison, that's a very big deal. Thinking before acting – brilliant! Mind you, one of the chaps said, 'We know you play a French Defence so we are well prepared for you.'

I replied, 'Very good but you have made one big mistake – you have revealed your hand before we have even pushed a pawn. Now that you have told me that I am not going to play a single French Defence today.'

One of the chaps was furious 'Fucking blabbermouth,' he said to the other bloke.

There's a lesson here just as much in chess as there is for example in business negotiations. Prepare by all means, but do not reveal your cards too early.

On another occasion I visited a women's prison and a big fight kicked off in front of me. That ruined the day because I was due to have about ten women for my chess coaching session, but several were locked up for bad behaviour as a result of the brawl. In the end I only had three ladies attend but they were very keen to play chess. One of them was a very small, slim Scottish woman with barely a tooth in her head, but she had beautiful big blue eyes that reflected like marbles.

As we played she suddenly asked, 'Why are women not as good as men at chess?' Crikey, how was I to field that one? Honesty is the best policy so I said, 'I will tell you what ex-world champion Garry Kasparov once said – women lack the killer instinct.'

She looked at me and in a flash said, 'I fuckin' didn't though' and she smiled. We both giggled.

I believe that International Master and chess guru Malcolm Pein once visited HMP Wandsworth prison for chess business and he was the unfortunate recipient of a bucket of excrement that had been thrown from an upper wing down to where he was standing. I have stood on that same spot at Wandsworth prison, but fortunately avoided such a fate so far. You've got to be on your guard at all times clearly, but it would take more than a bucket of poo to deter a stalwart like Malcolm from the task in hand.

I also recall the first time that a prisoner beat me at chess. He was a young and very quiet lad and he outplayed me in a fine attacking game. In a simul of twenty boards it is normal for me to lose two or three, and to draw at least two or three. That's fine. I have had days where I have lost none but I once lost four or five – so you take it as it comes.

This lad won a prize and I shook his hand in front of everyone and presented him with a chess book. I said, 'well done, you outplayed me and deserved to win.' His reply was, 'No I didn't.' I asserted that he certainly did, but he wasn't having any of it until I showed him the position on the board, and proved that he was better throughout. The penny dropped and suddenly he beamed.

His pals were congratulating him and (bless him) he asked me to sign a copy of my book which I did and I wrote that he had defeated a county champion at chess. A prison officer later told me that the lad had a brutal childhood, where no-one ever supported or loved him and literally no-one had ever said 'well-done' to him before. He was not used to praise, especially in front of his peers but that day will hopefully have changed a lot of things for him. Work hard and the rewards will come – and accept the praise for a job well done.

Another time, I played a group of quite strong players. One of them was an older gentleman, who wore a beret and Japanese sniper spectacles. As the play developed and I had my usual banter with the other players this man never said a word. He did not even look at me. All he did was focus on the game, which is perfectly fair. He was making the best moves out of the whole group and I was struggling to stay in the game. Sure enough, he was the last player to finish and I pulled up a chair opposite him and sat down so that we could play one-to-one.

It was another tricky endgame with rook and pawns, and it took all of my chess nous to hold him to a draw. When the game ended I said to him, 'Well, come on, who are you and how much chess do you play?' He looked at me and flashed a smile. In a thick Russian accent he said, 'I am Yuri (not real name) and I played chess in old Russia.' He was a bit of a hero to the other lads and they never let on who he was, so well done to them. It just goes to show that you can never take anyone for granted, nor should you in chess or in life.

People in general have fixed views about prisons and prisoners. I am often asked if I am worried about prisoners coming after me upon their release. Why should I be? Chess is a positive experience that brings people together. We all want the same thing – just to have fun and enjoy the game. I am not on the prison payroll and prisoners are totally appreciative of the fact that I am giving up my own time. There's never a problem. In fact, in one well-known prison in London an inmate commented that if ever I had any issues with anyone on the outside I could always contact them and they would sort it for me. The funny thing is I have probably got more protection now that I had before I took the job!

I have been involved in several prison initiatives. I received a letter from America asking if the ECF would help with an England team to play in the first online world prison chess championships in 2019. I wanted to share the love and involve the Chess in Schools and Community charity. We hooked up with Peter Sullivan and Malcolm Pein, and jointly managed a team from Wandsworth Prison representing England.

England were competing with Armenia, Brazil, Belorussia, USA, Spain, Russia and Italy. It was the first time any of the lads had played anything like this, and the team would never be serious contenders to win it *but* these men had now represented their country at chess. What an achievement that was. I would suggest that on the CV it stands equally as good as any other qualification that could be attained behind bars – and it is a unique one at that.

My work and that of the ECF seems to have caught on around the globe. I had an email from a sheriff in Chicago who said he had two copies of my book on his desk and they were using some of my tips to teach chess in jail. The same can be said in Canada where they are using my book as part of a prison chess for life program, facilitated by Dr Lance Grigg, an Associate Professor at the University of Lethbridge in Alberta.

I received a call from the Wall Street Journal asking for information about chess in prisons and they had a few copies of my work shipped out to New York, which was nice.

In November 2019 I was invited to Oslo in Norway to speak about 'Chess Behind Bars' and about chess in prisons in general. I was interviewed on the couch as it were and alongside me sat a former prisoner who had also found and enjoyed chess. It goes to show that for prisoners the world over, from Tunisia to Tanzania, from England to Indonesia, chess unites.

I was delighted to have been invited by none other than Grandmaster Judit Polgar to speak at the sixth global chess festival in October 2020 which was based in Hungary but it would have to be online this time because of the Covid situation. Judit and I shared a couple of Zoom sessions to discuss the format and it all went well. Indeed, I received some nice feedback that the Hungarian version of the BBC liked my lecture very much.

I was lecturing in my capacity as the author of my book. Judit is the strongest female chess player in history but she is wonderfully down to earth and very engaging. She spends a great deal of time giving chess back to communities and works tirelessly encouraging juniors to play and improve.

I recorded my lecture a few days before the event and it can be found online on YouTube. I have to say that at the time I was feeling horribly ill. My aforementioned blood disorder was giving me grief and my haemoglobin levels had dropped to worrying levels. The day after I recorded the lecture with Judit I had to go to hospital for a blood transfusion. I still delivered my prison chess message regardless. When one is a chess crusader, one must not give up at the first hurdle.

I had spoken about mental well-being and as if to reinforce it, a few months later in December 2020 I received a letter from an inmate. Here is a quote from that letter:

In the nine months prior to lockdown after opening (the chess club) in June 2019 we were averaging fifty-sixty players a week. I have spoken to many inmates and virtually all have said that chess has improved their mental wellbeing as a result of playing every week.

I take great pleasure in this because it was sent from a prison that I had visited to support their chess club and boost numbers. Governors and government take note – why not at least give chess a try?

I need to emphasise that the vast majority of prisoners that I have worked with at chess have been outstanding. They have participated and shared their thoughts and views openly and honestly. I am very grateful to them for that. I receive letters and even Christmas cards telling me how much chess matters. I have seen enough to know that the game can provide not just the necessary intellectual stimulus for a human being in confinement, but that the disciplines and lessons it teaches can equip us all for future days.

It is my sincere view that no inmate should be denied the opportunity to discover and play chess. Think of it as The Holy Trinity. Three things are required for mental liberation. They are a chessboard, a chess set and a chess clock. This Holy Trinity can be taken into any cell and played on any wing. Surely it is worthy of a try.

There is so much more work to be done with chess and the prison community. I have done hardly work with Young Offender Institutes (YOI's) for example, or women's prisons. I would also like to see a prison chess league, or at the very least inter-prison matches in the UK. Some people are up for this – but for others it is all too difficult. Security and resources are often used as excuses for not doing it but I am not having it. They built pyramids 2000 years ago so these things can be overcome. I say try something at least. Give chess a trial (no prison pun intended) run and see if it makes a difference.

There are some 84,000 people locked up in the UK so there is certainly a (literally captive) audience to introduce to chess. It is after all not an event, it is a process. Covid has knocked us back significantly but chess will prevail as it has for around 1600 years.

The final words go to John Healy. Referring to my prison visits, I asked him what was the most important message that I could convey about chess to those men and women who have so much time on their hands?

He said, 'Tell them that if they take up chess, time will become their toy.'

A lovely card from GM Judit Polgar encouraging me to carry on with my prisons work.

My next move

Dear past, thanks for all the lessons.
dear future…
I am ready

Anon

Chess is my silent obsession and I have been on this crusade for most of my life, championing the great game to anyone who will listen.

It has been played in the back streets of Rangoon and Havana, and the great cigar divans in London and Paris in the eighteenth and nineteenth centuries. Who is to say that those playing in the back alleys did not derive as much pleasure as the cigar smoking, learned gentleman of the day in Europe? Chess belongs to no-one, we all belong to chess.

In this book, I have openly shared my experiences about the wonder of finding chess in my formative years and how it has shaped and influenced my life. The people I have met and the places I have visited have been wonderfully life-enriching, and the mental nourishment that the game provides is so powerful that I cannot quantify it.

What is the next chapter in my chess crusade?

Chess has played a significant role in my motivational thinking. When you achieve your goal do not stand still. Push on. I am still in my fifties and honestly don't consider myself to be old in any sense. The old saying, 'Life is too short for chess, but that is the fault of life, not chess' is quite true.

There is much more to be done and more to achieve. I need to continue to improve my own game and bring the joy of chess to a much wider community. After all, my best game is still to be played. That is my driving force. I shall continue with my chess in prisons work and enjoy writing and playing.

(l-r) Dickens, Raven and Darwin are a welcome distraction from the madness of life and I thank them for never judging me.

We live in fearful and challenging times. The Coronavirus pandemic changed the way that society functions, and the significant loss of life across the globe has put our very existence into sharp perspective. The old joke that bacteria is the only culture that some people have is too serious to be funny. True enough, there are currently no chess clubs open and therefore we are devoid of human interaction. It feels like being in a movie and it can feel rather desperate if you let it take a hold.

Yet I refuse to perpetuate any dystopian view of the future. On the contrary, I believe that when the sun shines once again upon humanity, as it inevitably will, then the doors to chess clubs everywhere will open wide and Caissa's children will come. With this new dawn we might even witness a greater appreciation of the value of chess and the social and mental benefits that it provides. It is so much more than just a game. The Dadaist artist Marcel Duchamp said of chess that every chess player is an artist, but not every artist is a chess player. I can relate to this and I still have a great appetite for painting new creations on the chessboard. As football needs the fans, so chess needs over the board combatants and it will be a great day when this returns across the globe.

I do have some concrete ideas about where I want to go next regarding publicising chess. There is one notion that I have been unable to get out of my head. I want to organise an event involving both amateurs and grandmasters, where games are played and both sets of players commentate.

Grandmaster v Grandmaster.
Amateurs commentate, then Grandmasters give their thoughts on the game afterwards. Then compare notes!

Amateur v Amateur
Grandmasters commentate then amateurs give their thoughts on the game afterwards. Then compare notes!

Grandmaster v Amateur
Amateurs and Grandmasters commentate.

It would surely be tremendous fun (one of the basic tenets of chess) and it would highlight the differences in critical and general thinking, serving as a unique training exercise discussing chess tactics and strategy. Such comments could be used in coaching classes for years to come.

I want to continue to introduce more people to the game. The skills and disciplines that chess develops can be critical factors for success and are instantly transferrable from chess board to boardroom. Thinking one step ahead in life has so many advantages. In 2020 I had a telephone conversation with none other than Ian Gillan, the singer with the rock band Deep Purple. He loves his chess. Curiously, he compared it to gardening. He said that we grow our plants according to the climate we live in. We anticipate! That is a perfect analogy. He also said that every politician should be made to learn chess to develop their ability to predict and respond to global events. I cannot argue with that notion.

Whilst the rules of chess are the same as when I was twelve years of age, the chess world itself has changed radically. We have advanced from having only books, magazines and newspaper cuttings as a learning resource to engaging in live streaming with Twitch and Zoom. The top tournaments are shown live online, and we have e-books and games, computer chess, private coaching (online and face-to-face) and so much more. There has never been a better time to take up chess, and to improve at the game.

Just imagine chess clubs in every school. Could chess appear on the agenda in every prison and Young Offender's Institute? Imagine chess in every care home to help the elderly keep their brains active. Could these things really happen? As the song goes, *You may say I'm a dreamer, but I'm not the only one.*

One final thing I want to have a go at is blindfold chess. This is where you play chess without sight of the board. One requires an excellent memory to do this and mine is iffy at the best of times, but it would be great to try it. Apparently it sent people to the mad house in the nineteenth century when they took on anything from five to twenty boards simultaneously. Harry Nelson Pillsbury (1872-1906) once played twenty-two simultaneous games of chess and draughts blindfold, whilst taking part in a game of whist.

Before he began he would ask the watching audience for a list of random words and on one famous occasion in London, two professors came up with a list of thirty words which included the likes of Antiphlogistine, Periosteum, Salamagundi, Oomisellecootsi, Madjesoomaloops, Manzinyama and Threlkeld. He successfully concluded all of his games and then recited the words perfectly many hours later – in reverse order! He did so again at breakfast the following morning. What a character. If I could do a fraction of that I would be delirious. Perhaps that will be one for my care home in later years.

Writing this memoir has been a labour of love. It has reminded me as if I needed it, that I share a remarkable relationship with this ancient game that cannot be diminished by time. There are sixty-four squares on a chessboard, and I was born in 1964. Maybe it was just meant to be.

Further, I am clear that the most wonderful thing about chess is the opportunity to play it, and it is my sincere hope that everyone reading this book finds something equally significant and enjoyable in their lives.

I urge every reader to either take up the game or improve.

I do not care less if you are an amateur, semi-professional or professional. These are just terms. What matters is what chess means to you and how playing and studying chess can positively affect your life – each and every day. You just have to want it. Just play your first move and see how the game goes. Begin your own crusade for Caissa. Remember the Holy chess Trinity.

I shall conclude with the wise words of former world chess champion Garry Kasparov:

At the end of the day we are all being challenged, sooner or later, by our destiny. It is up to us to make all the difference in this life.

If not you, who else?

Games selection

On the chess board, lies and hypocrisy do not last long

Emanuel Lasker

I have lost many games of chess. Let that be perfectly clear. Some of those losses have been so painful that I will never recover from them. Many of these games have been lost because I was either not good enough, or I made careless blunders. I have played thousands of games of competitive chess and there are very few that I would pick out as being truly memorable for the actual standard of my play.

However, there are many games that have given me immense pleasure and made spending thousands of hours of study worthwhile. These games were not necessarily victories, as many losses taught me a great deal about myself if only I was prepared to listen.

Is this not a life lesson?

I really wanted to include some actual chess. To this end, the reader will now find nine of my own games. Remember that these are not necessarily my *best* games, but they are significant.

I could have included some sexy quick wins but in the context of chess these were not of great educational value. It is better to remain objective.

I have also added one further game, which is the Bobby Fischer v Boris Spassky encounter that I referred to in chapter eight. It has great personal as well as historical value.

I was going to add detailed annotations to the games, but I believe there is much to be had by studying the moves of these battles for yourself, so I have made only a very few light comments. Please do not seek perfection, it does not exist. As a famous grandmaster, Savielly Tartakower once said, 'the mistakes are all there on the board, waiting to be made.'

What many readers might see before them may just be a series of letters and numbers, but in the context of my life these are mini stories. They are nine relationships between me and my adversary. It was our space, our time.

Chess players will know how to play through these games of course, but if you are new to this then it is my cherished hope that you will take up the game for yourself. Just try it. This way I will have introduced newcomers to the game, which is the very least that Caissa would expect of me.

Chess has existed for around 1600 years and that liberating flame of the past continues to throw its beautiful light across the modern world.

Bless you Caissa, I am yours forever.

Chess Notation

I thought it might be prudent to explain chess notation – especially for non-chess players reading this book. It might help if you wish to follow the games in this chapter or the snippets of games that I mention throughout previous chapters. This is a very basic guide, so feel free to check Wikipedia for detailed explanations.

In essence an alpha-numeric co-ordinate system is used to identify each square. Letters appear horizontally and the numbers appear vertically. Thus you can observe that the square at the uppermost top right is h8 and the one bottom left is a1.

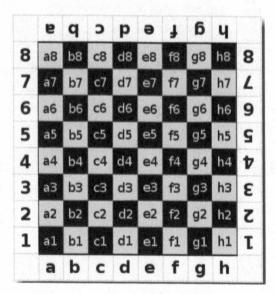

Board image taken from 'Hetricon' at chess.com

King   =   K
Queen   =   Q
Rook   =   R
Bishop =   B
Knight =   N

(note that we do not use K for knight, but for the king only)

Pawn   =   P

Notation for moves

Each move of a piece is indicated by that piece's uppercase letter, plus the coordinate of the destination square. For example, Be5 (move a bishop to e5), Nf3 (move a knight to f3). For pawn moves, a letter indicating pawn is not used, only the destination square is given. For example, c5 (move a pawn to c5).

Captures

When a piece makes a capture, an *x* is inserted immediately before the destination square. For example, Bxe5 (bishop captures the piece on e5). When a pawn makes a capture, the file from which the pawn departed is used to identify the pawn. For example, exd5 (pawn on the e-file captures the piece on d5).

Pawn promotion

When a pawn promotes, the piece it has promoted to is indicated at the end of the move notation, for example: e8Q (promoting to queen).

Draw offer

A draw offer is indicated by a = sign

Castling

Castling is indicated by the special notations 0-0 (for kingside castling) and 0-0-0 (queenside castling).

Check

A move that places the opponent's king in check usually has the symbol + appended.

Checkmate

Checkmate is represented by the symbol #

End of game

The notation 1–0 at the completion of moves indicates that White won, 0–1 indicates that Black won, and ½–½ indicates a draw.

Here is the notation for a series of moves.

A game or series of moves is generally written in one of two ways. Position after 1.e4 e5 2.Nf3 Nc6 3.Bb5 a6

You will get the hang of it, I promise. Do refer to Wikipedia.

Game 1 - my first big success

This was the first time in my life that I felt as if I had achieved something of genuine worth. Becoming champion of the school and therefore winning honours was a life-changing event. At that moment I was the best. Being number one felt good and I did it through my own efforts. I knew then that if I worked hard at something, and did not give up at the first hurdle I could achieve anything.

Carl Portman – Gary Cook
Charlton School Chess Championship final
March 18th 1980
Sicilian Defence

1. e4 c5 2. c4 e5 3. Nf3 Nc6 4. g3 Nf6 5. Nc3 b6 6. d3 d6
7. Bg2 Bb7 8. O-O Be7 9. a3 O-O 10. Bd2 a5 11. b3 Qd7
12. Nd5 Nxd5 13. cxd5 Na7 14. a4 Ba6 15. Qc2 Bd8 16.
Ne1 Rb8 17. f4 exf4 18. Bxf4 b5 19. axb5 Nxb5 20. e5 Nd4
21. Qd1 Re8 22. exd6 Ne2+ 23. Kh1 Nxf4 24. Rxf4 Qxd6
25. Qf3 f6 26. d4 c4 27. Re4 Rxe4 28. Qxe4 Bb6 29. bxc4
Bxc4 30. Nc2 Rd8 31. Ne3 Ba6 32. Nf5 Qd7 33. Bh3 Qe8
(diagram)

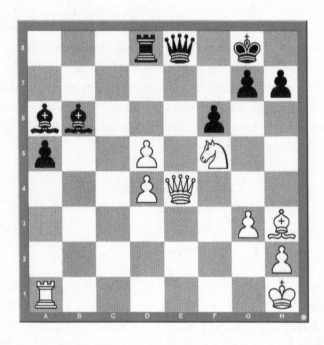

(This was the key moment) 34. Qb1!? (Trying to set a trap.) 34…Qb5? (The trap is sprung, 34… Rb8 is better.) 35. Qxb5 Bxb5 36. Rb1! (Winning one of the bishops.) 36…Bc4 37. Rxb6 Bxd5+ 38. Bg2 Bxg2+ 39. Kxg2 Rd5 40. Ne7+ Kf7 41. Nxd5 resigns. 1-0

Game 2 – in combat with a legend

Lev Polugayevsky was a legendary world-class chess player. He even has an opening variation named after him. This was the game we played in 1992 at a simultaneous exhibition in Shropshire which I organised.

Grandmaster Lev Polugayevsky – Carl Portman
Simultaneous Display Shropshire
September 13th 1992
Slav Defence

1.Nf3 Nf6 2.d4 d5 3.c4 c6 4.Nc3 h6 5.e3 Bg4 6.cxd5 Nxd5 7.Be2 e6 8.0–0 Nd7 9.Bd2 Be7 10.Rc1 0–0 11.h3 Bf5 12.Re1 Bh7 13.Bf1 Rc8 (It is a very solid game) 14.e4 Nxc3 15.Bxc3 Nf6 16.Nd2 c5 17.dxc5 Bxc5 18.Qf3 Bd4 19.Nb1 Bxc3 20.Nxc3 a6 21.Qe3 Qa5 22.a3 Rfd8 23.Red1 Bg6 24.f3 Nh5 25.Rxd8+ Rxd8 26.Rd1 Rxd1 27.Nxd1 Qa4 28.Nc3 Qb3 29.Qd2 Qb6+ ½–½

Final position

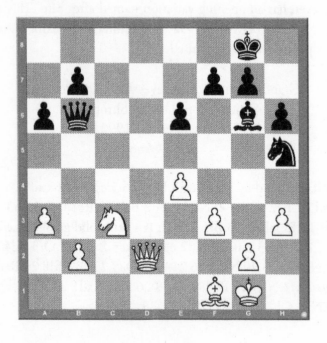

Game 3 – as Shropshire county champion

Success is one thing, but it brings its own pressure. Achieving the title of county champion was one thing, but I then became a target for others to beat. I was pleased to win this one (as champ) against a difficult opponent who still writes the chess column for the *Shropshire Star* newspaper.

Carl Portman – Toby Neal
Shropshire Chess Championship - Individual Round 4
February 2nd 1999
Classical Dutch

1. c4 d6 2. Nc3 f5 3. d4 Nf6 4. g3 e6 5. Bg2 Be7 6. e3 O-O 7. Nge2 Nc6 8. O-O Qe8 9. a3 Kh8 10. b4 e5 11. d5 Nb8 12. Bb2 a5 13. Qd2 axb4 14. axb4 Rxa1 15. Rxa1 Na6 16. Ba3 g5 17. b5 (diagram) both players are going for it.

17...Nc5 18. Bxc5 dxc5 19. Ra8 e4 20. Na4 b6 21. Qb2
Bd6 22. Bh3 Qe7 23. Qc3 Be5 24. Qd2 Rg8 25. Kf1 Qg7
26. Bg2 Qh6 27. h3 Nh5 28. Ke1 f4 29. exf4 gxf4 30. Bxe4
Qf6 31. g4 f3 32. gxh5 fxe2 33. Kxe2? (A mistake. I should
take with the queen). 33...Bd4 34. Kd3 Bxf2 35. Kc2 Bd4
36. Nc3 Qe5 37. Qh6 Bf5?? (The losing move when 37...
Qe7 was vital) 38. Rxg8+ Kxg8 39. Qg5+ Qg7 40. Qxg7+
Bxg7 41. Bxf5 1-0

Game 4 - when you lose, don't lose the lesson

This is my most memorable defeat, and it was also wonderfully instructive. My opponent left me twisting in the wind right from the off.

Carl Portman – Peter Hempson
British Chess Championships 2012
Bird's Opening

1. b3 Nf6 2. Bb2 d6 3. f4 e5 4. fxe5 dxe5 5. Bxe5 Ng4 6. Bg3 Qf6 (diagram) this is utter madness. After only 6 moves I am totally out of my depth. Black threatens mate on f2 if I were to remove my bishop from protecting it, and the queen also threatens my rook on a1.

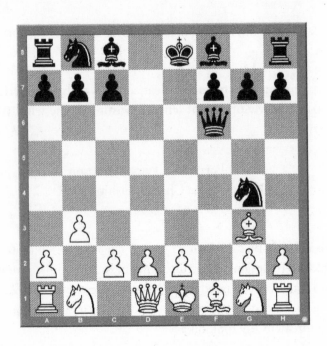

7. Nc3 Ne3 8.dxe3 Bb4 9. Nf3 Bxc3+ 10. Kf2 Bxa1 11. Bh4
Qd6 12. Qxa1 O-O 13. g4 f6 14. Bg2 Nc6 15. Rd1 Qe7
16. Nd4 Ne5 17. h3 c6 18. Qc3 Bd7 19. Kg1 Rae8 20. e4
g6 21. Bf2 c5 22. Nf3 b6 23. Nxe5 fxe5 24. Bg3 Bc6 25. b4
Bb5 26. Qb3+ Qf7 27. bxc5 Bxe2 28. Qxf7+ Rxf7 29. Rd2
Bc4 30. cxb6 axb6 31. Bf2 b5 32. a3 Rc7 33. Bb6 Rc6 34.
Ba5 g5 35. Bb4 Rf6 36. Bc5 Ree6 37. Be3 h6 38. Bf2 Rd6
39. Be3 Rxd2 40. Bxd2 Kf7 41. Bc3 Ke6 42. Bb4 Rf7 43.
Bc5 Kf6 44. Bb4 Rd7 45. Bf3 Ba2 46. Be2 Bc4 47. Bf3 Rc7
48. Kf2 Ba2 49. c3 Bc4 50. Bf8 Rc8 51. Bd6 Rd8 52. Bc5
Rd2+ 53. Kg1 Rd3 54. Be2 Rxc3 55. Bxc4 Rxc4 56. Bb4
Rxe4 57. Kf2 Rc4 58. Kg3 e4 0-1

Well done Peter!

Game 5 - when the stars align

This game was one I wanted to win, for several reasons. I played an opening that I rarely played and capitalised on my opponent's slow play. Chess strategy and tactics came together beautifully in this game at one of my favourite weekend congresses.

Carl Portman – Russell Goodfellow
Shropshire Congress
2016
Sicilian Defence

1.e4 c5 2. Nf3 e6 3. d4 cxd4 4. Nxd4 Nf6 5. Nc3 d6 6. Bb5+ Nfd7 (this cannot be good) 7. O-O a6 8.Bc4 Nf6 9. a4 b6 10. Bg5 Be7 11. Qe2 Qc7 12. Rad1 h6 13. Bh4 Ra7 14. Bb3 Qc5 15. Kh1 Bd7 (I really expected his queen to go to h5 here) 16. f4 Rb7? (Truly dreadful. Now I am going for the jugular.) 17. e5 dxe5 18. fxe5 Nh7 19. Qf3 Bxh4 20. Qxf7+ Kd8 21. Nxe6+ 1-0

Final Position

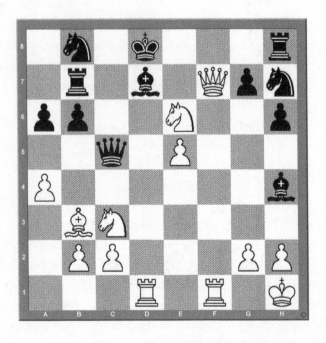

This final position shows pins and forks at their best. Note – The white king is safe in the corner, but his counterpart is exposed in the centre. Never good! Keep your king safe at all times.

Game 6 - if at first you don't succeed

I must be fair to Grandmaster Matthew Turner. This was the second game in a simultaneous display that he gave for the UK Armed Forces Chess Association in 2017. He had beaten me easily in game one and kindly allowed me to have another go. I include it not just because I won, honestly. I have beaten two other grandmasters (drawn with three others) in simuls, but this was just a fascinating game. In the end it was just Matthew and me playing one to one, so I had his sole attention and had to play correctly towards the end. Also, I play a certain opening as Black (The French Defence) and on his second move Matthew introduced a very unusual challenge.

Grandmaster Matthew Turner – Carl Portman
Simultaneous Exhibition
UK Armed Forces Chess Association
May 2017
French Defence

1. e4 e6 2. Qe2!? (The Chigorin Variation) b6 3. d4 Bb7
4. Nc3 Ba6 5. Qf3 Bxf1 6. Kxf1 Nc6 7. Nge2 Qf6 8.Qg3
Nxd4 9. Bg5 Nxe2 10. Kxe2 Qg6 11. Rhd1 f6 12. Qxc7
Rd8 13. Be3 Bb4 14. Qxa7 Ne7 15. Bxb6 Nc6 16. Qb7
Qxg2 17. Bxd8 Qg4+ 18. Kf1 Qh3+ 19. Ke1 Bxc3+ 20.
bxc3 Qxc3+ 21. Kf1 Qh3+ 22. Ke2 Qg4+ 23. Ke3 Qg5+
24. Kd3 Nxd8 25. Qc7 O-O 26. Qxd7 Nf7 27. Qxe6 Kh8
28. Ke2 Qh5+ 29. Ke1 Ng5 30. Qf5 Re8 31. Rd3 Qxh2 32.
Rad1Nxe4 33. Rd8 (This enables a nice little combination)

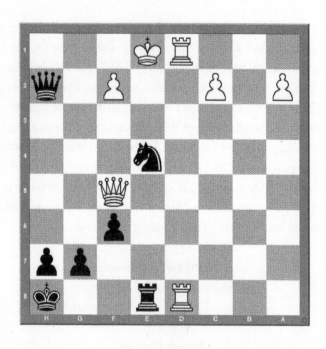

33...Qh1+ 34. Ke2 Ng3++ (double check, the queen is lost) 35. Kd3 Qxd1+ 36. Kc3 Rxd8 37. fxg3 Qd4+ 38. Kb3 Rb8+ 39. Ka3 Qa7+ 40. Qa5 Qxa5# 0-1

Game 7 - captain of my country

To captain one's country at any level is an achievement, and one to be rightly proud of. I had played as a UK member in France, but this was my first captaincy – the second would be in Texas, USA in 2018. Here I felt pressure to win and lead from the front so to speak, although no such pressure was put upon me by the team. My opponent was a stronger player, but I am pleased with how I fought this game, although he was better than me for much of the battle. To get a point on the board was very satisfying indeed.

Carl Portman - Pierre Christen
NATO Chess Championships – Hungary
2017
Nimzo-Larsen Opening

1. b3 e5 2. Bb2 Nc6 3. e3 d6 4. Bb5 a6 5. Bxc6+ bxc6 6. d4 e4 7. d5 Qg5 8. Ne2 cxd5 9. h4 Qh5 10. Qd2 c6 11. Qa5 Qf5 12. Nd2 Nf6 13. Ng3 Qe6 14. O-O-O Be7 15. Qc7 Bd7 16. Qa5 O-O 17. f3 Rfb8 18. Rdf1 Rb5 19. Qc3 exf3 20. Nxf3 c5 21. Ng5 Qg4 22. Rh3 Qb4 23. Nf5 (diagram)

The position looks complicated here, but Black has the better of it. Still a long way to go though.

23...Bxf5 24. Rxf5 Qxc3 25. Bxc3 d4 26. exd4 cxd4 27.
Rxb5 axb5 28. Bxd4 Rxa2 29. Rc3 Ra8 30. Rc7 Nd5 31.
Rb7 b4 32. Kd2 h6 33. Nf3 Re8 34. g3 Bf6 35. Kd3 Rc8
36. Rb5 Bxd4 37. Nxd4 Rc5 38. Rxc5 dxc5 39. Kc4 cxd4
40. Kxd5 f5 41. Kxd4 Kf7 42. c4 bxc3 43. Kxc3 g5 44. h5
Ke6 45. Kd4 Kd6 46. b4 Ke6 47. b5 Kd6 48. b6 g4 49. b7
Kc7 50. Ke5 1-0

Game 8 – from dreams to reality

Anatoly Karpov was my boyhood hero and one of the great World Chess Champions. I waited forty-three years to play him. Even though I lost, my preparation was good, and I was the last man to finish, being watched by a huge crowd in the city square in Chartres, France. I will never forget this encounter. I remain ever grateful to the French Chess Federation for making it happen and giving me the VIP treatment.

Grandmaster Anatoly Karpov - Carl Portman
Simultaneous Exhibition (Chartres France) 2019
Semi Slav

1. c4 e6 2. d4 d5 3. Nc3 a6 (diagram) This was what I had prepared at home. It is called the Janowski variation of the Queen's Gambit Declined.

4. cxd5 exd5 5. Bf4 c6 6. e3 Bd6 7. Bg3 Nf6 8. Bd3 Be6 9. Nge2 Bxg3 10. hxg3 Nbd7 11. Nf4 Qe7 12. a3 b5 13. Na2 c5 14. dxc5 Nxc5 15. Nb4 Nxd3+ 16. Qxd3 Qd7 17. Nh5 Nxh5 18. Rxh5 g6 19. Nxd5 Bxd5 20. Rxd5 Qe7 21. Rd1 O-O 22. Rd7 Qf6 23. Qd4 Qxd4 24. R1xd4 f5 25. g4 fxg4 26. Rxg4 Rf7 27. Rgd4 Ra7 28. Rxa7 Rxa7 29. Rd6 Kf7 30. Rb6 Ke7 31. g4 Kd7 32. g5 Kc7 33. Rf6 Kc8 34. Rf8+ Kb7 35. Rf7+ Kb6 36. Rxa7 Kxa7 37. Kd2 Kb6 38. Kd3 Kc5 39. b4+ Kd5 40. f4 Ke6 41. e4 Kd6 42. Kd4 1-0

Game 9 – sometimes you just have to go for it

League chess is brutal but hugely enjoyable. Occasionally we play a game that flies in the face of reason and this was one such example. I had read about the games of Emory Tate who played really wild chess and I had waited for the day when my opponent would allow me to play my rook to a3 on the fifth move. This was such a game and although it is far from *perfect*, I just went for it and began slugging it out from the off. It was also one of the last games I played over the board before the beginning of the Covid pandemic lockdown. I even showed it to Woman Grandmaster (WGM) Jovanka Houska, and she thought it was fun, playing it occasionally herself online.

Carl Portman – Simon Turner
Rugby A - Banbury A
2019
Alekhine's Defence

1. e4 Nf6 2. e5 Nd5 3. c4 Nb6 4. a4 a5 5. Ra3!? (This is the crazy looking move that I wanted to play for so long. The rook wants to go to g3 and add to the pressure on g7 and Black's king-side It is not sound, but it is fun.)

5...d6 6. exd6 exd6 7. d4 d5 8. c5 N6d7 9. Rg3 Nf6 10.
Nc3 g6 11. Bg5 Bg7 12. h4 O-O 13. Be2 c6 14. h5 (I was
in the mood for a bloodbath) 14...Bf5 15. hxg6 Bxg6 16.
Nh3 Qe8 (That rook on g3 is a nuisance, lining up against
the Black king) 17. Bxf6 Bxf6 18. Nf4 Nd7 19. Kf1 Qe7 20.
Bd3 Rae8 21. Ncxd5 cxd5 22. Nxd5 Qd8 23. Qh5 Bg7 24.
Bxg6 fxg6 25. Qxh7+ Kf7 26. Qxg6+ 1-0

Game 10 – sharing Bobby Fischer

This is not one of my own games, but the one I mentioned in chapter 8 where Lev Polugayevsky and I studied the Fischer-Spassky game 'live' by CEEFAX. To have analysed with such a chess legend – and it being a Bobby Fischer game as well has to be one of the highlights of my amateur chess life. That sort of opportunity will never come around again.

Robert Fischer – Boris Spassky
Yugoslavia 1992
Game 7
Ruy Lopez

1. e4 e5 2. Nf3 Nc6 3. Bb5 a6 4. Ba4 Nf6 5. O-O Be7
6. Re1 b5 7. Bb3 d6 8. c3 O-O 9. d3 Na5 10. Bc2 c5 11.
Nbd2 Re8 12. h3 Bf8 13. Nf1 Bb7 14. Ng3 g6 15. Bg5 h6
16. Bd2 d5 17. exd5 c4 18. b4 cxd3 19. Bxd3 Qxd5 20. Be4
Nxe4 21. Nxe4 Bg7 22. bxa5 f5 23. Ng3 e4 24. Nh4 Bf6
25. Nxg6 e3 26. Nf4 Qxd2 27. Rxe3 Qxd1+ 28.Rxd1 Rxe3
29. fxe3 Rd8 30. Rxd8+ Bxd8 31. Nxf5 Bxa5 32. Nd5 Kf8
33. e4 Bxd5 34. exd5 h5 35. Kf2 Bxc3 36. Ke3 Kf7 37. Kd3
Bb2 38. g4 hxg4 39. hxg4 Kf6 40. d6 Ke6 41. g5 *this was
the moment that I mentioned in chapter eight.*

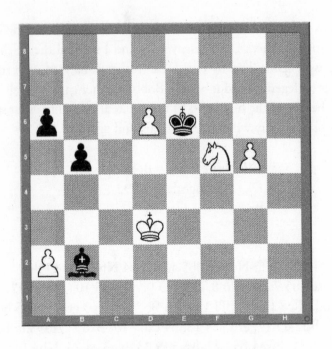

41...a5 42. g6 Bf6 43. g7 Kf7 44. d7 1-0

About the author

Carl is retired from the Civil Service and is now a co-director of his own management consultancy with his wife. He loves natural history – particularly arachnology, and he has written two books about his rainforest expeditions. However, his first love is chess. Whilst he describes himself as very much the amateur player, he has played chess at school, club, county and indeed International level. His proudest moments came representing the UK in France, Hungary and America in the NATO Chess Championships, being team captain at the last two. He is the author of the book 'Chess Behind Bars' and he works with chess in prisons for the English Chess Federation and is also a chess editor, columnist, coach, organiser and player. His achieved his dream when playing his childhood hero Anatoly Karpov in a simultaneous exhibition in Chartres, France in 2019. He lost – but was the last to finish in a good fight. He received the President's Award for Services to chess from the English Chess Federation in 2015 and he continues to take chess 'out to the people.' His life motto is 'Don't complain about the darkness, light a few candles.'

Bibliography and useful addresses

United Kingdom Armed Forces Chess Association
https://serviceschess.wixsite.com/home

NATO Chess Website
https://www.natochess.com/

Carlspix.co.uk
www.carlspix.co.uk

English Chess Federation
https://www.englishchess.org.uk/

Caissa Consulting Ltd
www.caissaconsulting.co.uk/

Chess coaching with Carl Portman (beginner to intermediate)
email me at: carl@caissaconsulting.co.uk

Books

S. O'Neill, *From Kosovo to Kandahar (A March Through the Ranks OR What the Hell – It'll be a Laugh.* Mrpinkster books 2019

Hooper and Whyld, *The Oxford Companion to Chess*. New Edition Oxford University Press 1992

C. Portman *Chess Behind Bars* Quality Chess 2017

J. Healy *The Grass Arena* 1988

D. Shabazz *Triple Exclam!!! The Life and Games of Emory Tate, Chess Warrior* The Chess Drum 2017

R.F.Green *Chess* Bell

J. Houska *The Mating Game* Conrad Press 2016

I. Chernev *The Golden Dozen* Oxford University Press 1976

Index of Names

A

Adams, Michael 220–222
Adams, Tara 221
Alekhine, Alexander 292–293
Allen, Woody 104
Anand, Vishy 199
Andrews, Norman 157–158, 248
Angelou, Maya 297
Archer, Richard 5, 78, 105, 149–151, 168
Arkell, Keith 167
Ashby, Tony 152, 223
Aubury, Ben 5, 288–292

B

Baldry, Tony 138
Bannister, Rose 31, 36–40, 220
Bannister, Sid 31, 36–40
Bates, William 170
Beckett, Richard 5, 138, 198–199, 201
Best, George 132
Betjeman, John 280
Betts, Timothy 5, 130–131
Bhokanandh, Tao 5
Blain, Gary 5
Boberg, Carl 265
Bogoljubov, Efim Dmitriyevich 63
Botterill, George 60
Botvinnik, Mikhail 288
Bricknell, Syd 76–77, 282
Brokenshire, Laurie 6, 264–265
Brooke, Rupert 159
Brotherton, Kevin 78

Brotherton, Trevor 5, 149, 157, 163
Brown, Pamela 23
Browne, Walter 60, 62
Buckland, Robert 300

C

Cadman, Chris 90
Cameron, Phil 149
Campling, Michael 292–294
Capablanca, José Raúl 292
Carlsen, Magnus 135, 230
Chandler, Murray 166
Cheesman, Colin 197–198
Chernev, Irving 26
Christ, Gerhard 193
Christen, Pierre 337
Churchill, Winston 122
Clements, Mr 28
Clemenz, Hermann 165
Conquest, Stuart 5, 222–223
Cook, Gary 63, 67–69, 71–72, 325
Cooper, Lawrence 166–167
Costello, Elvis 67
Cox, Jeff 5–6, 147–148
Cox, John 5, 66–67, 70, 147
Cox, Meyrick 5, 64–66
Cox, Nancy 6, 147–148
Cresswell, Les 144
Cromwell, Oliver 144
Crowhurst, Bernard 5
Crowhurst, Jean 5
Csecs, Gilbert 212
Curtis, Tony 38

D

Darmanin, Phil 78
Darwin, Charles 146
Davies, Mrs (English teacher) 53
Davies, Nigel 153
Dean, Roger 95
Derby, Abraham 146
Dickens, Charles 101, 291, 302
Dio, Ronnie James 35, 51, 96, 134
Donner, Jan Hein 60
Doudon, Marc 143–144
Duchamp, Marcel 316
Dumas, Alexandre 21

E

Emerson, Ralph Waldo 124
Essinger, James 6
Evans, Chris 138
Evans, Irene 138
Everington, David 6, 157–159

F

Ferguson, Sarah 139
Fischer, Bobby 32, 109, 135,
    154–156, 226, 321, 343
Footner, Andrew 167
Foulds, Andy 268–269
Frank, Anne 172
Freeman, Irfan 272
Freeman, Veronica 5, 134, 271–272
Freshwater, Keith 5
Fyodorovich, Anatoly 112

G

Gauke, David 300
Gemmill, Hugh 167
Gilbert, Ian 149
Gillan, Ian 317
Gilmour, Dave 134
Goodfellow, Russell 333
Gorbachev, Mikhail 108

Gove, Michael 298, 300
Graff, Ben 5
Gray, Andy 41–42
Grayling, Chris 299
Green, R.F. 58–59
Grigg, Lance 310
Gustaffson, Jan 191

H

Hagesæther, Arne 224, 226
Hale, Angela 5, 295
Hale, Ray 5, 295
Halford, Rob 90, 134, 147
Händel, Georg Friedrich 193
Harmon, Beth 117
Harris, Karla 5
Harrison, Tom 256
Hartston, William 60
Harvey, Marcus 199, 201–202
Harvey, Rob 201
Haslinger, Mandy 164
Healy, John 313
Hedges, Antonia 5
Hempson, Peter 331
Hendy, Jerry 258, 273–274
Henman, Tim 280
Hiddleston, Tom 280
Hitler, Adolf 71
Hoddle, Glenn 140
Hort, Vlastimil 60
Houseman, Alfred Edward 146
Houska, Jovanka 5, 9–11, 224–225,
    341
Howe, Steve 134
Howell, David 237
Hyde, Thomas 142

I

Iommi, Tony 35, 134
Ivanchuk, Vassily 222

J

Jones, William 26

K

Karpov, Anatoly 60–61, 67, 85,
    105–106, 218, 226–229, 339,
    346
Kasparov, Garry 218, 238, 260, 307,
    319
Kędzierski, Sławomir 277
Keene, Raymond 5, 226, 264–266
Keeve, Herr 190
Khalifman, Alexander 113
Khugashvili, Tamara 121
Kilmister, Lemmy 134, 199
King, Daniel 153
Klewin, Oliver 190
Knight, Alan 75, 149
Knight, Andy 63
Knight, Frederick 31–32
Koopmeiners, Karl 277
Korchnoi, Viktor 60, 135, 159–160
Kotov, Alexander 123
Krivlenkova, Natalia 111–116,
    119–123

L

Lagno, Kateryna 223
Lancaster, Penny 139
Larsen, Bent 60
Lasker, Emanuel 320
Laurie, Hugh 280
Lazarus, Simon 199
Lear, Edward 163
Lee, Robert E. 144
Lehrerin, Frau 174–175
Lenton, John 5, 24, 58, 63, 68–69,
    71, 73
Levy, David 106
Lidington, David 300
Llada, David 226

Lohse, Adolf 190
Lom, Herbert 51
Lord, Jon 135
Lucas, Julie 5
Lucas, Steve 5
Lynott, Phil 35

M

Maier, Sepp 55
Makwaya, Kiddy 149
Malinowski, Tomasz 277
Mandela, Nelson 302
Marshall, Janet 5
Mencken, Henry Louis 212
Messi, Lionel 136
Miles, Tony 60, 159, 223, 239
Moreton, Ian 198
Moore, Patrick 6, 214–216
Moore, Roger 38
Mushens, Arthur 154
Myers, Paul 56, 69, 73

N

Nakamura, Hikaru 238
Neal, Toby 151, 168, 329
Nelson, Mrs (Form teacher) 55
Nimzowitsch, Aaron 63
Norris, Kevin 96–97, 99–100
Norwood, David 161
Nunn, John 60, 153

O

O'Byrne, Danny 272
O'Connell, Kevin 105
O'Neill, Stephen 262
O'Reilly, Gerard 229
Oakley, John 91
Ocean, Frank 279
Onischuk, Alexander 260, 273
Onley, Dave 275
Osbourne, Ozzy 35, 94, 96, 133–134

Owen, Wilfred 146

P

Paice, Ian 134
Palliser, Richard 5
Peart, Neil 134
Pedersen, Finn 273
Pein, Malcolm 5, 308, 310
Pesch, Doro 134
Petrosian, Tigran 118
Phillips, Alan 73
Pigden, Caroline 5
Piggott, Terry 38–41
Pillsbury, Harry Nelson 318
Polgar, Judit 311, 313
Polugayevsky, Lev 153–159, 327, 343
Portman, Andrew 34–36
Portman, Fiona 37, 47
Portman, John (JTB) 36, 43–46, 60, 73, 82
Portman, Jonathan 47
Portman, Lawrence 24, 31, 34, 43, 48, 54–55, 73, 82
Portman, Sandra 31–33, 36–39, 43–49, 54, 57–60, 73, 80, 82
Portman, Su 160–161, 170, 186, 188–189, 202, 204
Portman, Susan (née Watson) 6, 11, 103–104, 126–128, 133, 139–140, 165, 200, 203–211, 214–217, 219, 224, 261, 272, 276–277, 287
Prescott, Lou 75
Pugh, Glyn 5, 78, 149, 168, 284
Pugh, Sandra 78
Purves, Peter 207

Q

Quinteros, Miguel 62

R

Rafferty, Mrs (Headmistress) 51
Rashford, Marcus 46
Regan, Natasha 153, 219–220
Richard, Cliff 40
Roberts, Colin 6, 168–169
Rooney, Mary 302
Roosevelt, Franklin D. 122
Ross, David 5, 261, 265–267, 274–276
Ross, Helen 5, 261
Ross, Ian H. 256
Rotstein, Arkadij 194
Rylance, Mark 297

S

Sachdev, Tania 153, 219
Sadler, Matthew 153, 219–220
Sayer, Leo 68
Schiller, Eric 223
Sedgwick, David 259
Shakespeare, William 306
Shamkovich, Leonid 67
Short, Nigel 60, 62, 153, 217–218
Singleton, Danielle 272
Smith, Dean 42
Smith, Jeremy 5, 46, 131
So, Wesley 223
Spassky, Boris 112, 135, 154–155, 321, 343
Speelman, Jon 60, 153
Squire, Chris 135
Stalin, Joseph 122
Staples, Neil 5, 211
Stewart, Rod 139
Suetin, Alexei 190
Sullivan, Peter 310

T

Taimanov, Mark 193
Tal, Mikhail 135, 165

Tarr, Steve 128
Tartakower, Savielly Grigoryevich 63, 225, 260, 321
Tate, Emory 341
Thatcher, Margaret 80–81, 83, 85, 94
Thomas, Jake 269
Thomson, Richard 164
Thurlow, Kevin 5, 151–153, 223, 259
Tierney, Sieglinde (Ziggy) 173, 182, 185–186
Tolkien, J.R.R. 95
Tomlinson, Ricky 302
Tromans, Roy 51
Truran, Mike 213
Truss, Liz 300
Tucker, David 259–261, 263
Turner, Gill 5
Turner, Matthew 259, 335
Turner, Simon 341
Turner, Terry 5
Tyson, Mike 122

U
Ufford, Reverend Edward Smith 44
Uhlmann, Wolfgang 190–191

V
Vida, Hieronymus 26
Viszokai, George 5, 77

W
Walker, Captain H.T. 256
Wallace, Alfred Russel 295
Wasmuht, Klaus 128
Watkiss, Ivan 63
Watson, Paul 255
Webb, Mary 146
Wells, Pete 271
Whittaker, Maria 94
Whittingham, Karen 69

Wood, Glenn 55, 63, 67
Wright, Billy 146

Y
Yeltsin, Boris 108
Yudovich, Mikhail 123

Z
Znosko-Borovsky, Eugene Alexandrovich 63

Other names
Amrik 91
Arthur 101–102
Barry 101–102
Bernard 89
Claire 100–101
Dave 93
Derek 101–102
Dieter 180
George 84–85, 96, 176
Gill 107, 111, 113, 115, 118–119, 123, 149–150, 155
Harry 84
Jackie 97–98
Jean 89
Kenton 42
Klaus 171, 176, 183–184, 186
Lance 93–95
Nicola 42
Pat 96–97
Ralph 111
Ray 135
Roy 96–97
Sandra 103
Stuart 56
Stuart 84
Sven 195
Valentina 227
Wolfgang 188–189, 195